The Call to Seriousness

IAN BRADLEY

The Call to Seriousness

The Evangelical Impact
on the Victorians

MACMILLAN PUBLISHING CO., INC.
New York

Macmillan Publishing Co., Inc.
866 Third Avenue, New York, N.Y. 10022

Library of Congress Cataloging in Publication Data

Bradley, Ian C
    The call to seriousness.

    Bibliography: p.
    Includes index.
    1. Evangelicalism—Church of England.   2. England—
Civilization—19th century.   I. Title
BX5125. B68   1976   269'.2'0941   75-44282
ISBN 0-02-514420-0

First American Edition 1976

Printed in Great Britain

For my Mother and Father,
with Love and Gratitude

Contents

List of Illustrations

9

between pp. 160 and 161

Acknowledgments

My interest in the Evangelicals was first aroused when, as a sixth former, I came across a handwritten Victorian family magazine in the Kent County Record Office in Maidstone. This experience I owe to the imaginative teaching of my two history masters at school, Geoffrey Parker and Colin Reid, both of whom encouraged me to develop my interest and helped me in the early stages of my research. Since then, I have had consistent guidance and support from my two main tutors at Oxford, Penry Williams and Garry Bennett. The Warden and Fellows of New College, by electing me to a Salvesen Fellowship, have made the two years in which I have been engaged in full-time research on the Evangelicals a particularly happy time. To all of them I am profoundly grateful.

Many people have helped me over the manuscript sources for this book. The Earl of Harrowby very kindly let me see the Harrowby papers at Sandon Hall. Mr C. E. Wrangham not only opened his collection of Wilberforce papers at Catterick to my inspection, but also offered me very generous hospitality while I was looking at them. I have met with unfailing courtesy and co-operation from the staff of the British Museum, the Bodleian Library, the Cambridge University Library, the Durham University Library, Balliol College Library and the Devon County Record Office, the curator of the Wilberforce Museum at Hull, the archivists of the Church Missionary Society and the British and Foreign Bible Society, and the secretaries of the Lord's Day Observance Society and the Church's Ministry to the Jews.

I have derived considerable benefit from conversations with Norman Vance, Elizabeth Jay, Michael Hennell, Norris Pope and

Geoffrey Rowell, all of whom have given me new insights on the Evangelicals. My greatest debt of all is to John Walsh, who supervised my D.Phil. thesis on Evangelicals in Parliament, read most of the chapters of this book in draft form, and has been a constant guide and companion in my wanderings through a world which he knows far more about than I ever will. For the errors which remain, I alone am responsible.

I. C. B.

New College, Oxford
December 1974

Introduction

'Nobody is gay now; they are so religious.'

Lord Melbourne's gloomy observation to Queen Victoria at the time of her accession to the throne in 1837 summed up the transformation which took place in English life in the first half of the nineteenth century under the impact of Evangelical religion. At least one of her subjects hoped that the new Queen might reverse the trend: Lucy Aikin wrote to an American friend, Dr Channing, that she felt sure that 'a gay, young, play-going Queen would make a formidable counteraction to the progress of the Evangelicals, whose doctrines make all the noise now.'[1] She was to be sadly disappointed. Victoria had been brought up by devout Evangelical parents from whom she had inherited many of the principles of 'vital religion'. The entry which she made in her journal on the day of her coronation forms a suitably earnest preface to a reign which was to display both the high sense of duty and the air of self-righteousness which character-ized the Evangelicals:

> Since it has pleased Providence to place me in this station, I shall do my utmost to fulfil my duty towards my country; I am very young ... but I am sure that very few have more real good will and more real desire to do what is fit and right than I have.[2]

The list of those Victorians who, like the Queen, had an Evan-gelical upbringing and who remained profoundly influenced by it for the rest of their lives, even when many of them renounced its creed, includes many famous names. Among them were Lord Macaulay, Sir Robert Peel, W. E. Gladstone, John Henry Newman, Henry

Manning, Archbishop Tait, Sir Henry Havelock, the legendary defender of Lucknow, General George Gordon of Khartoum, George Gilbert Scott, the architect, F. H. Bradley and T. H. Green, the philosophers, John Ruskin, Charles Kingsley, Samuel Butler, George Eliot, Wilkie Collins, Elizabeth Barrett Browning and the Brontë sisters. Literally hundreds of thousands of Victorians were brought up in Evangelical homes. For millions more the strong hold which Evangelicalism exercised throughout society made it a dominant and inescapable influence on their lives.

The Victorians themselves were well aware of the powerful part which Evangelical religion had played in shaping the attitudes and customs of their own age. In the year of Victoria's accession, Frances Trollope wrote a novel about a young clergyman possessed of an almost demonic desire to dominate everyone with whom he came into contact. The purpose of the book, which was called *The Vicar of Wrexhill*, was to show the terrible power of Evangelical influence in society. Evangelicalism was a favourite subject for later Victorian novelists. Dickens satirized it in *Bleak House*, and Thackeray in *The Newcomes*. Disraeli started a novel entitled *Falconet* about its influence on politics. The horrifying descriptions of Evangelical childhoods in Charlotte Brontë's *Jane Eyre* and Samuel Butler's *The Way of All Flesh* are among the most vivid and unforgettable passages in English literature. Two famous critics of conventional Victorian attitudes recognized the power of the Evangelical impact. John Stuart Mill identified Evangelicalism as the root cause of the cult of respectability and conformity against which he railed in his essay *On Liberty* in 1859, and Matthew Arnold regarded it as being responsible for the narrow philistinism and puritanism of the middle classes which he attacked in *Culture and Anarchy* in 1868.

Historians are generally agreed in seeing Evangelicalism as one of the most important forces at work in shaping the character of the Victorians. Commenting on the formative influences operating on a boy born in 1810 and attaining full manhood at the time of Victoria's accession, G. M. Young observed in the opening paragraph of his classic work, *Victorian England – Portrait of An Age*, that 'whichever way his temperament led him, he found himself at every turn controlled and animated by the imponderable pressure of the Evangelical discipline'. In his biography of the writer Leslie Stephen, another eminent Victorian to come from an Evangelical home, Noel Annan describes Evangelicalism as 'the single most widespread influence in Victorian England'. David Newsome in his book on Victorian public schools, *Godliness and Good Learning*, sees it as 'perhaps the most formative power behind the eminence of eminent Victorians'; while for Eric Stokes, writing about another important influence on the Victorians in *The English Utilitarians and India*, it is quite simply 'the rock upon which the character of the Nineteenth Century Englishman was founded'.

The origins of Evangelicalism lay in the religious revival which occurred in Great Britain in the middle of the eighteenth century. During the period between 1735 and 1760, a number of Anglican clergymen went through parallel but apparently spontaneous conversion experiences which involved an intense feeling of their sins being forgiven them and a personal assurance of salvation and which led them to devote the rest of their lives to preaching the Christian Gospel to the masses in a particularly powerful and compelling way. The most famous of these men was of course John Wesley, who dated his own conversion to a day in 1738 when he experienced the momentous sense of sins forgiven. Three years earlier, George Whitfield, who was to become a field preacher second only to Wesley in his capacity to move crowds of thousands to take up the Christian calling, had obtained 'mercy from God', and Howell Harris, who was to lead a religious revival in Wales, had experienced a sudden assurance of his personal salvation. In the ensuing decade several other Anglican clergymen independently underwent similar conversions. They included the Revd George Thomson, Vicar of St Gennys, who subsequently led a religious revival in Cornwall; the Revd William Grimshaw of Haworth and the Revd Henry Venn of Huddersfield, who together transformed the spiritual state of West Yorkshire; and the Revd William Romaine, lecturer at St Dunstan's, Fleet Street, who until the very end of the eighteenth century was the only clergyman preaching in London inspired by the spirit of the revival. All of them attracted large followings and were responsible for the conversion of substantial numbers of people.

The form of Christianity practised and preached by these founding fathers of the Evangelical Revival was intensely emotional and experiential. They themselves rather aptly described it as 'vital religion'. In essence, it centred around the doctrine of salvation by faith in the atoning death of Christ. This was the theme to which Wesley, Whitfield and the others returned again and again in their sermons. In part the practitioners of vital religion were simply returning to the central teaching of the Reformation and reviving the traditions of seventeenth-century Puritanism in Britain. In part they were reacting to the philosophies of deism and rationalism which prevailed in their own time. They themselves felt that they were simply living out in their lives and putting across through their preaching a purer and truer form of the Christian Gospel than that expressed by others. They saw themselves, in fact, essentially as 'evangelical' – the word literally means being imbued with the spirit of the Gospel.

In the early years of the Evangelical Revival those who felt the call to embrace the new 'vital religion' generally still remained within the Church of England. But well before the end of the eighteenth century a significant minority had broken away to form their own separate sect. They took the name that had been applied to John Wesley and his circle of serious young friends at Oxford in the 1730s, and called themselves Methodists. Those evangelicals who remained in the Church of England came to be called the Evangelicals. It is not clear whether they themselves first used the term, as the *Anti-Jacobin Review* suggested in 1799 when it talked of 'those who arrogate to themselves the title of Evangelical preachers' or whether it was first applied in a derogatory sense by others, as a writer suggested some years later when he commented: 'a certain number of their clerical brethren apply the epithet of Evangelical ministers as a term of reproach.'[3] What is clear is that by the beginning of the nineteenth century the Evangelicals were a distinctly recognized group of clergymen and laity within the Church of England who adhered to the principles and practices of vital religion.

This book attempts to examine the nature and the extent of the impact which the Evangelicals made on English life in the first half of the nineteenth century.* It is therefore confined in its scope to Anglican evangelicalism and does not deal with the specific, and very important contribution made by Nonconformity to British life in the nineteenth century. The time span which it covers is roughly

---

*Hereafter, the term 'Evangelicals' is used in this book to denote Anglican evangelicals, and 'evangelicals' to refer to all those, both Anglican and Nonconformist, who adhered to an evangelical form of Christianity.

that between 1800 and 1860, the period in which the vast majority of Victorians grew up and when the influence of Evangelicalism was at its height. Before 1800 the Evangelicals did not have a significant hold either on the Church or on society. After 1860 they declined into a narrow party. During the intervening sixty years there was hardly an area of life which they did not touch and affect.

Two men dominated the Evangelical world during the period covered by this book. From 1800 until around 1830 the acknowledged leader of the Evangelicals in England was William Wilberforce, the Yorkshire M.P. who was the central figure in that celebrated group of Evangelicals, known as 'the Clapham Sect' or 'the Saints', whose most famous achievement was the abolition first of the slave trade and then of all slavery from the British Empire. After Wilberforce's death in 1833 his mantle passed to Anthony Ashley Cooper, Seventh Earl of Shaftesbury, remembered chiefly for his championship of the cause of factory workers, and under whose leadership the Evangelicals considerably extended their philanthropic activities and consolidated their hold within the Church.* There were marked differences between Wilberforce and Shaftesbury, but they had one very important thing in common: they were both essentially positive figures, constructive in their behaviour and outward-looking in their attitudes. The same was broadly true of their Evangelical contemporaries and of the Evangelical movement as a whole during the time that they led it.

There are those who argue that the Evangelicals' legacy to the Victorians was a wholly negative one and that their enduring achievement was to create a spirit of violent anti-Catholicism in the country, a sense of bitterness and partisanship in the Church of England, and an equation of religious belief with obscurantism and cant in the minds of many earnest men and women. This is true, if it is true at all, only of the influence of Evangelicalism after 1860. The Second Evangelical Revival, which began around 1858, radically changed the character of the movement and inspired adherents who were more fanatical, more bigoted and more introverted than those who followed Wilberforce and Shaftesbury. In the period with which this book is concerned, Evangelicalism was essentially a

---

*Although he did not inherit the title until 1851, Ashley Cooper is referred to as Shaftesbury throughout this book.

dynamic movement and the influence which it exerted on society was, on the whole, a positive one.

Evangelicalism, of course, was only one of several forces at work in creating the ethos of the Victorian Age. The fact that this book is concerned with its contribution alone does not mean that the author is blind to the other influences which shaped the attitudes and habits of the Victorians. The role of that other great nineteenth-century ideology, Benthamite Utilitarianism, in moulding patterns of thought and behaviour, is acknowledged more than once in the following pages. The Evangelicals alone did not make the Victorians what they were. They did, however, play a very considerable part in helping to establish the peculiar temper of the age. The piety, the prudery, the imperialistic sentiments, the philanthropic endeavour, and the obsession with proper conduct which we think of as the distinctive characteristics of the Victorians can all be traced back to their influence.

Above all, Evangelicalism, more than any other single influence, was responsible for giving the Victorians their notorious seriousness and high-mindedness. In 1835, just over half-way through the period covered in this book, Samuel Butler had the Revd Theobald Pontifex christen his son Ernest since 'the word "earnest" was just beginning to come into fashion.'[4] In 1859, at the end of it, Charles Kingsley noted in the preface to his novel *Yeast*:

> One finds more and more, swearing banished from the universities, drunkenness and gambling from the barracks; one finds everywhere, whether at college, in camp, or by the cover-side, more and more, young men desirous to learn their duty as Englishmen and if possible to do it.[5]

The message that the Evangelicals had sought to get across through their own lives and deeds, in the tracts which they wrote and the sermons they preached, was one which the Victorians took to heart. 'It was', one of them commented, 'just a perpetual call to seriousness – to a sense of personal responsibility; taking the form of an appeal to be like Christ, to trust Christ, to be near Christ.'[6]

I

Vital Religion

The Evangelical Revival was a reaction against the worldliness and complacency of eighteenth-century England. Specifically, it was a protest against the prevailing attitude towards religion and morality. This attitude William Wilberforce outlined in his book, *A Practical View of the Prevailing Religious System of Professed Christians in the Higher and Middle Classes in this Country contrasted with real Christianity*, which was published in 1797 and which became the handbook of the Evangelicals:

> It seems in our days to be the commonly received opinion, that provided a man admit in general terms the truth of Christianity, though he neither know of nor consider much concerning the particulars of the system; and if he be not habitually guilty of any of the grosser vices against his fellow-creatures, we have no great reason to be dissatisfied with him, or to question the validity of his claim to the name and privileges of a Christian.[1]

It was against this vague, undemanding concept of Christianity, which pushed God and his commandments far into the background of man's consciousness, that the Evangelicals rebelled. In its place they preached what they called 'vital religion', an intense, urgent, all-consuming faith which, as Hannah More, the 'high priestess' of the Evangelical Revival put it, made Christianity 'the principle of all human actions, the great animating spirit of human conduct'.[2] In contrast to the religious viewpoint of the eighteenth century, which was almost entirely intellectual and rational, Evangelical Christianity appealed wholeheartedly and unashamedly to the emotions. There was, indeed, a strong measure of anti-intellectualism about it. 'God cares little for man's intellect,' the Earl of Shaftesbury once said, 'he cares greatly for man's heart.'[3] Significantly, one of the main sections in Wilberforce's *Practical View* dealt with the admission of the passions into religion. For the Evangelicals Christianity was something which involved a man in making a total commitment for life and not just in paying lip service to a series of dogmas. 'Religion is not, on the one hand, merely an opinion or a sentiment,' wrote Hannah More, 'so neither is it, on the other, merely an act or a performance; but it is a disposition, a habit, a temper: it is not a name but a nature: it is a turning the whole mind to God.'[4]

The theology of the Evangelical Revival was stark and simple. There was very little more to it than the 'Gospel Plan' which G. W. E. Russell, a late Victorian journalist and Liberal politician, remembered from his Evangelical childhood which taught:

> that all mankind were utterly sinful, and therefore in danger of Hell; that God had provided deliverance in the atoning death of Christ; and that, if only we would accept the offer of salvation so made, we were forgiven, reconciled and safe. That acceptance was conversion.[5]

The starting point of Evangelical theology was the doctrine of the total depravity of man. This concept, so different from the confident view of humanity which had prevailed in the eighteenth century, was the central theme of Wilberforce's *Practical View*. He devoted his longest chapter by far to discussing the inadequacy of prevailing conceptions of the corruption of human nature. The Evangelicals were preoccupied with the fate that awaited sinful man when he came face to face with a terrible and powerful God of Judgment. In this situation only one thing mattered; as Edward Bickersteth, who was later to become a leading Evangelical clergyman, wrote in his diary on his twenty-first birthday in 1807, 'Eternity is at stake, and I am trifling away the salvation of my soul. My soul asks the question, what shall I do to be saved?'[6] This was the urgent and insistent question which forced itself on every Evangelical mind. There was only one answer to it. To escape the eternal damnation which was the inevitable fate awaiting erring humanity, the individual must achieve regeneration of his soul by utterly repenting of his sins and fully accepting Christ's death as an atonement for them.

In this way, and in this way alone, was he converted to a saving faith.

The doctrine of conversion stood at the heart of Evangelical theology. Every Evangelical had personally experienced the 'great change' which occurred when, burdened down by his sense of sin and inadequacy, he had thrown himself on God's mercy and been made regenerate. Evangelical conversions were intense and dramatic. They often followed serious illness or the sudden death of a loved one but they could also result from apparently trivial incidents which were subsequently held up as sure evidence of the workings of Divine Providence. Those who had been converted almost invariably noted down their experiences in some detail and were generally able to give the precise time and location at which the 'great change' had occurred. A sure conversion was the badge of the Evangelical Christian. Those who felt that they had only partially undergone the conversionary experience often prayed for a dangerous illness which would bring them still nearer to God and complete the process. Those who felt certain that they were surely converted themselves looked eagerly for evidence that their friends and relatives had attained the same state. All that William Wilberforce could say to his son Samuel in a letter on the boy's ninth birthday was that he hoped soon 'to see decisive marks of your having begun to undergo the great change'.[7]

Once converted, it might seem that Evangelicals had nothing else to do but sit back and wait for their eternal repose. This was not, however, the case. Although good works played no part in the Evangelical scheme of salvation as such, they were regarded as the only sure evidence of a true conversion. Furthermore, the Evangelicals held that a regenerate man could have no pleasure in anything but striving to please his new Lord. The essential characteristic of the true Christian as opposed to the nominal one, Wilberforce pointed out in the *Practical View*, was that, 'relying on the promises to repenting sinners of acceptance through the Redeemer, they have renounced and abjured all other masters and have cordially and unreservedly devoted themselves to God.'[8] The doctrine of sanctification, or striving gradually to attain behaviour nearer and nearer to that of Christian perfection, was an important part of Evangelical theology. It was reinforced by a nagging fear which the Evangelicals could never entirely escape, and which prevented them from lapsing into complacency and the worst excesses of anti-nomianism, that, to quote Wilberforce again, 'they dare not believe their title sure, except so far as they can discern in themselves the growing trace of this blessed resemblance (to God).'[9]

The doctrines of the depravity of man, the conversion of the sinner, and the sanctification of the regenerate soul represent virtually the sum total of the theology of early nineteenth-century Evangelicalism. It is true that the Evangelicals also held a strong belief in the power of Providence and in the effectiveness of its workings on earth; as Charles Simeon, Vicar of Trinity Church, Cambridge, from 1783 to 1836 and known as 'the Old Apostle of Evangelicalism', told his congregation, 'He is no Christian who does not see the hand of God constantly.'[10] But this was less of a theological doctrine than a vivid sense of the power and imminence of God. Later in the century many Evangelicals took up the doctrine of the Second Coming of Christ and the literal authority of the Bible and in doing so did irreparable harm not only to their own cause but to the credibility of Christianity itself. But neither of these two positions was characteristic of any but a small minority of Evangelicals in the period up to 1860.

Important though its doctrines were, Evangelicalism was never really a theological system so much as a way of life. It did not present itself to its adherents as a logical set of beliefs but rather as a series of vivid and compelling personal experiences. The strongest of these experiences were associated with the anxiety and fear which had first caused the conversion to vital religion: a dread of the terrible power and presence of a Wrathful God; a perpetual sense of accountability for every lapse from the highest standards of Christian behaviour; and an ever-present consciousness of the fall from a state of grace which could so easily occur if an individual failed to live up to his calling – these were the dominant emotions which shaped the lives and determined the characteristics of Evangelical Christians.

Above all else, Evangelicals were obsessed with the judgment which awaited them at death and the account which they would have to give of the way in which they had spent their lives. They regarded their time on earth essentially as a preparation for the Day of Judgment when, as Sir Thomas Dyke Acland, a leading Evangelical who was M.P. for Devon from 1812 to 1857, told his son, they would face 'the awful decision of an all-wise, unerring judge who will require a strict account of every talent, every trust that he has at any time committed to your care – our time, health, strength, abilities and possessions are all included.'[11] Every Evangelical lived out his life in the knowledge that for every single thought and action within it he would be required to make a detailed account at death, and in dread of the terrible consequences which would ensure if this failed to satisfy the Almighty.

This perpetual fear of being found wanting when the Day of Judgment came led the Evangelicals into agonizing sessions of self-examination and soul-searching. Regularly they probed into the innermost recesses of their minds and indulged in an orgy of self-criticism. It was the most introspective feature of a highly introspective religion. Sarah Trimmer, a prominent lady in early nineteenth-century Evangelical circles, retired to her closet for two or three hours each week 'to reflect on the occurrences of the week that was just expired, and to examine into her past conduct and sentiments that she might stand with her lamp burning in her hand ready to obey the summons of her great Lord and Master whenever he should call her'.[12] To assist in the task of self-examination and to chart their spiritual progress nearly all Evangelicals kept diaries which contained detailed accounts of their daily thoughts and actions. These diaries make painful reading. They are almost invariably long – Mrs Sherwood, a celebrated Evangelical tract writer, constructed an autobiography of well over a million words out of the diary she had kept from the day of her conversion – and they are shot through with self-reproach and protestations of unworthiness. Henry Thornton, the famous Evangelical banker around whose home the Clapham Sect formed, opened his diary each year with a detailed enumeration of his faults: 'First, I lie idly in bed often and even generally longer than I need. 2. I am not steady and punctual enough in reading the Scriptures. 3. In my prayers I am idle. 4. In my secret thoughts and imaginations I am far from having learnt self-denial. 5. I am not self denying in my business.'[13] The degree of introspection, even of egotism, shown in such obsessive concern with one's own state may seem distasteful today, but for those who felt they would be held to account for every thought and deed of their lives, it was impossible to avoid.

This sense of accountability gave the Evangelicals a determination not to waste a moment of the time which had been given them on earth. For many years after his conversion in 1786, and whenever in later life he felt himself to be slipping, Wilberforce noted in his diary at the end of every week a precise account of how he had spent the past seven days, listing in tabular form the number of hours devoted to the following occupations: serious devotion; major application – study, serious reading and writing; minor application – study, reading with no great attention, family letters; House of Commons and business; requisite company and visits; dressing; relaxation sua causa and meals – 'the more this head can be reduced the better'; squandered; and bed. Other Evangelicals kept similar accounts of the way they spent their time and endeavoured to cram their days with useful activity. Nearly all of them were early risers. Zachary Macaulay, a leading member of the Clapham Sect and father of the famous Whig politician and historian, rose at 4 a.m. every day after just six hours' sleep and proceeded to get through the equivalent of a day's work on his own correspondence before breakfasting at nine. Edward Bickersteth got up at dawn every morning to a cold bath, breaking the ice with his own hands in cold weather, and by breakfast time had undertaken his private devotions, gone for a walk and heard his children repeat the Scriptures. Lying in late was an unpardonable sin in Evangelical eyes. Wilberforce told his son Samuel that 'there was scarcely anything else equally injurious ... he had seen many instances where from lying in bed late private prayers had been neglected and the soul always suffered in consequence.'[14]

The Evangelicals were determined to make full use of every opportunity given to them in their lives so that when the time came they would be able to give a satisfactory account of their stewardship. The parable of the talents was one of the passages in Scripture they quoted most often. Their time, their opportunities, their influence over others – all these were given to men by God for a purpose and He would require a strict account of how they had been used. At the dreadful judgment seat, a Yorkshire Evangelical clergyman warned his parishioners in the 1830s, 'a man shall not only be called to answer for his own direct violations of the law of his Maker, but he shall be equally responsible for the indirect influence of his conduct and pursuits upon his neighbour.'[15] The Evangelicals' greatest dread was that they would waste their talents and neglect their opportunities of doing good. Their constant aim was to exploit their chances to the full and live to a purpose. After his conversion, Wilberforce resolved not only to draw up an account of how he spent his time, but also to keep a notebook on the character and circumstances of his friends to make his dealings with them more useful. When one of Bickersteth's children asked him if there was anything that she could do for him in the village, he replied 'Yes, my love, all the good thou canst.'[16]

That they might be privileged to live useful lives was the most sincere prayer of all Evangelicals. 'I wish God would give me something to do for Him,' wrote the eminently serious Lady Victoria Buxton at the age of twenty in 1859, 'I feel so useless and not living for a purpose.'[17] The quality of usefulness in a person's life was more highly regarded than any other. David La Touche, an Evangelical banker and M.P. from Dublin, published a series of letters to young men on the subject of Christian Usefulness in which he declared that 'the business of usefulness, in such a world as this, is an undertaking quite of sufficient magnitude and importance to occupy the thoughts, yea the life, of the highest and most intelligent of God's creatures.'[18] When Disraeli died in 1881, the Earl of Shaftesbury remarked to a friend, 'He was a wonderful man in his generation. But was he a useful one?'[19] Such was the criterion by which the Evangelicals judged other men and by which they expected themselves to be judged.

It is not difficult to see why the quality of usefulness appealed so strongly to the Evangelicals. It was only by leading a useful life, filled with good works and application to occupy every minute, that they could hope to escape from the promptings of their restless consciences and the dread of being found wanting. Ceaseless activity provided the only refuge from the horrors of self-examination. Shaftesbury commended it as such in a lecture to the young men of the Bristol Y.M.C.A. in 1861 when he told them that nothing was more likely to keep them from mischief of all kinds, and especially from the mischief of speculation, than to be permanently engaged in some great practical good work. Evangelical Christianity was nothing if not practical and it was its practical aspect, and particularly the intense activity and industry which it inspired in its adherents, that often struck non-Evangelicals most. A colleague of Thomas Fowell Buxton, the Evangelical M.P. who took over from Wilberforce the leadership of the movement to abolish the slave trade, said that he never went into his study without standing rebuked before the mountains of documents which stood on the desk. One of Shaftesbury's characteristics which most impressed his contemporaries was his phenomenal capacity for work which continued well into his old age. Once, in his seventy-sixth year, he chaired meetings for more than nine hours on a single day. For both of these men, as for Mrs Jellyby, the formidable Evangelical female in *Bleak House* who used her meal times to dictate answers to the voluminous correspondence which she daily received about her plans to help the Negroes, this almost obsessive dedication to business and work was an essential aspect of leading a useful life.

Addiction to hard work was not the only feature of the Evangelicals which struck their unregenerate contemporaries. The characteristic which was most commonly commented on was their excessive seriousness. As someone remarked of a conversation with Simeon, 'it partook of the solemnity which one would feel in the presence of a spirit come down from Heaven.'[20] The accusation that they were excessively serious was not one that the Evangelicals themselves wished to refute. For them seriousness was the one unmistakable sign of an Evangelical faith and was, therefore, a quality to be fostered and encouraged. They looked eagerly for signs of seriousness in themselves and in others as sure evidence of a true conversion to vital religion. Although the concept of becoming serious had a certain specifically theological connotation for the Evangelicals, it also involved the assumption of those attributes which their critics felt made them gloomy and solemn.

The seriousness of the Evangelicals was a favourite theme of their opponents. W. M. Thackeray, who detested Evangelicalism, made considerable play of it in his description of Clapham society in the second chapter of *The Newcomes*:

As you entered the gate, gravity fell on you; and decorum wrapped you in a garment of starch. The butcher-boy who galloped his horse and cart madly about the adjoining lanes and common, whistled wild melodies and joked with a hundred cook-maids, on passing that lodge fell into an undertaker's pace, and delivered his joints and sweetbreads silently at the servants' entrance. The rooks in the elms cawed sermons at morning and evening; the peacocks walked demurely on the terraces; the guinea-fowls looked more quaker-like than those savoury birds usually do.

Thackeray's picture of the solemnity of the Clapham Sect was, of course, a grossly exaggerated one. It did, none the less, highlight an aspect of the Evangelicals' behaviour which profoundly disturbed their contemporaries. The friends of Sir Andrew Agnew, a Scottish M.P. who became an Evangelical in the late 1820s, probably came nearest to an accurate definition of Evangelical seriousness when they tried vainly to persuade him not to undergo the great change. It would, they argued, lead to enthusiasm, separation from the world, hyper-sanctity and censoriousness. These four qualities were certainly a feature of the Evangelical character.

It would have been odd if Evangelical seriousness had not embraced a certain degree of religious enthusiasm. The Evangelical Revival was, after all, a protest against the coldness and rationalism of eighteenth-century Christianity and it was only to be expected that its adherents should express their own intense emotions in ways which others found excessive and embarrassing. Those unsympathetic to the Evangelicals made much of what they regarded as their affected sentimentality and histrionic behaviour. In an essay published in 1805 a Baptist minister described the characteristics of Evangelicals as being a 'solemn uplifting of the eyes, artificial impulses of the breath, grotesque and regulated gestures and postures in religious exercises and an affected faltering of the voice'.[21] Charles Dickens gave much the same traits to Mr Chadband, the sanctimonious Evangelical preacher in *Bleak House*. It was true that the Evangelicals often expressed themselves in extremely emotional and dramatic terms which bordered on the fanatical and that their penchant for extempore preaching could lead to wild excesses. But as Rowland Hill, perhaps the greatest preacher of the Evangelical Revival, told one of his open-air congregations, theirs was a dramatic message:

> Because I am in earnest men call me an enthusiast. But I am not; mine are the words of truth and soberness. When I first came into this part of the country, I was walking on yonder hill; I saw a gravel pit fall in, and bury three human beings alive. I lifted my voice for help, so loud, that I was heard in the town

below, at a distance of a mile; help came, and rescued two of the poor sufferers. No one called me an enthusiast then; and when I see eternal destruction ready to fall upon poor sinners, and about to entomb them irrevocably in an eternal mass of woe, and call aloud on them to escape shall I be called an enthusiast now?[22]

Evangelical seriousness also involved a degree of separation from the world. Those who had undergone the 'great change' regarded themselves essentially as pilgrims and strangers on earth, in the world but not of it. Evangelicalism was a puritanical creed, life-denying rather than life-affirming and stressing the negative values of abstinence and self-control rather than the positive values of generosity and altruism. The Evangelicals imposed on themselves a régime of strict self-denial and shunned several apparently innocent worldly amusements. The Reverend Henry Venn, son of the chaplain to the Clapham Sect and himself a leading Evangelical clergyman, had been one of the finest cricketers of his generation at Cambridge. At his ordination in 1820 he gave up the game which he loved, never to play it again, because he felt it did not accord with the gravity of his calling. Visits to the theatre, card games, dancing and even singing were taboo in many Evangelical homes. So too was the reading of fiction: on the rare occasions when they turned from their serious books to lighter works, Evangelicals regretted their weakness. Wilberforce once chided himself for bestowing on Scott's *Heart of Midlothian* some eyesight and time which could have been better employed, while Arthur Young, an Evangelical pamphleteer and agriculturist, noted after reading a novel that 'it has unhinged my mind and broken my attention to better things which shows how strongly pernicious this reading is and what a powerful temptation to vice such productions are sure to prove. Oh the number of miserables that novels have sent to perdition.'[23]

The Evangelicals often seem unnecessarily puritanical in their abstention from worldly pleasures. For some of them the very fact of enjoying something was good enough reason to stop doing it. Sir James Stephen, the son of a member of the Clapham Sect, who became a prominent civil servant in the 1830s, once smoked a cigar and found it so delicious that he never smoked again. Often their efforts to avoid pleasure affected other people as well as themselves.

Wilberforce would not even let up on his rigorous régime of self-denial during his honeymoon and insisted on turning it to serious purpose by taking his bride on a tour of Hannah More's Sunday schools. When he was asked by one of his children why, given his love of the Lake District, he did not buy a house for the family there, he replied coldly 'I should enjoy it as much as anyone, my dear, but we must remember we are not sent into the world merely to admire prospects and enjoy scenery.'[24] The stern régime which the Evangelicals imposed on themselves on the Sabbath, which involved a total prohibition of almost every activity other than church-going and serious reading, applied equally to their families and even to their sweethearts, as Henry Thornton found out when he was careless enough to post the letter in which he proposed marriage to his future wife, Marianne, on a Saturday so that it arrived on Sunday. She dispatched an immediate reply declining his proposal and sharply rebuking him for sending so important a letter on a day when her thoughts ought properly to be far from the concerns of the world. Only on the following Tuesday, after a decent interval had elapsed, did she write accepting the proposal.

There were certain common exceptions to the general rule of self-denial which the Evangelicals imposed on themselves. Unlike most Nonconformists, very few of them were teetotallers. Nor did they shun the pleasure of good food. The stress on the lavishness and frequency of the dinner parties given at Clapham in *The Newcomes* and in Disraeli's unfinished novel, *Falconet*, is not unfair, although, as the latter book points out, these occasions 'generally led to some religious ceremony and were always accompanied by psalmody'. Frances Trollope noted in *The Vicar of Wrexhill* that 'it is a remarkable fact, that the serious Christians of the present age indulge themselves bodily whenever the power of doing so falls their way exactly in proportion to the mortifications and privations with which they torment their spirits.' G. W. E. Russell put it more succinctly: 'Debarred from worldliness, the Evangelicals went in for comfort.'[25]

Self-denying though the Evangelicals were, they were not otherworldly. It is true that their thoughts were fixed ultimately on the solid joys and lasting pleasures of eternity to which they hoped themselves to be journeying rather than on the more transitory concerns of life on earth. But the business which they had to do lay entirely in this world and they could not lead useful Christian lives without participating in it. Evangelicals had no sympathy with those who hid themselves away in the hermitage or the cloister. 'Action is the life of virtue' wrote Hannah More in one of her most influential tracts, 'and the world is the theatre of action. Perhaps some of the most perfect patterns of human conduct may be found in the most public stations, and among the busiest orders of mankind.'[26] Pitt could hardly have been more wide of the mark when he expressed the fear that Wilberforce's conversion to Evangelicalism would lead to a withdrawal from public life and a retreat into seclusion. In fact, few careers have embraced more participation in public causes. Wilberforce himself reflected shortly after his conversion: 'my shame is not occasioned by my thinking that I am too studiously diligent in the business of life; on the contrary, I then feel that I am serving God best when from proper motives I am most actively engaged in it.'[27]

Although they participated so actively in the affairs of the world, the Evangelicals regarded themselves as a group apart from others. The sanctity which Agnew's friends felt that he would fall prey to was a conspicuous feature of Evangelical seriousness. In being so certain of their own salvation, and so deeply pessimistic about the condition of others, the Evangelicals could hardly avoid a certain self-righteousness and spiritual pride. Their sense of being an elect group tended to make them behave as a sect. Evangelicalism had its own special language in which terms such as 'truly religious', 'acceptable', 'gracious' and, of course, 'serious' carried particular meaning. Evangelical terminology could often lead to misunderstandings on the part of those who were not privy to it. Readers of *Bleak House* may remember that Mr Chadband's habit of referring to himself as a vessel caused him to be mistaken by strangers as a gentleman connected with navigation when, in fact, it was an indication of his spiritual capacities. A celebrated passage in *The Pickwick Papers* has Mr Weller in similar difficulties over the doctrine of regeneration that his wife has picked up from Stiggins:

> She's got hold o' some invention for grown-up people being born again, Sammy; the new birth, I think they calls it. I should very much like to see that system in haction, Sammy. I should very much like to see your mother-in-law born again. Wouldn't I put her out to nurse! (Chapter XXII)

The Evangelicals were concerned to preserve themselves from being tainted by too much contact with those who had not yet undergone satisfactory conversions. The refusal of the Evangelical attorney, Mr Corbold, to travel in the same coach as the unregenerate, and the advertisement placed by the Revd Mr Cartwright for 'a serious footman' which occur in the *Vicar of Wrexhill* were by no means far-fetched examples of this. An Evangelical periodical, the *Record*, regularly contained advertisements calling for household servants of serious disposition and Evangelical sentiments. Sir George Gilbert Scott, the great Victorian architect whose father and grandfather were Evangelical clergymen, remembered in his youth visiting a boarding house which 'had a preference for those of the Evangelical party, and a still more particular preference for missionaries'.[28] While he was at school at Charterhouse, Henry Havelock insisted on sharing a dormitory only with serious boys like himself who were accustomed to reading religious books. In 1823 the Evangelical clergy founded a special school for their own daughters at Cowan Bridge in Yorkshire to ensure that their offspring should not be contaminated by contact with the unregenerate. The sentiment which was uttered by Mrs Falconet when it was suggested that her son Joseph might lodge at a club when he went to work in London was one that must have been echoed by many Evangelical parents. 'We had hoped', she said, 'that Joseph might have found an abode with some *serious* family.'

Together with the Evangelicals' determination not to mix too much with unregenerate members of the population went a certain censoriousness in their attitude towards them. Readiness to reprove any defect which one might observe in others was one of the hallmarks of true Evangelical seriousness. This was an understandable tendency on the part of those who were so used to searching out their own failings; it must at least have been a welcome change to find fault with others. The Evangelicals were fearless in their censure of the behaviour of others. When Zachary Macaulay met a young lady whose ostentatious clothes he took as 'striking marks of a vain mind' he had a conversation with her the tone of which may be guessed from the fact that, as he subsequently recorded, she discarded 'her monstrous, mis-shapen dress, and reverted to the use of plain and simple attire, and her lowly looks were, I hope, no fallacious indication of a humbled mind'.[29] The woman who rushed out on a Sunday to buy tea and sugar when she heard that Hannah More and her sister Martha would be calling received no thanks from her visitors but only a sharp lecture from Martha on the probability that in profaning the Sabbath she had endangered the eternal prospects of all three of them. When William IV invited Sir George Sinclair, an Evangelical M.P., to dinner on a Sunday in January 1832 he not only had the invitation returned, but for the next few weeks he received a series of letters and addresses instructing him on the importance of observing the Sabbath.

It is, at first sight, difficult to see how a movement with the characteristics of Evangelicalism could have had a major influence on society at large. It was hardly calculated to appeal to any more than a few religious zealots let alone to change the prevailing attitudes and customs of the entire population. Yet this is precisely what it did. In part the Evangelicals' success is to be explained by their own drive and determination. A group of people so determined to fill every moment of their lives with useful activity and to seize every opportunity which came to them could hardly fail to make some impression on their contemporaries, if only because their behaviour contrasted so strongly with the indolence and apathy of the majority. The Evangelicals were all out to make an impact. The great object in life which Frances Trollope attributed to the Vicar of Wrexhill, 'to touch, to influence, to lead, to rule, to tyrannise over the hearts and souls of all he approaches', represents a fair summary of the Evangelicals' purpose which was nothing less than a frontal assault on virtually every prevailing assumption and habit of their time and their replacement by the principles and practices of vital Christianity. Labouring under an intense sense of mission, they believed that their task was to call their fellow men to seriousness. It was to this end that they bombarded their contemporaries with sermons and tracts, set about attacking all those influences in the world which they believed to be evil, and consciously lived out their own lives as examples to be followed.

The fact that so much of their message got home and that they did make a substantial impact on their contemporaries the Evangelicals themselves attributed to the workings of Providence. In our sceptical age, we would probably prefer to look for an explanation in terms of social and psychological factors. To a large extent, Evangelical principles and practices triumphed and came to be adopted generally in nineteenth-century England because they answered directly to the existing fears and aspirations of the age and fitted the demands of a rapidly developing and increasingly complex industrial society. The success which the Evangelicals had in propagating their ideas depended much on purely secular factors. This was especially true in respect of their first and most urgent task, the conversion of their fellow countrymen to vital religion.

2

Converting the Nation

An early historian of the Evangelical Revival observed that during the eighteenth century the great mass of Englishmen had been unmoved by the power of Christianity. It was, of course, an exaggerated claim, but one not wholly without foundation. The practices of daily Bible reading and of regular attendance at public worship which had formerly been customary among many Englishmen declined markedly during the eighteenth century, and several churches closed down altogether in the face of dwindling or even non-existent congregations. The Evangelicals were determined to reverse this trend and to ensure that no such remark would be made by historians about their own age. The conversion of their fellow countrymen was their first and foremost aim, inspired both by a horror of the fate which awaited those who failed to heed the call to vital religion during their time on earth, and by a fear that they themselves might be found wanting when they came before the judgment seat, if they had failed to extend their own saving faith to others. To the task of converting the nation to vital religion the Evangelicals directed their energies and talents.

The Evangelicals were prepared to try anything if there was some chance that it might lead to a soul being saved. Lady Olivia Sparrow, an aristocratic confidante of Wilberforce, regularly spent her holidays on the French Riviera in an effort to convert the Jewish and Catholic population there. Annabella Milbanke, the pious niece of Lady Melbourne, actually went as far as accepting Lord Byron's proposal of marriage in 1812 and remained with him for a year although she did not love him in the hope that by doing so she might be able to enlist him to the ranks of the regenerate. Wilberforce, who was an acknowledged expert in the art of conversion, prepared 'launchers', or carefully arranged topics which would turn conversation insensibly towards the subject of religion, for use at dinner parties and other social occasions. No opportunity of putting across the saving message of vital religion was missed by the Evangelicals. Many carried tracts around with them which they deposited at strategic points on their travels. When the railway was being built through East Kent in the 1840s local Evangelicals appointed a scripture reader to minister to the navvies. The tremendous potential of the Great Exhibition of 1851 as a mission ground was early appreciated by Lord Shaftesbury and others: visitors to the Crystal Palace found themselves accosted by missionaries and tract distributors in the grounds and confronted by a large Bible depot which had been erected next to the Exhibition Hall.

Securing the conversion of royalty had a special appeal to the Evangelicals. They believed that it would have an important influence on the community as a whole, quite apart from its effects on the converted monarchs themselves. George III, with his rigorous standard of morality and his famous statement that nothing gave him more pleasure than to think of every cottager in England earnestly reading his Bible, was as pious and serious as the Evangelicals themselves and they regarded him as an ally in their great work of converting the nation. But, despite his efforts to propel his eldest son in a godly direction as a child, or perhaps because of them, George IV proved resistant to all attempts to save his soul. This was certainly not for want of trying on the Evangelicals' part. George IV's private chaplain, the Revd Charles Sumner, was a strong exponent of the principles of vital religion. He had managed to infiltrate the royal closet through the good offices of Lady Conyngham, one of George's mistresses, whose son he had saved from an unsuitable match by marrying the girl in question himself. While Prince Regent, George had been the subject of a major conversion attempt by Wilberforce who wintered in Brighton in 1815 for the purpose. On their first encounter, the Prince recalled that they had first met each other at the Duchess of Devonshire's ball in Wilberforce's unregenerate days when he had entertained the company in song. 'We are both I trust much altered since, sir', came the stiff reply. The Prince immediately retorted, 'Yes, the time which has gone by must have made a great alteration in us'. 'Something better than that too, I trust, sir', the relentless Wilberforce continued.[1] George concluded the conversation by asking Wilberforce to dine, adding a hasty assurance that he would hear nothing at his table that would give him offence. The invitation was accepted but did not lead to any perceptible change in the Prince's spiritual condition.

William IV proved as indifferent to the compelling claims of vital religion as his elder brother. Not so their younger brother, Edward, the Duke of Kent, and the father of Queen Victoria. Both he and his wife were strong Evangelicals and were determined to bring their daughter up in the same faith. The tutor chosen for Victoria was an Evangelical clergyman, the Revd George Davys, who afterwards became Bishop of Peterborough. In 1833 a tourist in the Isle of Wight came across the Princess, then aged fourteen, reading to her mother *The Dairyman's Daughter*, a popular Evangelical tract about a short but pious life written by the Revd Leigh Richmond, who had been her father's chaplain. She was seated on the grave of the young girl on whose life the story was based. Victoria never described herself as an Evangelical when she was Queen; to do so in the violently partisan religious climate which existed through most of her reign would have been the height of folly. But there was no doubt that in in her deep attachment to the Bible, her preference for plain unadorned services and fervent preaching and her own intense seriousness of mind, she inclined strongly towards Evangelicalism. Lady Barham, who had felt qualms at becoming a lady of the bedchamber in 1837 because she feared that she might be asked to take part in activities of which she disapproved, such as dancing or theatrical entertainments, was never once in her thirty-six years in the Queen's service to witness anything which offended her Evangelical conscience. On one occasion only did she feel it necessary to speak to the Queen on the subject of her insufficient seriousness, and that was when the Royal Family were intending to travel from Crewe to London on a Sunday. As a result of her protest, Victoria postponed the journey until Monday.

Next in importance to royalty the Evangelicals rated the conversion of the aristocracy. Winning the high-born to the cause of Christ had a strong appeal for them, apart from its intrinsic merits; they felt that it would influence those of lowlier station who took their cue in matters of attitude and behaviour from their betters. The Evangelicals believed that they had a special mission towards the upper classes in the same way that John Wesley had felt a particular call to awaken the hearts of the people. Since Methodist preachers had concentrated largely on ministering to the lower classes, the aristocracy remained virtually untouched by the Evangelical Revival at the end of the eighteenth century. This state of affairs led the Evangelicals to direct their efforts especially to evangelizing the upper classes. It was significant that two of their most important treatises were addressed to this section of the population. Wilberforce's *Practical View* dealt exclusively, as its full title made clear, with the prevailing religious beliefs of the higher and middle classes of the country. So did one of Hannah More's most influential books, *An Estimate of the Religion of the Fashionable World*, which appeared in 1790. Both works attacked the comfortable and undemanding religious ethic which prevailed in aristocratic circles in the eighteenth century and called for its replacement by the rigorous creed of vital religion.

The call did not go unheeded: by the middle of the nineteenth century there cannot have been more than a hundred or so upper-class families in which one member at least had not been converted to Evangelical Christianity. Contemporary observers noted with amazement the spectacular effects of its progress through the aristocracy. Church-going became fashionable. As early as 1798 the *Annual Register* had noted the novelty of seeing the avenues of churches thronged with carriages. In 1851 the national census on religion reported that both the middle and upper classes had vastly increased their attendance at services and that 'a regular church attendance is now ranked among the recognized proprieties of life.'[2] Private patronage of the arts and attendance at race meetings declined markedly as the interest of the aristocracy moved to more serious subjects. In 1824 a visitor to the home of Lord Derby, who had formerly been a noted patron of the turf and champion billiard player, reported that 'many hours were spent in Lady Derby's sitting room, in scriptural investigation.'[3] Towards the end of his life, in the 1840s, the society wit, Henry Luttrell, made a tour of the country houses of England and told his friends on his return that he had been quite put out by the theological talk that prevailed in every one of them. Perhaps the surest evidence of the progress of

Evangelicalism among the aristocracy came in the increasing custom of having family prayers in nearly every middle- and upper-class household in the first half of the nineteenth century. The Lord Lieutenant of one of the Midland shires commented to Lord Stanhope in 1850 that whereas when he came of age there had only been two landed gentlemen in the county who had family prayers, now there were only two who did not.

One of the more striking consequences of this transformation in the lives and habits of the English upper classes was that the older generation began to complain about the seriousness of the younger, and children to censure their parents for frivolity. This reversal of the usual battle between the generations disturbed the harmony of several families in the early nineteenth century. The Sixth Earl of Shaftesbury, who was a hard-drinking and haughty relic of the generation of Squire Western, was perplexed and disturbed by his son's sombreness and religious enthusiasm. He would have been even more annoyed had he known that when his son inherited the family estate in 1851 he would order the tap room to be closed at 9 p.m. and hire Scripture readers for each of the estate villages. Sometimes Evangelical children seem even to have effected the conversion of their parents. The biographer of Edward Bickersteth noted that at the time of his childhood 'both parents were ignorant of those deep truths of the gospel, which their own children were afterwards the means of bringing before them: his mother joined without fear the amusements of the ball-room and the card table and even sent her son to dancing classes.'[4]

The particularly high incidence of Evangelicalism among the children of upper- and middle-class families in the early nineteenth century provides a clue to identifying two of the main agencies through which vital religion seems to have spread in these circles. These were the nursery and the Universities. Non-Evangelicals did not have the same scruples about the beliefs of those employed in their households that Evangelicals had, and a considerable number of serious young ladies managed to find their way into the nurseries of unregenerate homes from where they set about converting their young charges. Shaftesbury owed his first experience of vital religion, in what one of his contemporaries euphemistically referred to as 'a difficult environment', to the teaching and influence of his nursemaid. So, in their middle-class homes, did Harriet Martineau and George Eliot. Those who escaped Evangelical influence in the nursery were quite likely to encounter it if they went up to university. Cambridge was renowned for its Evangelical leanings throughout Simeon's time at Trinity Church and for long afterwards. Unsuspecting freshmen were liable to find themselves lured by the promise of tea and cakes to the rooms of the 'Sims' who were eager for their souls. Samuel Butler's description of Mrs Cowey, the wife of a Cambridge Professor, in *The Way of All Flesh*, was based on his own memories of the Evangelical types he had himself encountered when he went up to St John's College in 1855:

> She was what was called a truly spiritually minded woman, a trifle portly, with an incipient beard, and an extensive connection among undergraduates, more especially among those who were inclined to take part in the great evangelical movement which was then at its height. She gave evening parties once a fortnight at which prayers were part of the entertainment. (Chapter IX)

That any undergraduates were actually converted by the likes of Mrs Cowey seems unlikely. But the influence of Evangelical tutors could be decisive in turning young minds to seriousness. Granville Ryder, the son of the First Earl of Harrowby, seems to have owed his conversion to vital religion around 1850 at least partly to Henry Venn Elliott, his Evangelical tutor at Cambridge, although the latter had plenty to work on as the boy came up to University obsessed with gloom about his eternal prospects and already in a highly serious state. At Oxford, St Edmund Hall became a breeding ground of serious young men at the beginning of the nineteenth century under a succession of Evangelical Vice-Principals and much to the dismay of some of the older fellows who sighed for the days when undergraduates preferred port and whist. Among those who graduated from St Edmund Hall in this period were Daniel Wilson, himself later a Vice-Principal of the college and subsequently Bishop of Calcutta, and Josiah Pratt, a future secretary of the Church Missionary Society. The motives of those undergraduates who attended the evening parties of John Hill, Vice-Principal of the College from 1812 to 1851, were not, however, altogether serious. One of them later recalled that although the parties were made up of 'tea and coffee, pietistic Low Church talk, prayer and hymnody of portentous length, they were yet palliated by the chance of sharing Bible or hymn-book with one of the host's four charming daughters.'[5]

The most important agents in the spread of Evangelical religion among the upper classes seem, however, to have been the female members of their families. It was nearly always through wives and daughters that seriousness was introduced into aristocratic households. At the time of Queen Victoria's succession at least twenty noble houses had Evangelical ladies at their head. They included some doughty fighters for the cause of vital religion. Lady Spencer had installed Sarah Trimmer as governess at Devonshire House at the beginning of the nineteenth century and so ensured an Evangelical upbringing for her two daughters, one of whom later became the Duchess of Devonshire and the other Lady Bessborough. Lady Caroline Lamb also came under Mrs Trimmer's tutelage. The Duchess of Gordon introduced morning prayers at Gordon Castle in the early 1830s and finally persuaded her reluctant husband to attend and sometimes even to lead them. The Duchess of Beaufort succeeded in bringing up all her eight daughters as strong Evangelicals, with the result that several of them later converted their husbands. She herself tried hard but unsuccessfully to win over to the ranks of the regenerate the unpromising figure of Charles Greville, the worldly diarist and wit, whom she forced into reading the whole of Thomas Chalmers' lectures on the Book of Romans in 1842.

The most determined attempt of all to introduce seriousness into an aristocratic household in the early nineteenth century was made by Emma Parnell, who married the Fifth Earl of Darnley in 1827. Like that other formidable female among the Evangelical aristocracy, Lady Olivia Sparrow, Lady Darnley was a product of the Irish Evangelical Revival which was, as might be expected, even more fanatical and puritanical than its English counterpart. On her arrival at the Darnley family seat at Cobham Hall in Kent she set about the business of converting her husband and family. When the Earl gave a party at the house to mark the seventy-second birthday of the distinguished actress, Sarah Siddons, which included the recitation of scenes from Shakespeare, she marched him out of the room and refused to let him return until he called off the entertainment. Subsequently she brought about a total transformation of life at Cobham Hall, putting an end to house parties and stopping the purchase of any more works of art, and reduced her husband to a nervous wreck. The effect which she had on her son, who succeeded to the title in 1835, was even more devastating. So influenced was he by his mother's puritanism that he destroyed some of the finest paintings in the house because of their indecent exposure of the human form, and so terrified by her warnings about Divine Judgment that he read the Bible even while shaving.

Vital religion did not make the same spectacular headway in the lower echelons of society in the early nineteenth century as it did at the top. Many working-class families remained untouched by its influence. It was they who made up the bulk of the fifty per cent of the population of the country who did not attend any church or chapel on the Sunday in 1851 when a national census was taken of all worshippers. The figures in the census have to be interpreted with some care as it counted attenders at morning, afternoon and evening services without distinguishing how many of them were present at more than one of these occasions, but historians are generally agreed that they show that roughly nine million people, about half the total population, attended a place of worship on Census Sunday. This total indicates, of course, that a considerable number of the working classes were practising Christians but other statistics in the census show that many more of them had been won by the Nonconformists than by the Anglican Evangelicals. The Evangelicals lacked preachers with the appeal to the masses that Wesley had had in the eighteenth century and C. H. Spurgeon was to have in the later Victorian period. The nearest rival that they had to these charismatic figures was probably the Revd Rowland Hill, whose preaching career spanned a spectacular sixty-six years between 1766 and 1832 and who secured many conversions among the poor. But although they were less well-equipped for it than the Methodists, the Evangelicals were by no means indifferent to the task of converting the working classes. The flood of tracts which they poured out to this end and the missions which they established in cities and slums were among the most enduring features of their legacy to the Victorians.

The main weapon in the Evangelicals' assault on the souls of the lower orders was the cheap tract or broadsheet. This simple device, destined to become the greatest single medium of mass communication in the nineteenth century, owed its origin to the determination of Hannah More to counter the dissemination of atheist and radical views in the aftermath of the French Revolution. Noting that 'the appetite for reading had been increasing among the inferior ranks in this country,' she informed the readers of her *Tales To The Common People* in 1819, she had judged it expedient, 'at this critical period, to supply such wholesome aliment as might give a new direction to their taste, and abate their relish for those corrupt and inflammatory publications which the consequences of the French Revolution have been so fatally pouring in upon us.'[6] In letters to serious friends, she expanded on her design: 'It has occurred to me to write a variety of things, somewhere between vicious papers and hymns, for it is in vain to write what people will not read ... I propose printing striking conversions, Holy Lives, Happy Deaths, Providential Deliverances, Judgments on the Breakers of Commandments etc.'[7] On March 3rd, 1795, she published the first of her *Cheap Repository Tracts*. These continued to appear at the rate of three a month and by the end of its first full year of operation, the association which had been set up to distribute them, with Henry Thornton as its Treasurer, had sold over two million tracts. Other Evangelicals soon moved in on the tract-writing business. In 1800 Rowland Hill embarked on a series of *Village Dialogues* and Leigh Richmond followed with *Annals of the Poor*. A year earlier, on the initiative of an Evangelical clergyman in Coventry, a national society was founded for the purpose of putting improving literature into the hands of the people. When it celebrated its fiftieth anniversary in 1849, the Religious Tract Society had circulated over 500 million copies of 5,000 separate titles and was issuing tracts from its central depository at the rate of 20 million a year.

The gigantic operation involved in the publication of these tracts was the first exercise ever undertaken in England which involved the mass production and distribution of reading matter. The techniques which the Evangelicals pioneered were later adopted by other groups who were interested in purveying cheap literature to the masses, like the Society for the Diffusion of Useful Knowledge. Their method of ensuring a wide circulation for the tracts was simple: the Evangelicals took over the extensive distribution network already provided by the hawkers of obscene ballads by paying them more than they were getting previously. The extremely high sales figures achieved for the tracts, which normally retailed at a penny each, suggest that this system worked well. It was supplemented by the activities of vendors employed by the tract-distributing societies and by the voluntary efforts of Evangelicals themselves, who, if they did not have the same experience in high-pressure salesmanship as the hawkers, were at least more committed to the spiritual interests of their potential buyers. Sometimes particularly altruistic Evangelicals bought up large supplies of tracts and distributed them free to all whom they met on their travels.

It is impossible to say how many people were converted by the Evangelicals' tracts. Their dramatic content, with sudden deaths and miraculous deliverances looming large, and their bold and simple message cannot but have made a considerable impression on those many newly literate people for whom the tracts must have provided almost their first encounter with the printed word. Two of the publications of the Religious Tract Society which put across the central Evangelical themes of redemption and conversion in a particularly direct and forceful way, *The Sinner's Friend* and *The Swearer's Plea*, both achieved a circulation of over one and a half million. The most popular of all the Evangelical tracts, Leigh Richmond's highly sentimental account of a young girl's death of consumption, *The Dairyman's Daughter*, sold a total of four million copies and was cited by many Evangelicals as having been instrumental in their conversion. The Religious Tract Society confidently proclaimed in 1849 that, as a result of its activities, 'sinners have been converted to God; Christians edified and comforted; backsliders mercifully restored; and numerous evils prevented by timely admonitions.'[8]

As well as through tracts, the Evangelicals tried to win the souls of the masses by establishing schools for them and their children. In an age when there was no state-provided education and when those of the poorer classes who wanted to become literate had to throw themselves on the mercies of the local Dame's School or the inadequate resources of the charity schools, this was a shrewd move. Once again, Hannah More was in the van of it. When Wilberforce made a day's excursion to the Cheddar Gorge in 1789 he told her that while he found the scenery delightful the spiritual degradation of the inhabitants had appalled him. The redoubtable Miss More needed no further encouragement to embark on the redemption of the people among whom she had recently come to live. By the turn of the century she and her sisters had set up over a dozen day schools and Sunday schools for adults and children in the villages of the Mendips, an area where there had hitherto been no educational provision for the poor. The Mendip schools became a model for the development of voluntary schools throughout the country. Other Evangelical ladies quickly followed the More sisters' lead. Within a few years Mrs Trimmer had established schools at Brentford and Lady Spencer had set up Sunday schools and adult classes at St Albans.

The Sunday school was the most successful of the agencies which the Evangelicals devised to convert the working classes. It was very largely their own invention, although Nonconformists were also active in the early days of the movement. Two specific factors inspired the Evangelicals to establish Sunday schools: the work discipline imposed by the Industrial Revolution which made Sunday the only day when those who laboured in the factories and mines were free to improve their minds and souls, and their own concern to make the Sabbath a day of serious study and not of play for the people. It was because he was shocked by seeing children playing on Sundays in the streets of Gloucester in 1780 that Robert Raikes, the Evangelical newspaper proprietor who is generally credited with being the founder of the Sunday school movement, engaged four women to hold a weekly class to instruct children in reading the Bible and saying the catechism. There were, in fact, Sunday schools established before Raikes' but he was the first man to publicize the system through articles in his own *Gloucester Journal* and in the *Gentleman's Magazine*. Before the end of the eighteenth century there were at least two Sunday schools in London, the first started by Rowland Hill in his chapel in Blackfriars Road and the second by a shoemaker who had walked to Gloucester and back to talk to Raikes about his plans. In 1785 a Sunday School Society was set up, again with Henry Thornton as Treasurer, and in 1820 it estimated that there were well over 5,000 schools in the country with nearly 500,000 pupils. The number steadily rose until by the end of the nineteenth century it was calculated that three quarters of all those aged between five and fifteen in England attended Sunday schools. This figure, of course, included those at Catholic, Anglican and Nonconformist schools but it is none the less a powerful testimony to the success of an Evangelical invention.

The effect of the schools and adult classes started by the Evangelicals, and especially of the Sunday schools, in raising the general level of literacy and culture of the English working classes in the nineteenth century was immeasurable. But for those who established them this was of purely secondary importance. The Evangelicals had only one aim in mind in setting up schools for the poor, and that was the conversion of their souls. This was why Hannah More taught reading but not writing in her Mendip classes; the former skill was relevant to the business of salvation, the latter was not. 'The grand object of instruction', she told a friend, 'is the Bible itself ... the great thing is to get it faithfully explained, in such a way as shall be likely to touch the heart and influence the conduct.'[9] In similar vein a manual of hints on establishing Sunday schools published in 1835 urged:

> Let all your instructions have some reference to religious improvement ... It is highly desirable to procure serious persons, if possible, as teachers ... those who have been called by Divine grace in early life will, in general, be found best qualified for addressing young people on the concerns of their souls; they feel peculiarly interested in youth and the ardour of their own feelings leads them to engage in the service with delight and energy.[10]

Delight the teachers may have had, but one suspects that for those pupils who had to endure the five and a half hours of instruction which was recommended on their one free day of the week it was the seriousness of Sunday school which came across more strongly.

The large concentrations of working people to be found in cities and manufacturing areas demanded special attention from the Evangelicals. In London particularly they set up special missions and schools in an effort to reach slum dwellers and down-and-outs. Individual Evangelicals were active throughout the nineteenth century in evangelizing particular groups in the metropolis. In 1819 the Revd George Smith began a lifetime's work with sailors by establishing a mission to seamen in the Port of London and setting up a floating chapel on a sloop in the Thames. W. J. Orsman, a civil servant, decided in 1861 to devote his leisure time to the task of evangelizing the costermongers and street traders of East London. Others concentrated on the watercress girls, the young matchsellers and the wretched crossing sweepers. In 1835 Anglican Evangelicals and Nonconformists joined together to establish the London City Mission. The declared object of the Mission, which had T. F. Buxton as its first treasurer and the Revd Baptist Noel as its chairman, was 'to extend the knowledge of the Gospel among the inhabitants of London and its vicinity – especially the poor – without any reference to denominational distinctions, or the peculiarities of Church Government', and its immediate aim was to supply every poor family in the capital with a Bible. By 1837 it had 64 paid missionaries, all laymen, working in the roughest parts of the city, regularly visiting gin palaces and public houses, making nightly tours of railway termini and all-night coffee stalls, and even evangelizing the pathetic creatures who scavenged on the refuse tips. Special missionaries were attached to each division of the Metropolitan Police and spent most of their time with drunkards, thieves and pickpockets. Two missionaries worked with the construction gangs employed on building the Crystal Palace and managed to dispose of 10,000 tracts in one month alone. When the Great Exhibition opened in May 1851 they were joined by another six evangelists who were instructed to 'do good by every means in their power to the people approaching and leaving its attractive display'.[11]

The most successful of the agencies established by the Evangelicals in their efforts to convert the urban poor were almost certainly the ragged schools. These were set up in the slum areas of large cities – a notice on a large building which proclaims it to be the Sharp Street Ragged School is still visible today on the approach to Manchester by rail from Leeds – to provide simple instruction in the Bible for those children who were turned away from more genteel day and Sunday schools on account of their filthy appearance and extreme poverty. Ragged schools were held wherever shelter could be found, in old storerooms, barns and covered railway arches, and functioned during the day for children and at night for adults. In 1844 a Ragged School Union was formed to co-ordinate the efforts of individual schools and by 1850 there were over a hundred ragged schools in the country, regularly attended by more than 100,000 children and by thousands of adults from the lowest and most wretched class in the community. 'I could tell you some wonderful stories of these rescued lives', the Earl of Shaftesbury told his biographer Edwin Hodder, alluding to the hopeless drunkards and thieves reclaimed and turned to vital religion, and often to missionary work among their own kind, by the ragged schools. As well as being the first President of the Ragged Schools Union, Shaftesbury was an active worker in the schools themselves and spent many evenings in the poorest quarters of London preaching the gospel. The vigour and emotion of his preaching seem to have won through the considerable barrier which separated the titled representative of one of the leading families of the land from the down-and-outs of the city slums. This is certainly the impression one gets from the description which Shaftesbury gave to Hodder of a magic lantern show on the subject of the Crucifixion which he gave to a group of over 400 vagrants in a ragged school in East London:

> The last picture represented our Lord standing beside a closed door, and the text at the foot of the picture was, 'Behold I stand at the door and knock'. The effect was startling – it seemed to bring the whole story home to every heart, and when I said 'What you see there, is going on at the door of every house in Whitechapel', they were moved to tears (and the eyes of the old Earl filled and his voice faltered as the scene came back to him again). It was a revelation to them, and when I told them that, if they would throw open the door, 'He would come and sup with them', there was something so cosy and comfortable to them in the idea of it that they came pouring round me and thanking me.[12]

The Earl of Shaftesbury was closely connected with another venture established in the early Victorian period in an effort to convert the working classes in the large cities. His diary for February 26th, 1846 records that he 'took chair at Young Men's Christian Association. Four hundred persons to tea, a very striking scene – young shopmen, with their mothers and sisters, attending really in a religious spirit.'[13] The Y.M.C.A. had been established two years earlier as 'a society which should have for its object the arousing of converted men in the different drapery establishments in the metropolis to a sense of their obligation and responsibility as

Christians in diffusing religious knowledge to those around them'.[14] With its sister foundation, the Young Women's Christian Association, founded in 1855, it came to be one of the most important agencies in spreading the principles and practices of evangelical religion among young people in Victorian England. It has, of course, survived to the present day. The Y.M.C.A.'s chief promoters in its early days were mostly Nonconformists, but it received valuable support from Anglican Evangelicals, notably, apart from Shaftesbury, Canon J. W. Reeve, who later became one of Queen Victoria's chaplains, and the First Earl of Cairns, who was to be Lord Chancellor in Disraeli's administration.

As in the case of the upper classes, the most active agents in the conversion of the working classes to vital religion seem to have been females. Most of the teachers in Sunday schools and ragged schools were women. Shaftesbury was alarmed to find a young woman in her mid-twenties in charge of a class of men in a ragged school in a particularly rough area of London, but the Superintendent told him that what worried him was not that they would molest her but 'that some day a man might drop in who, not knowing the habits of this place, might lift a finger against her, for if he did so, he would never leave the room alive.'[15] The Scripture readers and district visitors appointed by Evangelical clergymen to evangelize working-class areas of their parishes were generally female and it was entirely female initiative which lay behind the institution in the late 1850s of a group which was to make a vital contribution to the Evangelical mission to the poorer classes in the later nineteenth century, the Bible Women. One wet evening in 1856 an orphan girl named Marion, who eked out a meagre living by cutting fire papers and moulding wax flowers, took shelter in the doorway of a London mission hall. She went inside and, being given a Bible, she asked if she might go round the poorest areas of the capital and distribute the book there. Her offer was taken up by the British and Foreign Bible Society which paid her ten shillings a week to do this work in the Seven Dials area. Marion was soon joined by other women and by the late 1860s there was an extensive and highly organized network of Bible women going round the poorest areas of London and collecting a penny a week from those inhabitants who could be persuaded to buy a Bible for a shilling. Like many of the Sunday school and ragged school teachers and the district visitors, the Bible

Women were from the same social class as those with whom they worked. Middle-class ladies read the Bible to the sick and the elderly in the better areas of towns and in the countryside, encouraged by the example of Queen Victoria who was often to be found reading the Scriptures at the homes of those who lived on the royal estates.

Three Evangelical women devoted themselves with particular success to converting the working classes in the latter half of the nineteenth century. In 1862 Mrs Louisa Daniell established a mission to the soldiers stationed at Aldershot camp which provided them with recreation rooms and good hot dinners as well as suitable reading matter and Bible classes. Later she set up similar missions at other military bases in the country, so consolidating the pioneering work which had already been done by Evangelical officers in the 1850s in establishing an Army Prayer Union and Scripture Readers Society. Josephine Butler, famous for her work among prostitutes in the 1860s, secured the conversion of several of the girls whom she encountered on her tours round brothels. Sometimes she took girls into her own home, as with the nineteen-year-old prostitute whom she found lying in a Liverpool street having been thrown out of a brothel when she was discovered to be spitting blood. When the girl died three months later, having been converted to vital Christianity, Mrs Butler filled her coffin with white camellias as a symbol of purity. Perhaps most successful of all was Catharine Marsh, who worked among railway navvies and labourers in the 1840s and 1850s and who arranged for the Archbishop of Canterbury to confirm five workers employed on the building of the Crystal Palace whose conversion she had secured. In 1858 she wrote a best-selling book on her experiences, *English Hearts and English Hands*, which strongly criticized the indifference with which the upper classes regarded the moral and spiritual state of their inferiors and argued that the soul of every man, however vicious and depraved he might seem, was ultimately redeemable. The book probably inspired many of the efforts made to evangelize the working classes in the later nineteenth century. It ended with a plea to the privileged classes:

When navvies, or any other labourers either in fields or factories are within your reach, meet them with a frank and genial friendliness. Alleviate their discomforts as far as lies in your power. Provide some little innocent pleasure – a tea party for instance – from time to time, for their hard worked existence. Above all, seek to secure to them their Sabbaths; and hold forth to them the Word of Life. Give them Bibles or Testaments; and if the navvy's name be written therein, with a few words of friendly dedication, he will starve rather than part with it at any price.[16]

Catharine Marsh's confident belief that once he had been given a cup of tea and a Bible the conversion of the English working man was assured for all time was of course wildly over-optimistic. Thousands of members of the working classes remained unmoved by the saving message of Christianity when it was urged on them by missionaries and tracts, and many thousands more escaped it altogether. Yet there is no denying the tremendous impact which Evangelicalism, along with Nonconformity, had on the outlook and the condition of the English lower classes in the first half of the nineteenth century. Among the rural poor it had helped to achieve the transformation in life-style which Hannah More triumphantly reported to the female friendly society in one of her Mendip villages:

Where are the half-naked, poor, forlorn, wretched, ignorant creatures we used to find lying about on a Sunday upon this hill, swearing, gaming, reprobates, vagabonds, flying as it were in the face of the Almighty, a disgrace to their parents, a scandal to their country, a dishonour to their God, a prey to the devil – where are they now to be found? At school, at prayer, at church – serving the Lord, keeping his Commandments.[17]

In the towns and cities the ragged schools and the specialized missions had provided massive educational opportunities for factory workers and slum dwellers and had helped to raise their moral and intellectual condition. The Evangelicals may not have succeeded in their aim of converting the whole population of nineteenth-century England to vital Christianity, but at least they made a very brave try at it. The *Edinburgh Review* was generally a strong critic of the Evangelicals but when in 1853 it reviewed their activities over the past half-century it could not help but concede that 'they have not hesitated to preach in filthy courts and alleys, the haunts of vice and infamy to audiences which could not be tempted to listen under any roof but the sky' and conclude that it was chiefly thanks to their efforts 'that the profound darkness in which the English peasantry were enveloped at the beginning of the century has been gradually dissipated.'[18]

It was neither among the aristocracy nor the masses that Evangelicalism made greatest headway, however, but rather among the middle classes. Vital religion seemed to hold a particularly strong attraction for civil servants, officers in the Armed Services, bankers, merchants and members of the professions. The towns which were known as centres of Evangelicalism in the early years of Victoria's reign – Cheltenham, Bath, Tunbridge Wells, Hastings and York – were significantly middle-class strongholds. Most of the leading figures of the Evangelical Revival had solid bourgeois origins. Wilberforce's father had made his money out of the Baltic trade and his fellow 'Saints' in the Clapham Sect included three bankers (Henry Thornton and the brothers Samuel and Abel Smith), an East India Merchant (Charles Grant), a Chancery lawyer (James Stephen), a Company secretary (Zachary Macaulay), a naval officer turned civil servant (Sir Charles Middleton, later the First Lord Barham) and the head of a brewing firm (T. F. Buxton). Hannah More and Charles Simeon were from middle-class backgrounds; so were Bickersteth and Venn. Part of the reason why Evangelicalism did well among the middle classes was that many of them were already nominally Christian and therefore at least half-way towards a regenerate state. The call to seriousness which Evangelical pamphleteers had delivered to their countrymen at the beginning of the century was, so Hannah More said, directed chiefly 'to that decent class who while they acknowledged their belief of its truth by a public profession, and are not inattentive to any of its forms, yet exhibit little of its spirit in their general temper and conduct'.[19] Wilberforce likewise declared that he had written his *Practical View* for 'those who belong to the class of orthodox Christians' and not for 'absolute atheists and infidels'.[20] It was among the middle classes that the churchgoing and Bible-reading habit had persisted most strongly through the dark years of the eighteenth century and it was not surprising that their already nominally Christian ranks should respond most enthusiastically to the call of vital religion.

Serious reflection occasioned by reading a particular book seems to have been a leading factor in promoting conversions among the middle classes. Wilberforce was converted while reading Dr Philip Doddridge's *Rise and Progress of Religion* on a tour of Switzerland and John Newton, a slave ship captain who subsequently became one of the most effective Evangelical preachers in London, first felt prompted to undergo the great change after reading Thomas à Kempis' *Imitation of Christ* in the middle of the Atlantic. Wilberforce's own *Practical View* was held to be instrumental in the conversion of many middle-class Evangelicals, among them the Revd Leigh Richmond, and a spectacular success rate was claimed when 6,000 copies of the work were distributed by agents of the Religious Tract Society in the more respectable residential areas of London. Hannah More need hardly have bothered to write special *Stories for Persons in the Middle Ranks* since all her works seem to have appealed principally to a middle-class readership. Numerous letters to her testified to the power of her books in effecting conversions. In 1810, for example, John Venn reported to her that 'the aunt of a lady in this neighbourhood, whose excellent niece suffered much restraint and hardship in consequence of her seriousness, is now, from having read *Coelebs*, no longer prejudiced, and herself reads the books which her niece recommends.'[21]

Although they probably had a firmer intellectual foundation, the conversions to vital religion which were achieved among the middle classes in the first half of the nineteenth century were no less spectacular than those which occurred among the aristocracy and the poor. Nor are they any easier to explain. The question still remains unanswered as to why so many people should have given up their existing life-styles to embrace the rigorous and demanding code of Evangelicalism. The evidence is clear that they did so in very considerable numbers; by 1850 there were probably between two and three million people in England who regarded themselves as Evangelical Christians. What was it that had made the call to seriousness so compelling in the previous fifty years?

It is important not to underestimate the persuasive powers of the Evangelicals themselves. Their message of damnation for all who did not repent of their sins and turn to God was a powerful enough one in itself and it became doubly so when hammered home with the fiery eloquence of Rowland Hill or the dramatic prose of Hannah More. It is not difficult to appreciate the influence that Evangelical nursemaids could have on their young charges, nor in their very different way that the young women who taught in Sunday schools and ragged schools could gain over the roughest of their pupils. Numerous conversions were attributed by those who had experienced them to the personal influence and example of Evangelical friends and associates. For women Evangelical influence sometimes presented itself in a particularly beguiling and disarming form, through the attentions of a handsome young Evangelical clergyman. Mrs Sherwood, the wife of an Indian Army captain and later to become a best-selling author of children's books, was converted to vital religion in 1807 by the Revd Mr Parson, the English clergyman resident at Berhampore, 'a good, serious young man' with whom she spent a good deal of time. One day she betrayed her ignorance respecting the doctrine of total depravity and so paved the way for her regeneration at his hands. From her account of her conversion it is clear that she was strongly attracted to the young clergyman. Many other women had similar experiences. Provided that they were neither too old nor too ugly, Evangelical preachers and missionaries did not need to have the tyrannical designs of the Vicar of Wrexhill to win over the hearts of at least one group among the unregenerate.

The influence of Evangelicalism was all the greater when it operated on minds which were already anxious and ill at ease. As much as the power of its message, the condition of those who were brought into contact with it seems to have been crucial in effecting conversions to Evangelicalism. It has already been noted that conversion very often followed a serious illness or a grave emotional trauma which brought people face to face with death. The deep gloom and consciousness of sin which Evangelicals almost invariably mention as the prelude to their conversion seem often to have been the result of brooding during a long and dangerous illness. Mrs Sherwood was very much more susceptible to Mr Parson's teachings for having just lost her eighteen-month-old son and having herself been in a fever since arriving in India. The death of a close relative often led to conversion; Captain Hedley Vicars, a young artillery officer who was later to become an Evangelical hero after his early death in the Crimean war, turned to vital Christianity in the late 1840s after the sudden death of his brother had inspired him with the fear that he himself might die young.

The emotional effects of serious illness and sudden bereavement seem to have played a large part in bringing about Evangelical

conversions. Evangelicalism was a religion which appealed essentially to those who were already anxious and disturbed about their own
state. It gave them at once an explanation for and a relief from their
anxiety. But serious illness and sudden deaths were not peculiar to
the first half of the nineteenth century. They had been a feature of
life in England for centuries without inducing men and women to
adopt fervent and puritanical religious beliefs at their occurrence.
The massive number of conversions to Evangelicalism achieved in
this particular period requires a more specific explanation which
takes account of the circumstances of the time. So does the fact
that it was more than fifty years after Englishmen had first been
called to seriousness by George Whitfield and the early Evangelical
preachers that they began to show any signs of responding to it in
significant numbers.

The main reason for the large number of conversions to Evangelicalism which occurred in England in the first half of the nineteenth
century is, perhaps, to be found in the anxiety and social dislocation
which accompanied the country's emergence as the world's first
modern technological society. Contemporary accounts leave no
doubt that there existed throughout England in this period widespread concern and uncertainty about the new forces at work in the
country which, although they were only half-understood, seemed to
be threatening its social and political stability. A rapid rise in
population, the full-scale emergence of the factory system and the
consequent transition from a rural to an urban living pattern, and the
emergence of class conflict and popular movements of protest and
unrest – these were the inevitable consequences of the Industrial
Revolution which England had yet to experience at the end of the
eighteenth century but which dominated its history during the next
fifty years. They were all forces which induced anxiety and fear
among people and, as the Evangelicals were to discover, which
excited a spirit of dependence on God.

The call of Evangelicalism to self-discipline and seriousness
seemed a temptingly straightforward, if hardly easy, antidote to the
chaos and anarchy which many people felt was not far off. Its moral
absolutes and certainties offered welcome release in an age which was
becoming increasingly plagued by doubts and fears. Part at least of
the appeal of Evangelicalism must have lain in the fact that it
provided an escape from a troubled world. There were probably

many people who embraced vital religion because they felt like William Cowper, the only poet of note produced by the Evangelical Revival, that:

> 'Tis pleasant through the loop-holes of retreat
> To peep at such a world; to see the stir
> Of the great Babel, and not feel the crowd;
> To hear the roar she sends through all her gates
> At a safe distance, where the dying sound
> Falls a soft murmur on th' uninjured ear.[22]

It is significant that the period in which most of the great leaders of early nineteenth-century Evangelicalism had themselves been converted to vital religion was one of extreme gloom and despondency in England. The decade in which Wilberforce had forsaken the prospect of political advancement to devote himself to the abolition of the slave trade and the reformation of the nation's morals, and Hannah More had renounced the salons and the stage to devote herself to tract writing and good works in the Mendips, was also the decade in which England had lost the American colonies, suffered unprecedented national debts, first experienced the power of the organized mob and witnessed with horror the events of the French Revolution. It was not difficult to believe in times like this that the hand of God was at work in the world. The Evangelicals developed a theory which explained the succession of disasters besetting England, and offered a way out of them which was anything but escapist in its implications. The country was suffering, they argued, because it had incurred the anger of God. Divine judgment had already fallen on France for the atheism and infidelity for which it had been notorious throughout the eighteenth century: it would soon fall on England if there was not a massive return on the part of the people to God. In one of the most perceptive contemporary analyses of the reason for the advance of Evangelicalism in the early nineteenth century, an Anglican clergyman writing in 1817 noted that 'England was alarmed by the judgements, of which, without feeling them, she was a close spectatress, and panted for an opportunity to take the lead in restoring erring man to his allegiance to his Heavenly Sovereign.'[23]

Such was the urgent message which the Evangelicals drew from the stormy years at the end of the eighteenth century and which spurred on their efforts to convert their countrymen in the succeeding fifty years or so. They were to find that many people felt anxieties and doubts about the state of the world similar to those which had led them to take up vital religion themselves. Evangelicalism made such headway in England in the first half of the nineteenth century because it matched the mood of many people as they experienced life in a rapidly changing society and saw traditional attitudes and habits threatened and swept away by powerful new forces. 'In such times', one Evangelical clergyman told his congregation, 'the Scripture characters fasted and prayed. The old puritans did so. I think we ought to.'[24] Many people agreed with him.

When England returned to more stable and certain conditions around 1850 and entered what one historian has called the 'Age of Equipoise', the appeal of Evangelicalism did not diminish.[25] But it was a different kind of appeal which now attracted recruits to vital religion. Evangelicalism had become fashionable. The wheel had turned full circle from the days when Wilberforce and Hannah More had lambasted their countrymen for their merely nominal Christianity and had struggled hard to win them to the difficult and challenging faith which they called vital religion. Now dramatic conversions and experiences of regeneration were all the rage. The seriousness was going out of Evangelicalism and in its place were coming in affectation and cant.

3

Assault on the Church

The most obvious agency open for the Evangelicals to use in their efforts to convert their fellow countrymen was, of course, the national church. Yet, loyal members of the Church of England though they were, they did not accord it a primary role in their scheme to achieve the conversion of the country. It is not difficult to see why Evangelicals were happier working outside the Church of England than within it. They preferred the spontaneity and flexibility of voluntary missionary efforts to the formalism of the Church's services and the rigidity of its structure. Even when the Church of England was dominated by Evangelical clergy, in the late 1850s, the Earl of Shaftesbury was still railing against its inability to preach to the heart and was involved with other Evangelicals in starting religious services in theatres and public halls. Like all extreme Protestant doctrines Evangelicalism had a low regard for the part played by priests in effecting the salvation of souls and was strongly anti-clerical in tendency. It is significant that most of the leading figures of the Evangelical Revival were laymen. Those Evangelicals who were in the Church were deeply contemptuous of their fellow clergy, accusing them of not providing the proper Gospel ministry that they regarded only themselves as being able to discharge. The exclusivism of the Church of England was a further complaint of many Evangelicals who felt themselves closer both in theology and temperament to Nonconformists than to other Anglicans. As we have already seen, they often co-operated with Dissenters in missionary ventures. William Wilberforce once told his son Samuel that:

the differences between Churchmen and dissenters were in his eyes of very small consequence. They were but the scaffolding ... when the building was complete no one would ask what sort of scaffolding it had been ... He nowhere found in Scripture that it would be asked at the last day 'Were you Churchman or dissenter?' but 'What were your works?'[1]

The Church Establishment for its part regarded with strong disapproval the indiscipline and irregularities of the Evangelicals, who were perennially referred to as Methodists. In 1800 the curate of Blagdon in Somerset launched a fierce attack on the school which Hannah More had set up there on the grounds that the schoolmaster was trying to turn it into a private conventicle by inviting his students to describe their spiritual experiences. Twenty years later Lord Barham was fined £40 for holding religious services at his home when he was unwell and several more similar prosecutions were brought against Evangelicals under the Conventicle Act of 1670, until in 1855 Shaftesbury successfully carried through Parliament a Religious Worship Act which permitted religious meetings in places other than churches or licensed chapels. Evangelical clergy were often denied access to Anglican pulpits. Arthur Young could not persuade a single vicar in the vicinity of his home to allow Charles Simeon to preach when he came to visit him in 1805. He commented bitterly: 'Oh! for the dumb dogs of our clergy who will neither preach the Gospel themselves nor let others do it.'[2] Some Evangelical clergy were even driven out of the Church for their views and activities; this was the ultimate fate of Rowland Hill and also of Thomas Charles, a Welsh clergyman who was instrumental in founding the British and Foreign Bible Society and subsequently led the Welsh Calvinistic Methodists. Hannah More once reported to Lady Middleton that she had taken up the cause of a clergyman who had been removed from a good curacy because he had preached the doctrine of redemption on an ordinary Sunday, in contravention of the orders of his rector who had told him that the subject should only be mentioned on the three principal festivals.

Despite their low opinion of the Church, the Evangelicals could hardly afford to ignore it, given its potential as an instrument in the task of converting the land. Indeed, the contempt which they had for the existing state of the Church of England and the hostile reaction which they met from most of the clergy served only as a spur to them to reform it. So successfully did they infiltrate the Church that by 1850, and according to some contemporary observers even by the time of Queen Victoria's accession, Evangelicals formed one of the largest groups among the clergy. The enduring legacy of Evangelicalism in the Church of England was to be a spirit of divisiveness and party feeling. But its more immediate achievement was the total revitalization and transformation of church services and of the role of the clergy. Nothing less could be expected when Evangelical seriousness confronted the complacency of eighteenth-century Anglicanism.

There is no doubt that the Church of England went through the worst phase of its history in the late eighteenth century. It was during this period that pluralism and non-residence among the clergy were at their highest point ever. A Parliamentary inquiry in the early years of the nineteenth century revealed that more than a quarter of all beneficed clergy were not resident in their parishes and that one parish in ten was without any minister of the Established Church at all. Partly in consequence of this state of affairs, and partly because of a general decline in church attendance, services were discontinued and churches often remained closed on Sundays. Many of those people who did go to church regarded it largely as a social occasion, coming in and out during services as they pleased and chatting with their friends during the intoning of prayers and psalms. Although there were notable exceptions, the general calibre of Anglican clergymen was low. Many of them were the younger sons of landed families who had opted for 'the fat slumbers of the Church' which Edward Gibbon regretted in his later years that he had not chosen for himself. At best, this tended to make for an uninspired ministry. At worst it could lead to serious scandals. G. W. E. Russell remembered from his childhood an Anglican clergyman dropping the chalice while he was administering communion because he was too drunk to hold it.

This state of affairs in the national church horrified Evangelicals. Wilberforce was appalled to find on a tour of his native East Yorkshire in 1796 that many parish churches had no Sunday services and that the practice of churchgoing had all but died out in the region. Hannah More's labours in the Mendip villages were largely inspired by her discovery that in twelve adjacent parishes there was not one resident incumbent. At Cheddar, for example, the rector was 'something at Oxford University' and was never seen near the parish; his curate lived twelve miles away at Wells, and the prebendary who lived in the rectory was intoxicated on average six times a week. Evangelical clergymen strongly attacked those of their colleagues who had taken orders to earn a comfortable living much as they might take up any other gentleman's profession and, as the Revd Thomas Gisborne put it, 'without a serious purpose of habitually striving to exhibit to those whom they shall be appointed to guide in the way of salvation an edifying example of piety and virtue'.[3] 'What opportunity, or what desire for watching over his flock', the Revd B. W. Mathias asked a meeting of Evangelical clergymen in 1802, 'can that clergyman have whose hours are employed in the routine of the drawing room or assembly, at the receptions of the great, in political studies and parties, at the hunt or the racecourse and whose days are dedicated to the business of their farms or the pursuit of philosophy and "belles lettres"? Such persons may be polite gentlemen, they may be good jockies and farmers, they may be deep philosophers or elegant poets; but they are not, they cannot be Watchmen.'[4]

The Evangelicals were determined to put things right in the Church of England by filling it with 'serious' clergymen and so ensuring a proper Gospel ministry in every parish in the land. In an effort to achieve this aim they established funds to support through University young men of promise and piety who intended to become ordained but whose finances were limited. The largest of these funds were those administered by the Elland Society in Yorkshire and the London Clerical Education Society. Training serious young men for the ministry was, however, not much use if they could not subsequently get livings within the Church because of the hostility of most patrons to those clergymen who held Evangelical views. To counter this problem, the Evangelicals set about obtaining ecclesiastical patronage for themselves by buying up advowsons (the right to present a clergyman to a particular living). The greatest of the lay Evangelical patrons, the Second Earl of Dartmouth, purchased the advowsons of nearly a dozen livings which he subsequently gave to Evangelical clergy, including Huddersfield which went to Henry Venn and Olney to which he presented John Newton. John Venn owed his position as rector of Clapham from 1792 to 1813 to the patronage of Henry Thornton, who held the advowson there, and Edward Bickersteth was able to find a parochial ministry after his retirement from the secretaryship of the Church Missionary Society in 1830 through the good offices of Abel Smith, an Evangelical banker and M.P., who presented him to the living of Watton in Hertfordshire. In 1817 Charles Simeon set up a trust to buy livings and so secure them for Evangelical incumbents. By the time he died in 1836, the Simeon trustees held the advowsons of twenty-one livings, including Cheltenham, Bath, Derby, Macclesfield, Bridlington and Beverley.

Where they could not get hold of the patronage of livings to introduce 'serious' clergymen as incumbents, the Evangelicals tried to ensure that there were at least serious curates appointed wherever possible. In this task they were actually assisted by the non-residence and pluralism prevailing in the Church since they were often able to introduce Evangelical curates into parishes which were held in plurality with others or in which the incumbent was not resident. From 1836 onwards Evangelical efforts to increase the number of 'serious' curates in the Church of England were concentrated largely on the activities of the Church Pastoral Aid Society which was set up in that year with Shaftesbury as Chairman. The ostensible purpose of the society was to raise money to provide curates for large and understaffed urban parishes, but its primary aim was to increase the specifically Evangelical element among the clergy. When approached by an incumbent for a grant for an additional curate, the Society, which was entirely Evangelical in its membership, had the power to say who should be appointed. So alarmed were High Churchmen by the aims of the Society, and by its keenness to put lay workers into parishes, that they established a rival organization, the Additional Curates Society, in 1837. The Church Pastoral Aid Society was by far the more successful of the two ventures. Within thirty years of its establishment it was supporting nearly 500 curates and over 150 lay agents in parishes covering a total population of around four million people.

As a last resort, Evangelicals who were unable to secure a Gospel ministry in any other way built a church or chapel themselves and appointed a 'serious' clergyman to it. The erection of proprietary chapels by individuals or groups who subsequently retained the right to present clergymen to them was allowed, albeit reluctantly, by

Church authorities in the early nineteenth century since it eased the severe shortage of church accommodation in the country while avoiding the complicated legal and financial difficulties in creating new parishes. One of William Ewart Gladstone's earliest memories was of going to Cambridge in 1815 with his Evangelical father, who had just built a proprietary church at Seaforth and who wanted to ask Charles Simeon if he could recommend a suitably serious young clergyman to be incumbent there. Proprietary chapels provided several leading Evangelicals with a base from which to establish a Gospel ministry. In London Daniel Wilson was at St John's Chapel, Bedford Row, from 1812 to 1824, Thomas Scott, the grandfather of George Gilbert Scott, and the author of a major commentary on the Bible, at the Chapel of the Lock Hospital from 1785 to 1803, and Josiah Pratt, the first secretary of the Church Missionary Society, at the Wheler Chapel in Spital Square from 1824 to 1826. Henry Venn Elliott, a grandson of Henry Venn and himself the head of a distinguished Evangelical family, was incumbent of St Mary's proprietary chapel in Brighton, the most fashionable place of worship in the town, from 1827 until 1865.

It was not always possible for Evangelicals to keep the chapels they had built within the pale of the Established Church. When the Revd W. B. Cadogan died in 1797 after twenty years as vicar of Reading and was not replaced by an equally 'serious' successor, his Evangelical parishioners built their own chapel, for which they were forced to secure the services of a minister from the Countess of Huntingdon's connection. Rowland Hill was instrumental in securing the establishment of several proprietary chapels, all of which held services according to the Anglican prayer book but none of which the Church authorities would license. They included the Surry Chapel near Blackfriars, which he had set up with the help of Henry Venn and Thomas Scott in 1782 and where he himself ministered for the next fifty years, and a chapel in Cheltenham which he had established in 1808 because of the inadequate church accommodation in the town. In 1832 Hill helped to establish a chapel in Leamington Spa for a group of Evangelicals who were anxious to open their pulpit to Nonconformist preachers. Although they proposed using only the Prayer book in the chapel it was not allowed to remain within the Anglican pale.

Despite the difficulties and hostility which they encountered, the

Evangelicals managed to infiltrate a sizeable number of 'serious' clergymen into the Church of England. By the late 1820s, according to W. E. Gladstone's calculations, an eighth of the Anglican clergy were Evangelicals. A survey of the ninety-three principal clergy of London carried out in 1844 for the editor of *The Times* listed forty-six Evangelicals, twenty-five High Churchmen and twenty-three moderates. Nine years later the *Edinburgh Review* computed that of the 17,000 clergymen in the Church of England, 6,500 were Evangelicals, 7,000 High Churchmen and 3,500 Broad Churchmen. Other contemporary accounts agree in suggesting that by the middle of the nineteenth century Evangelicals made up between a half and a third of the clergymen of the Church of England.

What were the characteristics of the Evangelical clergy? Their portrayal in Victorian fiction is not generally a very flattering one. We have already encountered the terrifying, almost demonic figure of William Cartwright, the Vicar of Wrexhill, created by Frances Trollope and based on the Revd J. W. Cunningham, who was Vicar of Harrow from 1811 to 1861. Then there are Slope, the scheming curate in *Barchester Towers* who 'perpetually exudes a cold and clammy perspiration', and Charles Honeyman, the sanctimonious and hypocritical incumbent of Lady Whittlesea's fashionable proprietary chapel in Brighton, in Thackeray's *The Newcomes*. Mr Brocklehurst, the cruel and insensitive headmaster of Lowood School, in *Jane Eyre*, was based by Charlotte Brontë on the Revd William Carus Wilson, headmaster of the school for Clergy Daughters at Cowan Bridge which she had herself attended. Finally George Pontifex, the hero's father in the *Way of All Flesh*, represented all that was tyrannical and heartless in Samuel Butler's own upbringing in an Evangelical vicarage. To counter this formidable gallery of villains and hypocrites, I can find only three Evangelical clergymen who receive sympathetic portrayals in Victorian novels – the sincere and well-meaning old Mr Clare in *Tess of the d'Urbervilles* and the poverty-stricken and saintly Amos Barton and Edgar Tryan in George Eliot's *Scenes from Clerical Life*.

There is no doubt that there were, particularly in the latter part of the nineteenth century, Honeymans and Brocklehursts among the Evangelical clergy in the Church of England. But there were more Bartons and Tryans. The characteristics most generally displayed by the Evangelical clergy before 1860 were strong and simple piety, self-sacrificing devotion to the service of others and unceasing labour and activity. Few of them showed any intellectual brilliance but they nearly all had a keen and compassionate concern for the welfare, both temporal and spiritual, of the souls committed to their care. The remark which the author of the 1844 survey on the London clergy made about the Revd Montagu Villiers, the well-connected Rector of St George's, Bloomsbury, who was virtual leader of the Evangelical clergy in the Church of England in the early years of Victoria's reign, could have equally well been made of most of them: 'he does an immense amount of good in his parish. His exertions are unceasing; his Church crowded.'[5]

Wherever Evangelical clergymen became incumbents, they transformed the life of the parishes under their care. First and foremost, they literally opened the church to the people by abolishing the system of pew rents whereby wealthy parishioners rented seats which they often did not use, leaving poorer worshippers to stand in the aisles. When, as a young vicar, John Bird Sumner, who later became the first Evangelical Archbishop of Canterbury, stopped a service to ask why many of the congregation in his church were standing in the aisles when the pews were empty, he was told that the pews were private property and the owners had shut them up. 'There can be no such thing', he replied, 'in the House of God. Send for a blacksmith to take off the locks. We will sing a hymn while he does it.'[6] Having thus established the church as a place of worship rather than as a showplace of social advancement, Evangelical incumbents introduced early morning communion and six o'clock evensong on Sundays where previously there had been generally only Mattins and occasionally a mid-afternoon service. Weekday evening services and nightly lectures during Lent and Holy Week were also started. Evangelicals made no alterations to the form of service prescribed by the Prayer Book although they laid particular stress on the place of the ministry of the word in church services, introducing a morning and evening sermon every Sunday, each often up to one and a half hours in length.

The most important new feature which the Evangelicals introduced into the services of the Church of England was the practice of hymn-singing. During the eighteenth century congregational singing was virtually unknown in Anglican churches. Metrical psalms were usually chanted by a choir while the congregation remained sitting.

1 William Wilberforce

2 The Earl of Shaftesbury

3 The Revd Edward
Bickersteth

4 The Revd John Bird
Sumner

5 Sarah Trimmer

6 Mrs Sherwood

7 Lady Victoria Buxton

8 'Evangelical Influence.' Illustration from *The Vicar of Wrexhill*

9 Bible distributors at work in London

Evangelical clergymen introduced into the Church the Methodist practice of getting the congregation to stand and sing tuneful hymns at various points during the morning and evening services. They compiled hymn books which were soon adopted by non-Evangelicals; one of the most successful, Edward Bickersteth's *Church Psalmody*, sold 150,000 copies within a few months of its publication in 1833. Some of the most celebrated hymns in the English language were written by Evangelicals in the late eighteenth and early nineteenth centuries. John Newton and William Cowper collaborated to produce the Olney Hymn Book which included *Glorious Things of Thee Are Spoken*, *Amazing Grace*, *How Sweet the Name of Jesus Sounds*, *God Moves in a Mysterious Way* and *O For A Closer Walk With God*. *Oh, Worship the King* was written in 1833 by Robert Grant, a son of Charles Grant of the Clapham Sect and himself a prominent politician, *Just As I Am* by Charlotte Elliott, a sister of Henry Venn Elliott, three years later, and *At the Name of Jesus* in 1870 by Caroline Noel, the grand-daughter of the First Lord Barham. In 1847 H. F. Lyte wrote the hymn which was to become more popular among the Victorians than any other, *Abide With Me*.

The major effect of the efforts made by Evangelical clergy to revitalize church services was a massive increase in the number of people who attended church. Some of the estimates of the congregations attracted by Evangelical clergymen are almost unbelievable. Three thousand people are said to have crowded into Rowland Hill's Surry Chapel on one occasion in 1803, to sing a hymn which he had composed to the tune of *Rule Britannia* which began 'When Jesus first, at heaven's command'. When Leigh Richmond preached at Sheffield parish church in 1814, 3,500 people managed to get into the church to hear him, leaving many others outside, and when he subsequently preached at three services in Bradford the congregations were estimated at two, three and four thousand respectively. These were exceptional figures occasioned by the visit of a particularly powerful and popular preacher, but in a less spectacular way, most Evangelical clergymen built up the size of their regular congregations and contributed considerably to encouraging the churchgoing habit in Victorian England. Particularly impressive was the achievement of those who took over derelict urban parish churches and turned them into thriving centres of worship. In

1851, after fourteen years as vicar at Whitechapel, the Revd William Champneys had built up regular congregations of 1,500 for morning service, 800 in the afternoon and 1,600 for evensong, in what had previously been a defunct parish. Especially marked in churches which had Evangelical incumbents was an increase in attendance at communion. Charles Simeon noted on one occasion in the last year of his ministry at Trinity Church, Cambridge: 'Yesterday I partook of the Lord's Supper in concert with a larger number than has been convened together in any church in Cambridge since the place existed ... so greatly has the Church of England been injured by myself and my associates.'[7]

The Evangelical clergy were almost more interested in promoting activities which went on outside the Church than they were in revitalizing the services and the form of worship within it. Nearly all of them were ardent supporters of Sunday schools and evening institutes and many of them carried the Gospel into the homes of their parishioners. In one of the most memorable scenes in *The Vicar of Wrexhill* the Revd William Cartwright holds an extempore service in the drawing room of one of the more genteel homes in the village for the benefit of the regenerate daughter of the house and for 'some of the more promising of the domestics'. This practice was common among Evangelical clergy in well-to-do neighbourhoods. Those with poorer parishes held services in cottage kitchens, as did the Revd Edgar Tryan in *Scenes from Clerical Life*. Two Evangelical clergymen distinguished for their work in city centre parishes in the mid-nineteenth-century, Hugh Stowell, Vicar of Salford from 1831 to 1851, and J. C. Miller, Vicar of St Martin's, Birmingham from 1846 to 1866, held open-air services and established special industrial missions in an effort to reach their working-class parishioners.

Hardly surprisingly, the activities of Evangelical clergymen often provoked considerable opposition among their parishioners. Readers of *Barchester Towers* will remember that Slope's determination to turn an old men's hospital into a Sunday school caused a large part of Barchester society to turn against him. George Eliot's *Scenes from Clerical Life* include a particularly vivid and detailed account of the build-up of local opposition to an Evangelical clergymen in the story of *Janet's Repentance*, which is largely about the reactions of the parishioners of Milby to the activities of Mr Tryan, their new curate, once they discover that 'he held peculiar opinions; that he preached extempore; that he was founding a religious lending library in his remote corner of the parish; that he expounded the Scriptures in cottages; and that his preaching was attracting the Dissenters, and filling the very aisles of his church.' The story opens with a gathering of leading villagers in the bar of the local public house bemoaning the activities of the new curate and deciding how best they can put a stop to them. They get their opportunity when Tryan announces his intention of starting Sunday evening lectures in the parish church. On the first evening that these are scheduled to begin, a large and noisy procession leaves the pub to demonstrate against this Evangelical innovation. Carrying placards saying 'Down with cant' and generously supplied with free beer, the crowd is addressed by Mr Dempster, a local lawyer who leads the anti-Evangelical protest:

> we are not to have a preacher obtruding himself upon us, who decries good works, and sneaks into our homes perverting the faith of our wives and daughters! We are not to be poisoned with doctrines which damp every innocent enjoyment, and pick a poor man's pocket of the sixpence with which he might buy himself a cheerful glass after a hard day's work, under pretence of paying for Bibles to send to the Chicktaws!

Tryan braves the protesters and eventually establishes his Sunday evening lectures as a regular feature in the Church, but not before he has faced further violent opposition and the whole parish has divided into pro- and anti-Evangelical factions.

Similar opposition to that which Tryan met with among the parishioners of Milby was experienced by many Evangelical clergymen in the early nineteenth century as they tried to introduce a serious Gospel ministry into their churches. When John Venn announced his intention of instituting Sunday evening services with a sermon at Clapham parish church, a stormy protest meeting was held at the local public house by members of a card club which met there on Sunday evenings and who were alarmed by the advent of a rival attraction. Considerable efforts were made to thwart Charles Simeon's plan to hold Sunday evening lectures at Trinity Church, Cambridge. On at least one occasion the churchwardens bolted the doors of the church to prevent him entering it and undergraduates often came into the church to break up the services. But the old

Apostle of Evangelicalism was not to be deflected from his purpose; when the doors were locked against him he called for a smith to force them open, and to deter student hecklers he had men with truncheons stationed in the aisles during services and forced those who caused a disturbance to stand up and make a public confession. Evangelical clergy were often publicly reviled and socially ostracized for their views: the Victorian churchman, H. C. G. Moule, recalled that when his father, Henry Moule, Vicar of Fordington in Dorset, was found to be a 'Methodist' — 'that is to say, in the sense of those days, the preacher of a Gospel of definite and personal change of heart and consequent devotion of life; groups of villagers regularly congregated at the churchyard gates at the end of every service to shout abuse at him and virtually no one called on him at the vicarage.'[8]

It is easy to understand how the activities of Evangelical clergymen could provoke such opposition and why, as in Milby, parishes were regularly split into warring factions by the arrival of a Gospel minister. It was not simply that people saw their easy-going lives disturbed by the rigorous demands of Evangelical seriousness. The trouble was also that the power and emotion of vital religion tended either to attract strong adherents determined that theirs was the only true form of Christianity or to repel people utterly by its narrowness and puritanism. It was very difficult for those brought into contact with Evangelicalism to feel indifferent towards it; the natural reaction was to become violently partisan about it in one way or the other. The problem was further exacerbated by the tendency of Evangelical clergymen to attract a strong and rather partisan following of personal supporters in the parishes in which they ministered. For this they themselves were at least partly responsible.

Two groups of people were particularly prone to congregate around Evangelical clergy on their arrival in new parishes and to establish a local party to support them in their dealings with the unregenerate. The first were members of local Dissenting churches, especially Methodists, for many of whom it was only the absence of a serious Gospel minister in the parish church which had kept them away from it. Often the arrival of an Evangelical clergyman in a parish was sufficient to make several Nonconformists join the Church again. It was significant that Tryan's most constant ally in his struggle to secure Sunday evening lectures in Milby Church was a Dissenter, Mr Jerome, who tells the new curate: 'You are the fust man i' the Church to my knowledge as has brought the word o' God home to the people; an I'll stan' by you sir, I'll stan' by you. I'm a Dissenter, Mr. Tryan; I've been a Dissenter ever sin' I was fifteen 'ear old; but show me good i' the Church, an' I'm a Churchman too.'

The other group who almost invariably formed a personal following around Evangelical clergymen were the more susceptible of the female members of their congregations. As has been pointed out, Evangelical preachers and missionaries achieved particular success in winning over the hearts of the fairer sex. This was even more the case with Evangelical clergymen. It was no coincidence that both Tryan and Slope drew their strongest support from females. Like Charles Honeyman, doted on by the ladies of Brighton, who invited him to tea to compliment him on his delicious sermons, they derived considerable benefit from being pale young curates. It was not, one feels, simply Tryan's religion, pure and selfless though it undoubtedly was, which inspired the group of ladies who met regularly to bind books for the new circulating tract library to make him a black silk case to hold his clerical bands in, or to compose an address to him which began 'Forward, young wrestler for the truth'. Many Evangelical clergymen were themselves well aware of their attraction to the ladies and assiduously cultivated their female following. Frances Trollope noted perceptively in an aside in the *Vicar of Wrexhill*:

> Those who are at all acquainted with the manner in which the 'Church Methodists', as they were called, obtain the unbounded influence which they are known to possess in their different parishes, particularly over the female part of their congregations, must be aware, that great and violent as the effect of their passionate and extempore preaching often is, it is not to that alone that they trust for obtaining it.[9]

The strong and often excessively partisan support which certain Dissenters and females gave to Evangelical clergy does much to explain why they often encountered strong opposition in their parishes. The most violent opponents of Evangelical clergymen were almost always local churchmen who were disturbed at their connections with Nonconformists, and husbands perplexed, like Dempster in *Janet's Repentance*, about the effect which vital religion was having on their wives and daughters. Many loyal Anglicans regarded the Evangelicals as traitors in their midst who were bent on destroying the Established Church and in league with Dissenters to overthrow it. Those men whose wives and daughters had been converted to vital religion, and who had themselves remained resistant to it, felt that it was a profoundly disruptive force in the family. A common criticism levelled against the Evangelicals in the early nineteenth century was the one which is currently made against the Scientologists: – that they broke up families by encouraging those whom they converted to shun the company of those who remained unconverted. It was a fair allegation. Evangelical clergymen almost always counselled those whom they converted to consort only with other serious people and not infrequently encouraged them to forsake their unregenerate families and leave home.

There is no doubt that the presence of an Evangelical clergyman in a particular parish often had a disruptive effect on the life of the local community and encouraged it to divide into opposing factions. Evangelicals could not help but create party feeling and division by their insistence on the rigid barrier which must exist between the serious and the non-serious elements in the population. Admittedly very few seem to have gone as far as the Vicar of Wrexhill, who ejected the existing schoolmaster and the leading traders in his parish from their posts because they were not Evangelicals and introduced suitably serious replacements. But many Evangelical clergy would associate only with those whom they considered regenerate among their parishioners. In doing this they at least showed a refreshing disregard for social status which so obsessed many of their less serious colleagues in the ministry. The Revd Thomas Scott, for example, who refused to let his son George Gilbert play with the children of non-Evangelicals, would not entertain many of his wealthiest parishioners to dinner because he considered them insufficiently serious, but often had Evangelical farm labourers to the vicarage for Sunday lunch.

What individual Evangelical clergymen did for their local parishes, the body as a whole did for the Church of England: they revitalized it but at the same time they left it bitterly divided and split into warring factions. It is difficult to say at exactly what stage the Evangelicals came to see themselves as forming a distinct party within the Church of England, rather than as being simply the serious element among the clergy. There was never a time when they had not betrayed certain partisan tendencies in dismissing those of their clerical colleagues whom they did not regard as gospel ministers and in associating almost entirely only with fellow Evangelicals. The regular meetings of local Evangelical clergy which were established in every county at the beginning of the nineteenth century may have begun by being organized, as H. C. G. Moule claimed that the Dorset meetings which his father attended were, 'not on any narrow party test but by a law of spiritual sympathy'.[10] It was not long, however, before they became party gatherings. Almost certainly the single factor which did most to confirm the growth of party spirit among the Evangelical clergy was the emergence of the High Church Oxford Movement in the 1830s. The High Church Tractarians themselves share some of the blame for the petty squabbling and bitter divisions into which the Church of England was plunged for the major part of Queen Victoria's reign. But ultimately it is the Evangelicals who must take most of the responsibility for this squalid chapter in the history of Anglicanism which did so much to discredit Christianity in the eyes of the later Victorians.

The battle between High and Low in the Church of England reached its climax in the famous Gorham case of 1850. The Revd George Gorham, a West Country Evangelical vicar, had first incurred the disapproval of his High Church Bishop, Henry Phillpotts, when he had advertised in the Ecclesiastical Gazette in 1846 for a curate 'free from Tractarian error'. Phillpotts was disturbed by the party spirit that this displayed and when Gorham applied for transfer to another living in 1848 he took the chance of examining him on his beliefs, which he found to be heretical. The Court of Arches confirmed that Gorham held a doctrine contrary to that taught by the Church of England and that he was therefore debarred from holding a living within it. Gorham, however, appealed successfully to the Privy Council and continued as an Anglican clergyman. The episode was a vital test case of the position of the Evangelicals in the Church. The doctrinal point on which Gorham had been found to be heretical, that of baptismal regeneration, was a major point at issue between Evangelicals and High Churchmen. The Evangelicals held, of course, that regeneration was not given to the individual in the sacrament of baptism, while the

High Churchmen insisted that the Prayer Book declared that it was. Had the final judgment gone against Gorham, no Evangelical clergy-man could have conscientiously remained within the Church of England. 'I have been called by Providence', Gorham himself declared, 'not merely to maintain my personal right, but virtually to struggle for purity of doctrine, and for liberty of conscience, on behalf of a very large body of clergy.'[11]

The decade which began with the Evangelicals establishing their right to be in the Church of England at all in the Gorham judgment, ended with them reaching the summit of their influence within it. By 1860 the Evangelicals could count well over a third of the Anglican clergy as 'serious' and, what was even more important, they had for the first time more than merely a token representation in the episcopacy. Vital religion had been slow in invading the hierarchy of the Church of England. Before Victoria's accession there had been only two Evangelical prelates, Henry Ryder, Bishop of Gloucester from 1815 to 1824 and afterwards Bishop of Lichfield, and Charles Sumner, Bishop of Llandaff in 1826 and then at Winchester from 1827 to 1869. The breakthrough came first in 1848 with the translation of Charles Sumner's brother John to the see of Canterbury, where he remained until 1862, and subsequently with Palmerston's accession to the premiership in 1855. On the subject of ecclesiastical appointments Palmerston sought the counsel of his father-in-law, the Earl of Shaftesbury, with the result that virtually all of the exceptionally high number of bishoprics which fell vacant during his premiership went to 'serious' clergymen. By 1860 there were seven Evangelicals on the Episcopal Bench.

The Evangelicals had achieved their dominant position in the Church of England at the cost of dividing it and establishing within it an atmosphere of party warfare. The result of the Gorham judgment had infuriated High Churchmen and driven some of them, including William Wilberforce's son Henry, to join the Roman Catholic Church. At the time that they were at their most powerful within the Church, the Evangelical clergy were also at their most partisan and petty. By the late 1850s, they had even developed a distinct style of clerical dress to differentiate themselves from High Churchmen; Evangelicals wore cut-away tailcoats, white shirts and high collars while the Tractarians had long black frock coats, cassock waistcoats and collars similar to those worn by Anglican clergy today. But if there was more worldliness and narrowminded-ness to be found among the Evangelical clergy than there had once been, there was still also much simple piety and quiet devotion. Archbishop Sumner himself was a gentle and saintly figure who is remembered chiefly for wandering through the streets with an umbrella over his arm. Not for him the opulent trappings of a prince bishop; like most of the Evangelical clergy he believed in leading a stern and simple life. A narrow party they might have become, the *Edinburgh Review* reflected in 1853, but of all the clergymen in the Church of England, it was still the Evangelicals who exhibited the noblest and purest lives and who showed those qualities which had led them to make a unique and positive contribution to the Church:

> They may not perhaps be men of the most comprehensive understanding; nor the fittest teachers for inquiring minds, nor qualified to refute the learned infidelity of Strauss or Newman. But upon the middle and lower ranks of their parishioners, they often have a stronger influence than their intellectual brethren. The attraction of their personal character, shown forth in a daily life of self-sacrificing love, gradually wins many to righteousness, and turns the hearts of the disobedient to the wisdom of the just.[12]

4

A Mission to the Heathen

The Evangelicals did not confine their attentions to their fellow-countrymen. Their zeal to secure converts to vital religion extended to the entire population of the world and led them to concentrate especially on those countries which still dwelt in spiritual darkness. It was the most fervent prayer of many Evangelical mothers that their sons would grow up to be missionaries in some benighted heathen land. Missionary zeal was perhaps the strongest single characteristic of the Evangelicals in the early nineteenth century, and it was certainly one of their most powerful legacies to the Victorians. Indirectly it was to shape Britain's attitude to the countries under its dominion and play a major part in determining imperial policy. More immediately it inspired hundreds of men and women to forsake the comfort and security of home and journey to the farthest corners of the world, with the same conviction as that held by the archetypal Evangelical missionary, St John Rivers, that in taking the Gospel to the heathen lay:

> my vocation; my great work; my foundation laid on earth for a mansion in heaven; my hopes of being numbered in the band who have merged all ambitions in the glorious one of bettering their race. It is dearer to me than the blood in my veins. It is what I have to look forward to, and to live for.[1]

Evangelical missionary activity owed its origin to a discussion in the Eclectic Society in 1799 on the question 'What methods can we use more effectually to promote the knowledge of the Gospel among heathens?'. As a result of this discussion a society was formed, first called the Society for Missions to Africa and the East and later,

74

as it still is today, the Church Missionary Society (C.M.S.), which was to be the main agency in the Evangelicals' efforts to convert the heathen. Missionary work was by no means an exclusively Anglican enterprise; the Nonconformists had, indeed, been earlier in the field – the Baptists established their own missionary society in 1792 and the Calvinistic Methodists were involved in setting up the London Missionary Society three years later. The most famous of all Victorian missionaries, David Livingstone, was, of course, a Scottish Presbyterian. But it was the missionary work of the Anglican Evangelicals, channelled through the Church Missionary Society, which represented the largest single effort to convert the heathen in the nineteenth century.

Few corners of the globe were left untouched by Evangelical missionaries. In 1786 Wilberforce had made sure that a chaplain accompanied the first batch of convicts sent out to Botany Bay. The man appointed to the role was a fervent Evangelical and worked a good deal among the Maoris in New Zealand as well as with the convicts. In 1890 the Church Missionary Society established an Australasian Mission which subsequently extended its operations to the South Sea islands. By 1850 it had mission stations in Malta, Greece, Egypt, Abyssinia and in North and South America. Two more specialized Evangelical agencies concentrated on missionary work in Europe. The Continental Society, which was set up at the end of the eighteenth century to bring vital religion to the Catholic countries of Europe, had several missionaries in the field and in 1816 it even sent two Evangelicals to Geneva in the hope that they could rescue the city from the atheistic influence of Voltaire and Rousseau and restore it to the true seriousness of Calvin's time. The London Society for the promotion of Christianity among the Jews, founded in 1809, and known as the Jew Society, had mission stations in Holland, Poland and Germany as well as extensive operations in London which included several schools, an Operative Jewish Converts' Institution, and a missionary college, all sited in a single compound in Bethnal Green known as Palestine Place. By 1835 it had a permanent mission in Jerusalem itself and six years later, thanks largely to Shaftesbury's eloquent advocacy of the cause in Parliament, an Anglican bishopric was created there.

Two parts of the world particularly attracted Evangelical missionary interest. The twenty million inhabitants of India, sunk deep in

Hindu idolatry, seemed to cry out for conversion. So did the benighted tribes of Africa, whose status as human cargo in the transatlantic slave trade had already aroused Evangelical consciences. In both areas Britain had major commercial interests: in India through the extensive operations of the British East India Company, and in Africa through participation in the dreadful trade across the Atlantic. It was not surprising, therefore, that the English Evangelicals should regard the conversion of the native races of these two particular lands as in some way their own special charge.

The great obstacle to missionary endeavour in India at the beginning of the nineteenth century arose from the East India Company's conviction that missionaries would only excite the natives and disturb its profitable trading activities. Because of this it refused them entry to the sub-continent. In this situation there was only one thing for the Evangelicals to do, if they wanted to secure the triumph of vital religion in India, and that was to infiltrate the higher echelons of the Company themselves so that they could change its policy. Their take-over of the Company's directorate in the early nineteenth century was spectacular: there was no year between 1807 and 1830 when either the Chairman or the Deputy Chairman of the Board of Directors was not an Evangelical. As early as 1789 Charles Grant, the leader of the Evangelical assault on the Company boardroom, had managed to get five 'serious' clergymen, all pupils of Simeon at Cambridge, out to India ostensibly as chaplains to East India Company servants but effectively as missionaries to the natives. One of them, Henry Martyn, translated the New Testament into Urdu in a version which is the basis of that still used today. Meanwhile vigorous activity by the Evangelical M.P.s, led by Wilberforce, obtained a clause in the East India Company's Charter of 1813 which allowed missionaries into the sub-continent and provided for the establishment of Indian bishoprics. This was the signal for a period of major Evangelical missionary effort in India which reached a peak under the influence of Reginald Heber, not himself an Evangelical though a vigorous supporter of missionaries. Heber was Bishop of Calcutta from 1822 to 1826 and author of that most celebrated of all missionary hymns, *From Greenland's Icy Mountains*.

In Africa the Evangelicals had a rather freer hand. To begin with, most of their interest was focused on the colony of Sierra Leone, which had been set up in 1791 by members of the Clapham Sect as a refuge for freed slaves under the governorship of Zachary Macaulay. Two years after its foundation, Hannah More reported to a correspondent that there were 'very pleasant accounts from Sierra Leone, 300 black children in a good train of education, behaving orderly and singing their hymns quite delightfully'.[2] In 1807 the C.M.S. established a mission among the Susoo tribe in the North of the colony, and twenty years later it opened a training college at Fourah Bay to educate native Africans. The first student on its books was Samuel Crowther, an emancipated slave who in 1864 became the first black bishop in Africa. There was little Evangelical interest in other parts of Africa until 1840, when T. F. Buxton succeeded in persuading the Government to send three ships with C.M.S. missionaries in them up the River Niger. The expedition itself was a disaster but it was the first of those combined enterprises of evangelization and exploration which were to open up Africa to outside influences and which came to a climax in David Livingstone's great trek across the continent in the mid-1850s.

By 1850 the C.M.S. alone had over 200 missionaries in the field and there were probably at least another hundred Evangelicals engaged in evangelistic work overseas. By the end of the century the total number of English missionaries working abroad had increased to 3,500. They were not very successful in achieving their aims. Although it is difficult to estimate how many people were converted by missionaries, the number was certainly not large. The great Evangelical dream of a world freed from heathenism and populated entirely by 'serious' converts to vital Christianity came nowhere near to materializing. In indirect ways, through their education and medical work, missionaries undoubtedly had a lasting effect on the lives of those whom they had gone out to convert. But more important was the impact which they made on their own countrymen. The activities of the missionaries captured the excitement of the nation and for the first time aroused the hearts and minds of the British to the plight of those beyond their shores.

It is not difficult to see why there was so much interest in missionaries in the early nineteenth century. Their exploits had all the romance and excitement of good adventure stories. The Evangelicals were not slow to capitalize on this. They issued cheap missionary biographies which dwelt on the most sensational aspects of their subjects' careers. One such biography featured a missionary in the Fiji Islands whose first task on his arrival had been to gather up and bury the heads, hands and feet of eighty earlier visitors who had been cooked and eaten by the natives. The C.M.S. was particularly keen on instilling what it described as a 'missionary spirit' into the young. It devised special games like 'Missionary Outposts' and 'Missionary Lotto' and distributed numerous jigsaws, picture painting books and magazines on missionary subjects. 'Tell the missionary story to your little ones', the Revd Melville Horne, Chaplain to the C.M.S. training college at Bledlow in Buckinghamshire, told the Christian mothers of England in 1811, 'until their young hearts burn, and in the spirit of those innocents who shouted "Hosanna" to their lowly King, they cry "Shall not we also be missionaries of Jesus Christ?".'[3] For adults, there were regular missionary sermons preached by a team of leading Evangelical clergy who went round the country on behalf of the C.M.S., and a network of local missionary associations covering the whole country. To raise money the Society operated a pledged gift scheme extremely similar to that run by Oxfam and other charities today. Voluntary collectors went round their neighbours and friends, collecting a penny every week and giving them in return the quarterly *Missionary Register* which 'conveyed, in plain language, intelligence of the Proceedings of the Society, with Engraved Representations and Printed Accounts of the ignorance and miseries of the unhappy objects of their kind solicitude'.[4]

The public responded generously to appeals for money to promote the missionary cause. In a single tour of Yorkshire for the C.M.S., in which he preached fifty sermons on missionary themes, the Revd Basil Woodd raised over £1000 and initiated twenty-eight missionary support societies. By 1826 over 120,000 people were regularly subscribing to the C.M.S.'s pledged gift scheme and receiving the Missionary Register. The Society's early records are full of accounts of spontaneous gifts of money even from the poorest sections of the community. An orphan boy saved up his allowance of a penny a week and sent it for promoting missions to New Zealand. A pauper woman whose only beverage, and often only meal of the day, was tea, gave up sugar so that she could contribute to the missionary cause. A lame labourer walked nine miles to attend the 1820 annual meeting of the Staffordshire County Missionary Association and hand in the three shillings which he had saved up over the past five years. In the same year a Welsh clergyman raised £23. 1s. 6d. on a forty-mile journey on horseback round the homes of his poor parishioners. Many middle-class families kept a missionary box into which children paid a penny if they did anything wrong. By the middle of the nineteenth century the C.M.S. had an annual income of over £100,000.

It was not only financial support which was forthcoming for the missionary cause. Those people whose compassion and converting zeal were fired by the terrible stories of native superstition and suffering brought home by the missionaries, often took it upon themselves to organize schemes of relief and betterment. There were not a few Evangelical ladies who could claim, like Mrs Jellyby, the indefatigable supporter of the cause of foreign missions in *Bleak House*, that:

> the African project at present employs my whole time. It involves me in correspondence with public bodies, and with private individuals anxious for the welfare of their species all over the country. I am happy to say it is advancing. We hope by this time next year to have from one hundred and fifty to two hundred healthy families cultivating coffee and educating the natives of Borrioboola-Gha, on the left bank of the Niger. (Chapter IV)

The lengths to which the 'nigger worshippers', as the Evangelicals were called, took their concern with the condition of people millions of miles away was often ridiculed by contemporaries. Dickens' caricature of Mrs Jellyby is a portrait of a woman who ignores her family and household duties in pursuit of her wild obsessions with far-off lands; the chapter in which she is introduced is entitled 'Telescopic Philanthrophy'. In a more serious criticism of the supporters of foreign missions in 1844 *Punch* commented acidly that 'just as connoisseurs take a backward step truly to consider the beauties of a picture, so do many of these good folks require distance to see the miseries of human nature through an attractive medium. They have no taste for the destitution of the alley that abuts upon their dwelling-place, but how they glow – how they kindle at the misery somewhere in Africa.'[5] The charge is not entirely an unfair one; it is difficult to avoid the impression that for several early nineteenth-century Evangelicals Christ's commandment to love their neighbour only took effect outside the British Isles.

The interest which the British public came to have in the missionary cause in the early nineteenth century had a more important effect than the raising of funds or the activities of the likes of Mrs Jellyby. It shaped an attitude to the rest of the world, and especially to those two areas where missionary activity was most concentrated, which was decisively to influence British imperial policy. When British people thought about Africa and India they thought in missionary terms, as was only natural when it was the activities of missionaries which had given them an interest in these areas of the world in the first place. This attitude was to make Britain approach the native races of Africa and Asia with whom it came into contact in the nineteenth century in a way which was different from any other European country. It was also to give the Evangelicals a supreme opportunity to influence national policy in this sphere.

The outstanding example of what the Evangelicals achieved with public opinion behind them was, of course, the ending of the British slave trade in 1807 and the total abolition of all slavery in British colonies twenty-six years later. Recent attempts to debunk the Abolition Movement and to call into question the motives of those engaged in it have failed to provide any substantial evidence to support their case.[6] The traditional view is, for once, the right one — the abolition movement was a supremely altruistic crusade carried out almost entirely under Evangelical leadership and inspiration, with the sole object of securing legislation in the interests of humanity. It was first and foremost a missionary effort. The Evangelicals wanted slavery abolished because they believed that it was a practice directly condemned by Christian morality and a condition incompatible with salvation. Treat men as heathen savages, brutalize and exploit them, and heathens they would remain; regard them as your brothers, showing respect and charity, and they would behave as such and become Christians. It was this simple but revolutionary message that the Evangelicals sought to get their fellow countrymen to accept in the first three decades of the nineteenth century.

The Evangelicals succeeded in getting slavery abolished because they persuaded and shamed the British Parliament and people into accepting that they had a responsibility towards the temporal and eternal well-being of the Negro workers in the West Indian sugar colonies. They were equally determined to see Britain accept the same responsibility towards the native population of India, with whom it already had such extensive commercial dealings, and towards the Negroes of Africa, for whose shameful treatment in the past it owed reparation. The Evangelicals wanted Britain to assume the role of missionary to these two parts of the world and to adopt the attitudes and policies towards their native populations that this entailed. It was a role which they believed was providentially ordained for the country to play. It was also a role which suited and benefited a great many people apart from them. The Evangelicals did not find it difficult to convince Britain of its missionary destiny. Their attitudes provided the inspiration and the basis of Government policy towards India and Africa throughout the first half of the nineteenth century.

The leading exponent of the Evangelical view on India was Charles Grant of the Clapham Sect. In 1792, having spent thirteen years in the sub-continent, Grant published his *Observations on the State of Society Among the Asiatic Subjects of Great Britain*. The theme of the work was such as might be expected from a man who two years earlier had been converted to vital religion. Taking as his starting point the utter depravity and corruption of the Hindu race, Grant argued that only a total transformation of Indian society through the introduction of the values and practices of Christianity could bring true happiness to the natives and could justify Britain's continued involvement in the country. 'What is needed', he wrote, 'is a change in the moral and intellectual state of the inhabitants', something which could be accomplished only if Britain assumed the task of instructing the Indian population in Christian civilization which Providence had so clearly ordained for it, by putting the country under British control. The most important thing, to Grant's way of thinking, was to ensure that England's conquest of India 'shall have been made in our hands, the means, not merely of displaying a government unequalled in India for administrative justice, kindness, and moderation, not merely of increasing the security of the subjects and prosperity of the country, but of advancing social happiness, of meliorating the moral state of men, and of extending a superior light.'[7]

Grant's view of Britain's role in India contrasted sharply with that of his contemporaries. Three main attitudes towards India and its people then prevailed in Britain at the beginning of the nineteenth century. The East India Company regarded the country simply as a trading base and conceived Britain's relationship with it in purely commercial terms. Military opinion, represented most forcefully by the Duke of Wellington's younger brother, the Marquess of Wellesley, who as Governor-General had led several spectacular campaigns against the natives, regarded India primarily as so much territory to be conquered. Intellectuals and humanitarians respected and cherished the customs of the natives. Common to these three views of India was the insistence that Britain's interference with the native population should be minimal, or at the very most that it should be the interference merely of a conquering army. Anything more than this, it was felt, would only prejudice British trading interests and destroy native customs. Grant argued for Britain's interference with the Indian population to be maximum. His *Observations* were a call for the anglicanization of India and the total transformation of its values and social structure along the lines of Western Christianity.

The Evangelicals were determined to get their countrymen to respond to Grant's call. In 1809 the *Christian Observer*, the influential monthly journal of the Clapham Sect, ran a series of articles 'on the probable design of Providence in subjecting India to Great Britain' which argued for the urgent assumption by the mother country of its missionary task. This was to be the constant theme of Evangelical pronouncements on India for the next fifty years. As late as 1866 Sir Herbert Edwardes, one of many Victorian Evangelicals who had felt the call to go out to India and confer on it the blessings of Western civilization and Christianity, told a meeting of the Vernacular Education Society, 'I believe from my heart that India has been placed in our hands to be Christianised, and that we shall not be allowed to leave it till we have done our work.'[8] Meanwhile, Evangelicals in the East India Company and in Parliament campaigned for the acceptance of the missionary principle by their colleagues.

Gradually Grant's view of Britain's role in India won acceptance in official circles. The inclusion of a clause in the East India Company's Charter of 1813 which stated it to be the nation's duty to introduce useful knowledge and religious and moral improvement to the native inhabitants of India and, to that end, allowed missionaries free access to the country, was the Evangelicals' first major triumph.

The next was the appointment fifteen years later of Lord William Bentinck as Governor-General. Bentinck was strongly influenced by Evangelicalism and was an ardent disciple of Charles Grant, believing that 'the first duty of the Imperial Government is the moral regeneration of the immense mass of our fellow creatures.'[9] During his rule over India, which lasted until 1835, he abolished the Hindu customs of thuggee (assassination for religious reasons), suttee (the burning of widows on their husbands' funeral pyres) and female infanticide which Evangelical missionaries had long protested about but which previous administrators had been reluctant to interfere with. The Charter Act of 1833, which was drafted by Grant's son, Charles, together with another son of Clapham, Sir James Stephen, ended a long-standing Evangelical grievance by stopping British support for Hindu temples and shrines which had previously been forthcoming through a pilgrim tax levied on those who attended these places. The 1833 Act marked the final abandonment of the toleration and non-interference in native affairs which had characterized the rule of the East India Company and the eighteenth-century moguls, and confirmed Britain's acceptance of its new role in India as Christian missionary and harbinger of Western civilization. It placed the entire civil and military administration of India under a Governor-General and Supreme Council and established a Law Commission to produce a uniform law code for the country. Two years later Lord Macaulay's celebrated education minute insisted that instruction in Indian schools should be carried out in the English language and so put into effect one of the main recommendations that Grant had made in his *Observations*.

During the first two decades of Victoria's reign the Evangelical view of Britain's role in India reigned triumphant. These were the years when hundreds of Englishmen went out to India, certain, like the earnest young hero of W. D. Arnold's novel, *Oakfield* (published in 1853), that 'nothing less than Christianity, in the Cromwell or some other shape, will have any effect on the awful vis inertiae of Asiaticism', and determined to help in the work of raising the country 'from the depths of immorality to a state of comparative Christian earnestness'.[10] It was a period of unbounded optimism about the likely effects of Britain's Christianizing and civilizing mission, when many people seriously believed that within a short space of time the entire population of the Indian sub-continent would be made up of respectable, God-fearing Christians who spoke English and were actively engaged in the government of their country. What in fact happened was rather different: the Indians rebelled. The Indian Mutiny of 1857 was a protest against the attempt, which the Evangelicals had initiated, to mould the country to a British way of life. This was not, of course, the way that the Evangelicals interpreted it. To them the mutiny was a Divine punishment on Britain for not being active enough in promoting its vital work of converting the natives. But the Government realized that the optimism which had characterized the Evangelicals' approach was misplaced – the Indians were clearly beyond redemption. From 1858 a new spirit infused British relations with India. The desire to rescue and convert the erring natives was replaced with a cold bureaucratic arrogance. What remained of the missionary role which the Evangelicals had taught the country to adopt was a firm conviction that the continued government of the sub-continent remained Britain's solemn and inescapable duty.

The Evangelicals felt as certain about Britain's responsibility towards the natives of Africa as they did about its mission to convert the Indians. India might seem more clearly marked out by Providence as a mission ground through its existing subjection to Britain, but Africa had an almost more compelling claim for attention. The C.M.S. early singled it out as the most important area for missionary activity because of:

> the mental darkness and superstitious delusions into which the Natives of this extensive Continent were sunk; the miseries which had been entailed upon them by the Slave Trade; the duty of making some recompense for the injuries and wrongs, which by our participation in that nefarious traffic, we had inflicted on Africa; and the very little that had been done to meliorate the unhappy condition of her degraded sons and daughters.[11]

The Evangelicals' attitude towards Africa was dominated by their determination that Britain should make reparation for its leading part in the slave trade. In their concern with the victims of slavery, they formulated a concept of trusteeship and protection of native peoples which was to form the basis of British policy towards Africa in the Victorian period, and which was to lead to the colonization of much of the continent.

Just as Charles Grant was the leading spokesman for the Evangelicals' ideas on India, so Thomas Fowell Buxton expounded their view of Africa. More than any other individual, Buxton developed the concept of Britain's role in the continent as that of guardian and protector of the native peoples. He did so first and foremost by completing the work that had been started by Wilberforce to end for ever the system of Negro slavery. In 1828, acting on the request of missionaries in the areas, he was responsible for securing from the Government the ordinance which outlawed unpaid labour in South Africa and which led to the Great Trek North by the Boers who could not face living in a society where Negro slavery was outlawed. Five years later he introduced and carried through Parliament the bill abolishing slavery in the British colonies and emancipating thousands of Negroes in the West Indies. In 1835 it was Buxton who chaired the Parliamentary Select Committee on Aborigines which set out to examine injustices committed against natives in every country of the world under British dominion. This Committee was instrumental in forging the notion of imperial trusteeship, producing in its reports, as Buxton himself modestly put it, 'a sort of manual for the future treatment of aboriginal nations in connection with our colonies'.[12]

Like Grant, Buxton believed that Britain's role in the areas of the world that came under its influence was a maximum one, involving the assumption of a Christianizing and civilizing mission to their inhabitants. He told the first meeting of the Aborigines Protection Society, which he founded in 1837 to safeguard the interests of native peoples, that 'The complete civilization and the real happiness of man can never be secured by anything less than the diffusion of Christian principle.' Nowhere did Buxton feel that there was a greater need for Christian principle to be diffused or for the rights of natives to be guarded than in Africa. The unhappy inhabitants of that continent remained in total ignorance of the Christian religion and, even after the abolition of slavery by Britain, they suffered at the hands of those nations who still continued the practice and of those settlers like the Boers who regarded Negroes as an inferior race fit only for serfdom and bondage.

Buxton expressed his views on the plight of Africa, and Britain's responsibilities towards it, in *The African Slave Trade and Its Remedy* which was published in 1840, the same year that he founded a society for the extinction of the slave trade and for the civilization of Africa. His aim was simple – to eradicate from the African continent the trade in human beings which was, he pointed out, now twice as extensive as it had been when Wilberforce had first embarked on his great crusade. But it was not so simple to devise an effective way of stamping out slavery. Initially Buxton had pinned his hopes on the anti-slaving patrols of the Royal Navy which regularly sailed round the African coast. One-sixth of the Royal Navy's total fleet was already being used on these operations at a cost of three-quarters of a million pounds a year. Even if the Government had committed Britain's entire defence budget to this altruistic cause it is unlikely that it would have proved an effective deterrent to the slavers. The expedition of gun boats which Buxton persuaded the Government to send up the Niger in an effort to suppress slavery was a fiasco. It was clear that more than brute force was required to end a practice which so many Africans themselves indulged in to their own considerable profit.

The remedy which Buxton proposed in his book was the establishment of an alternative form of commerce in the continent. The Africans must be persuaded to trade in the produce of their own country rather than its inhabitants. 'The real remedy, the true ransom for Africa, will be found in her fertile soil,' Buxton wrote, 'it is the Bible and the plough which must regenerate Africa.'[13] There was nothing new in this call for the agricultural and commercial development of Africa as an antidote to the slave trade; it had been a constant theme of Wilberforce's speeches in Parliament. As early as the 1780s, James Ramsay, an Evangelical clergyman who spent nineteen years in the West Indies and was one of the earliest and most determined fighters against the slave trade, had advocated it. What was important about Buxton's restatement of the point was that, coming as it did after slavery had been abolished, it acted as a clarion call to Englishmen to take up their responsibilities to bring the benefits of commerce and Christianity to the African people. At one level, Buxton's cry inspired great missionary figures who went out to Africa in the 1840s and 1850s, determined not only to convert the natives to Christianity but also to animal husbandry, double-entry book-keeping and all the other accomplishments of

Western civilization. At a deeper level, it helped to generate the policy of colonization in Africa.

Common to the Evangelicals' attitude towards both India and Africa was a conviction of the desirability of establishing and extending direct British rule over these areas of the world. Grant's *Observations* argued for the permanent subjection of India to British rule as the only way in which the native population could be liberated from its moral and spiritual darkness. The whole theme of his work was that there was no foreseeable future 'in which we may not govern our Asiatic subjects more happily for them than they can for themselves'.[14] Buxton's ultimate point was the same: if gunboats and commercial missions failed, then Britain must assume direct responsibility for protecting the Africans, and teaching them an alternative life-style to that of slavery. This might well involve the colonization of the continent. By the time Buxton wrote his great work on the *African Slave Trade*, three British colonies – Sierra Leone (founded in 1798), Gambia (1816) and the Gold Coast (1821) – had already been established in Africa as a direct result of Evangelical pressure to provide refuge for ex-slaves and security for others who might be sold into slavery, and Britain had consolidated her hold over the South African Cape after agitation by missionaries about the treatment of Negroes had driven the Boers out. Vital religion, it seemed, went along with territorial expansion.

Again and again in the later nineteenth century missionaries proved to be the strongest advocates of colonization and annexation of native lands by Britain. On occasions they played a decisive role in ensuring continued British dominion over an area. British withdrawal from the Gold Coast in 1865 was prevented largely by the argument of the missionaries that it would involve the abandonment of the area to slavers. In 1894 pressure from missionaries wanting to see the suppression of the Arab slave trade in north-east Africa was instrumental in persuading the Government to make Uganda a British Protectorate. It is significant that when New Zealand was annexed to the British Empire in 1840, the keenest proponents of the move were the C.M.S. missionaries in the islands who helped to bring it about by persuading the Maoris to sign a declaration accepting the Queen's supremacy over them.

There is no doubt that the missionary purpose which the Evangelicals preached for Britain in the early nineteenth century helped to inspire the colonialist and imperialist sentiments associated with the Victorian Age. It was not only the Evangelicals, of course, who felt the nation had a missionary role towards the underdeveloped part of the world. No group of people were keener to spread their gospel of civilization and progress than the Utilitarians. In India Evangelicals and Utilitarians worked hand in hand to further the cause of anglicization. Many nineteenth-century Englishmen, who were in no way affected by Evangelicalism, believed in the value of extending the virtues of the steam engine and representative democracy to those parts of the world unfortunate enough not to know them. What gave the Evangelicals' view particular potency and influence was the noble and altruistic purpose which it gave to colonization and imperialism. Grant's *Observations* provided a convenient and high-sounding justification for the continuation and extension of British rule in India. In the same way the task to which Wilberforce and Buxton had committed Britain, of campaigning against slavery throughout the African continent and protecting the rights of native races throughout the world, could provide a useful pretext for schemes of territorial ambition and aggrandizement.

The Evangelicals themselves vehemently eschewed imperialistic sentiments. The whole theme of their argument was against the colonialist, settler mentality of the Caribbean slave owners, the Boers of the Cape Colony and the moguls of the East India Company who treated native people with indifference and cruelty. Evangelical propaganda came out firmly against notions of the inferiority of black men and argued strongly for racial equality. Henry Venn, Secretary of the C.M.S. from 1841 to 1873, insisted that the purpose of missionary work was not to establish a church with a European hierarchy, but to train up native men for the ministry and eventually for the episcopate. The Evangelicals were totally opposed to the extension of territory carried out for reasons of profit or aggrandizement. The strongest protests against the Marquess of Wellesley's policy of conquest and forced annexation of territory in India in the first decade of the nineteenth century came from the Clapham Sect. In 1876 the Earl of Shaftesbury took the lead in opposing the Bill to make Queen Victoria Empress of India on the grounds that the proposed title would have 'an air military, despotic, offensive and intolerable'.[15]

It was almost reluctantly that the Evangelicals found themselves to be advocates of imperialism. The fact was that their concern to convert the peoples of India and Africa and to abolish Negro slavery led them inevitably to call for the consolidation and extension of British rule over these areas of the world. The fight which Wilberforce had taken up against slavery broadened itself into a general crusade on behalf of the rights of native peoples and so involved Britain in the extensive annexation of territory to protect them. The Aborigines Protection Society became one of the major pressure groups campaigning for the extension of the British Empire, though Buxton had hardly conceived it as such when he founded it. Sir James Stephen entered the Colonial Office in the early 1830s so that he could help to achieve the abolition of slavery and so complete the great work which had been begun by his father, James Stephen, and his fellow members of the Clapham Sect. Gradually he came to see that only direct rule by Britain could secure the natives of Africa against slavery and exploitation and he ultimately became so strong an exponent of colonial rule that during his time as Under Secretary for the Colonies from 1836 to 1847 he was known as Mr Mother Country.

The role of trustee and tutor to native peoples to which the Evangelicals called their countrymen was their most significant contribution to the development of the Victorian imperial idea. Samuel Wilberforce, the eldest son of the great abolitionist, summed it up when he told the Government that it was 'the vocation of the British people to leave as the impress of their intercourse with inferior nations marks of moral teaching and religious training, to have made a nation of children see what it was to be men.'[16] His remark illustrates another attitude that the Evangelicals had very largely been responsible for implanting in the Victorians, namely their curiously ambivalent view of the native peoples of the Empire as, in Kipling's famous phrase, 'half-devil and half-child'. Evangelical missionary propaganda portrayed the natives as depraved and corrupted, yet with immortal souls which were not beyond salvation. This notion of unregenerate but potentially redeemable humanity characterized Britain's view of the native peoples under its care, and contrasted sharply with the more cynical, and more respectful view of the African and Asiatic races taken by other European countries. For the Victorians, the overwhelming purpose of empire was the conversion of the native inhabitants within it, whether to the doctrines of free trade, representative government or revealed religion. This was the enduring legacy of the missionary outlook which the Evangelicals had given to nineteenth-century Britain.

Evangelicalism helped to foster the notion that Britain had an imperial destiny. As early as 1812, in its twelfth annual report, the C.M.S. had reflected on the country's powerful position and extensive influence in the world and concluded that this could not but indicate that Divine Providence was at work:

> It is not from political greatness and extended dominion, that we would augur anything whatever in our own favour: but from dispositions which God has been pleased to put into our hearts, we humbly hope that our country has been exalted among the nations for nobler purposes; that the empire of Britain shall be an empire of mercy; and that no shore shall echo to the thunder of her power but what shall smile also under the blessings of her beneficence. Judging from the events passing around us, the signs of the times, is it presumptuous to indulge the humble and pious hope, that to Great Britain may be entrusted the high commission of making known the name of Jehovah to the whole earth?[17]

Thirty-one years later the Earl of Shaftesbury confidently reported that:

> the moral condition of England seems destined by Providence to lead the moral condition of the world. Year after year we are sending forth thousands and hundreds of thousands of our citizens to people the vast solitudes and islands of another hemisphere; the Anglo-Saxon race will shortly overspread half the habitable globe. What a mighty and what a rapid addition to the happiness of mankind, if then thousands should carry with them, and plant in those distant regions, our freedom, our laws, our morality, and our religion.[18]

The urge to participate in the country's Christianizing and colonizing mission to the heathen world was one of the most powerful forces operating on English men and women throughout the nineteenth century. It was felt most strongly and directly by those who volunteered to become missionaries. Every year the C.M.S. received hundreds of applications from people prepared to give up their homes and friends in their desire to carry the Gospel to distant lands. They came from every walk of life; in 1820 the Society received a letter from a butcher's boy who already had 600 sermons prepared for use among the natives and another from an Oxford don who wanted to preach the Gospel on the shores of the Carnatic. 'I am at your service as a schoolmaster, catechist, builder or in any way you please,' wrote a typical applicant to the C.M.S. in the same year. 'As to my sentiments, I believe that all are sinners by nature without exception, and that Jesus Christ has tasted death for every man.'[19]

It was not only a desire to redeem sinners which impelled people to become missionaries. The lure of adventure and excitement in distant lands was probably just as strong a factor in the case of several of the applicants to the C.M.S. Charlotte Brontë suggests that this was a major reason for St John Rivers' determination to be a missionary when she has Jane Eyre reflect that his restless personality was better suited to the Himalayan ridge, or even the swamps of Guinea, than to English drawing-rooms. For single women, missionary work offered a rare opportunity to make an independent career, and this may explain why by the end of the nineteenth century women considerably outnumbered men as missionaries. Many girls, inspired by Evangelical propaganda, must have had the same thoughts as Anna Hinderer, who recalled that as a child in a Norfolk vicarage, 'I longed to do something, I had a strong desire to be a missionary,' although few actually fulfilled their childhood longings, as she did when she went out to Nigeria in 1852 with her missionary husband.[20] Quite often, those who had initially felt strongly attracted to a missionary career realized after they had begun training, and reflected a little on what lay ahead, that their motives were not all they should have been. The C.M.S. received a steady stream of letters from those who wished to withdraw their applications to be missionaries. Typical of them was the one sent by a student at the Society's Training College in 1830 which concluded:

I have no doubt but that it was a degree of zeal, or other enthusiasm, together with a vague sense of duty, which led me to desire Missionary work; but I have too much reason to fear that that zeal sprang very little, if at all, from love either of Christ or to the souls of sinners. Of these latter motives, I must confess myself to have so small a share that I cannot with confidence affirm that I have any.[21]

It was not only by becoming Christian missionaries, of course, that Englishmen responded to the call to fulfil their imperial destiny. The thousands who went out to the Empire as soldiers and administrators were inspired with an equal sense of purpose. It was significant that the colonial armed forces and the imperial civil service attracted large numbers of Evangelical recruits. An Evangelical clergymen commented in 1858 that 'the Indian Army has been rich in good men. Both among officers and private soldiers has there been a remarkable number of intelligent and earnest disciples of the Lord.'[22] The roll call of serious army officers in India was particularly impressive: it included Captain Sherwood, the husband of Mrs Sherwood, and himself the centre of a large group of Evangelical soldiers in Calcutta; Captain Charles Acland, Sir Herbert Edwardes and Brigadier-General Sir John Nicholson among the leading military figures in the country in the 1840s; and, of course, General Sir Henry Havelock, whose death at the siege of Lucknow in 1857 made him a national hero. There were many Evangelicals among the servants of the East India Company as well as among its directors. The famous group of soldier-administrators who brought order to the Punjab after it had been annexed to Britain following the Sikh War of 1849 were almost all strong adherents to vital Christianity. Significantly, they had learned the principles of firm but fair government that were to make the 'Punjab system' the showpiece of the English administrative achievement in India, from James Thomason, Lieutenant-Governor of the North West province from 1843 to 1853. Thomason was the son of one of Charles Simeon's curates who had gone out as a missionary to Bengal.

The Punjab system was the supreme example of the application of the Evangelicals' idea of Empire. The men who created it, Henry and John Lawrence, Sir Herbert Edwardes, Sir John Nicholson and Sir Robert Montgomery, were the epitome of Evangelical seriousness. They laboured under an intense sense of mission and duty, often working a fourteen-hour day, to subdue an area ten times the size of Britain and to give its inhabitants the framework of civilization and the protection of the rule of law. Their Cromwellian certainty that they had been called to their task by God was summed up in the statement of their leader, John Lawrence, who in 1864 was to become one of the most famous Victorian Viceroys of India, that 'we have not been elected or placed in power by the people, but we are here through our moral superiority, by the force of circumstances, by the will of Providence. This alone constitutes our charter to govern India. In doing the best we can for the people, we are bound by our conscience and not theirs.'[23] Evangelicalism had given to Victorian imperialism both the air of self-righteousness and the overpowering sense of duty which pervade this remark. It had transformed the wholly secular and voluntary business of annexing territory and administering colonies into a great religious crusade and an inescapable moral imperative. No one heeded the Evangelicals' call to seriousness in the nineteenth century more closely or conscientiously than those thousands of English men and women who went out to the swamps or the jungle to bear the white man's burden and who were determined, as Lawrence was, 'to exhibit that uniformity of conduct which befits a Christian nation trying to do its duty'.[24]

5

The War Against Vice

'God Almighty has set before me two great objects;' Wilberforce noted in his diary on October 28th, 1787, 'the suppression of the slave trade and the reformation of manners.'[1] The Evangelicals had an overwhelming desire to reform the morals of their fellow-men quite independent of their wish to convert them. Like all puritans, they were obsessed with loose and immoral behaviour and determined to impose on others the rigorous régime of self-denial and abstinence from pleasure to which they subjected themselves. The crusade against vice which was launched by Anglican and Nonconformist evangelicals at the end of the eighteenth century continued well into Victoria's reign and produced effects in terms of social habits and legislation which are still felt in Britain today. It is the reason, for example, why public houses open only for a few hours each day and why most shops are closed on Sundays. No other aspect of the Evangelicals' activities affected as many people as their attempt to clean up the country's morals; nor was anything else they did quite so successful or so unpopular. Having managed to remove from British life many of the loose habits of the eighteenth century before Victoria came to the throne, they went on to establish through prohibitory legislation their right to force people into behaving as they thought proper.

It did not take a Saint to feel that English society stood in need of reform at the end of the eighteenth century. Indeed, one of the main reasons why the movement for the reformation of manners was so successful was that it got enthusiastic support from many non-Evangelicals who were shocked at the cruelty and lewdness of their age. There can be little doubt that there was something depraved about a society whose favourite country pastimes included hurling stakes at chained cocks and setting dogs on cats thrown into ponds, where townspeople regularly complained of being kept awake by the screams of victims of assault and rape and the cries of prostitutes, and in which an eighth of the deaths in the capital were attributed to excessive spirit drinking. The eighteenth century was probably no more vice-ridden than any other but no other age has ever paraded its weaknesses quite so openly or excessively. Sir Robert Walpole spent over £1,000 on the trimmings for one bed at his country house in Houghton, and went through over 552 dozen bottles of wine there in one year alone. Charles James Fox had piled up gambling debts of £140,000 by the time he was twenty-four and thought nothing of journeying right across France simply to buy a waistcoat which he fancied. Like James Woodforde, the Anglican clergyman who nightly ate his way through seven-course meals, they believed in gratifying their appetites on a gross scale. So, at a more squalid level, did their poorer contemporaries, like the wretched women who killed their children in order to sell their clothes for gin money and the working men regularly driven to ruin, and sometimes even to suicide, by losing all on the lottery.

The Evangelicals began their war on vice by persuading George III to issue a proclamation for the encouragement of piety and virtue in 1787. In it the King declared his resolve 'to discountenance and punish all manner of vice, profaneness and immorality, in all persons of whatsoever degree or quality, within this our realm'.[2] The proclamation was sent by the Home Secretary to every magistrate in the land and ordered to be read aloud four times a year from all pulpits. The Evangelicals had been characteristically shrewd in obtaining royal blessing and official sanction for their activities, especially since what they were demanding was nothing less than that the people of England should take upon themselves the role of common informer and spy on the activities of their neighbours. The proclamation commanded all the King's subjects to be 'very vigilant and strict in the discovery, and the eventual prosecution and punishment of all persons who shall be guilty of excessive drinking, blasphemy, profane swearing and cursing, lewdness, profanation of the Lord's Day, or other dissolute, immoral or disorderly practices'. It was certainly a comprehensive catalogue of vices.

Although it was addressed to the entire population, George III's proclamation against vice was directed primarily at those who had a specific responsibility for maintaining law and order in the country. Its main aim was to ensure greater vigilance and attention towards public morality on the part of the magistracy. Local justices were charged to suppress 'all public gaming houses, and other loose and disorderly houses, and all unlicensed public shows, interludes and places of entertainment ... and all loose and licentious prints, books and publications', and to put into execution statutes enforcing Sabbath observance. The magistracy rose to the challenge. A new vigour overtook the easy-going world of the county justices in the early nineteenth century. Benches up and down the country convened special meetings to determine how best they could put the proclamation into effect. Parish officers, constables and churchwardens were briefed on existing legislation and enjoined to go out and apprehend those who transgressed it. Long-defunct laws against swearing and Sabbath breaking were suddenly revived and invoked to bring offenders to court. Licences which had for years been issued to disorderly houses in return for a small consideration were recalled and refused. Public houses which had hitherto been allowed to stay open all night were made to eject their last customers at nine or ten in the evening and to close completely on Sundays. Warrants were issued to constables to search booksellers' and stationers' shops and to seize any obscene matter they might find there.

This new-found zeal and severity in matters of public morality which came over the magistracy was not simply a consequence of the royal proclamation. It was also a result of the infiltration of county benches by Evangelicals. Many magistrates in the late eighteenth century were only too keen to promote the movement for the reformation of manners in the hope that it would curb the high incidence of crime and disorder in the community. But there were others, the trading justices so familiar in the novels of Smollett and Fielding, who derived considerable profit from bribes which they took for granting licences to disorderly public houses and for letting offenders off punishments. So determined were the Evangelicals that these men should not be allowed to frustrate their planned reformation of the nation's morals, that they became magistrates themselves to ensure that the proclamation was applied with vigour throughout the country. In Leeds, for example, Evangelicals completely took over the town council and the magistrates bench in the 1790s and instituted a massive clampdown on immoral behaviour which included the prosecution of citizens caught cursing and swearing.

Although they were happy to see them take a major part in forwarding the campaign against vice, the Evangelicals were not content to leave the work entirely to the existing forces of law and order. They had themselves set up a society to enforce the King's Proclamation in 1787. In 1802 this became known as the Society for the Suppression of Vice, or the Vice Society for short. For the next thirty years the Vice Society was the spearhead of the Evangelicals' crusade to raise the level of public morality. Its members acted as moral policemen, informing on anyone they found to be transgressing the law. The Society employed paid agents who attached themselves to local police stations or went round the country looking for areas particularly steeped in vice. Within twelve months of its institution it had brought 678 offenders before the courts. Usually the Society was able to find some long-since-forgotten statute to cover the vice for which it wanted to bring a prosecution. When it could not, it campaigned vigorously for new legislation and acted in close co-operation with Evangelical M.P.s and peers who took up its request in Parliament. It was through this combination of prosecuting offenders under existing statutes, and pressing for legislation to create new offences where they felt it was needed, that the Evangelicals set about reforming the morals of the nation.

Like all puritans, the Evangelicals were particularly interested in sexual morality. They attempted unsuccessfully to stamp out both adultery and prostitution. A bill promoted by Evangelical M.P.s in the last years of the eighteenth century, which sought to prevent adultery by prohibiting the marriage of a divorced person to the co-respondent cited in the divorce case, failed to get a majority in Parliament and although Spencer Perceval, England's only Evangelical Prime Minister, promised to reintroduce it in 1800, he never did so. The Vice Society campaigned vigorously against prostitution but operated under the considerable disadvantage that the law required proof of use before a prosecution could be brought for illegal brothel-keeping, and this meant one of the Society's members visiting a bawdy house and availing himself of its services, something which Evangelical consciences would not permit, even to obtain evidence. What the Evangelicals were able to do, however, was to force those who were involved in adultery or prostitution to keep their activities private and not to indulge in them quite so publicly as they had in the eighteenth century.

Even if they could not ban all irregular sexual activity, the moral reformers could at least make sure that no references to it were allowed to intrude into literature. Their most famous achievement in this area was the production of Thomas Bowdler's edition of Shakespeare in which 'those words and expressions are omitted which cannot with propriety be read aloud in a family'.[3] This cleaned-up version of the Bard became extremely popular in Victorian homes and schools. An Evangelical poet, Robert Pollok, had the grandiose scheme of subjecting the whole of English literature 'to the standard and test of Christianity' and compiling a massive anthology containing those works which made the grade, but he died long before the project was completed. However, the Evangelicals were able to operate their own form of censorship through Charles Mudie's Select Circulating Library which started in 1842 and became by far the biggest and most popular of the Victorian circulating libraries. By 1860 it had over 25,000 subscribers. Mudie was a strong Evangelical and made sure no impure works were offered to his readers. W. H. Smith, who was a staunch Methodist, exercised an equally rigorous censorship over the books sold from the railway station bookstalls of which he had a monopoly through most of Victoria's reign. Evangelical standards of taste gradually came to predominate among publishers and authors. Hippolyte Taine, the French critic, noted in 1863 that in England there was only one literary rule, and that was to be moral.

Indecency and obscenity came high on the list of vices which the Evangelicals wished to eradicate. The Vice Society brought several convictions for offences against public decency. Early in the nineteenth century it ordered the owner of a house in Piccadilly to remove the classical bas-reliefs on the front of the building on the grounds that they represented 'a gross and filthy exhibition'. In 1809 it successfully prosecuted a young man who bathed naked within view of houses on the cliffs at Brighton. The unlucky offender had to find surety of good behaviour for two years. Six years later, Wilberforce protested in Parliament that the Thames Bathing Bill then before the Commons 'would go to sanction the indecency frequently committed on the banks of the Thames, and would be a declaration of

Parliament that it was expedient that persons should expose their bodies on the banks of the river.'[4] Shaftesbury persuaded the organizers of the 1851 Great Exhibition to cover up nude statues on display in the Crystal Palace.

The Vice Society waged a particularly successful campaign against the sale of obscene articles and publications. In 1808 its Bristol Branch reported that 'a variety of devices, in bone and wood, of the most obscene kind, particularly those representing a crime, which ought not to be named among Christians' were being offered for sale outside a prison in the city.[5] The articles, which were made by French prisoners of war, were seized and the trade suppressed. Shortly afterwards the Vice Society uncovered the existence of an extensive trade in obscene prints being carried out by a gang of over sixty Italian hawkers. The principal market for the prints, it discovered, was girls' boarding-schools, to which the salesmen gained admission under the pretence of buying cast-off clothing. By 1817 George Pritchard, the Society's Secretary, reported that the gang had been smashed and the plates from which they made their prints seized. Three years later the *Christian Guardian*, an Evangelical periodical, triumphantly reported that the Vice Society had 'checked the sale of toys and snuff boxes with abominable devices, which were imported in immense quantities from France'.[6] In 1833 Evangelical pressure in Parliament was instrumental in obtaining legislation outlawing the display of obscene pictures in the public highway. Later it helped to put on the statute book the Customs Consolidation Act of 1853, which prohibited the import of obscene material, and the Obscene Publications Act of 1857, which empowered magistrates to order the destruction of obscene books and authorized the grant of warrants to police to search the premises of suspected dealers.

The Evangelicals were naturally as much concerned with blasphemy as they were with obscenity. Wilberforce, who intended throughout his Parliamentary career to introduce a bill to outlaw profane oaths, proudly told the House of Commons in 1823 that the Vice Society had already made thirty-two prosecutions for blasphemy, not one of which had failed. Many of the books which the Society attacked as blasphemous were acknowledged works of pornography but they also included atheist tracts and pamphlets which 'either suggest doubts respecting the truth of Revelation or infuse principles unfavourable to virtue'.[7] In 1821 the Vice

Society caused a major sensation by prosecuting Mary Ann Carlile, a London bookseller, for blasphemous libel for selling an Appendix to the theological works of Thomas Paine. Mrs Carlile's defence was silenced from the Bench before she had read a tenth of what she had prepared to say and she was sentenced to a year's imprisonment and a £500 fine. As she had no money to pay the fine, she was ordered to remain in prison after the year was up. In 1823 a radical M.P., Joseph Hume, raised the case in Parliament and declared that the only parallel to Mrs Carlile's treatment by the Vice Society was to be found 'in times when individuals were brought to the stake and were otherwise outrageously punished for their religious opinions'.[8]

Gambling was a major object of Evangelical attack. There is a celebrated Clapham anecdote that on the night of the abolition of the slave trade, Wilberforce had turned to Henry Thornton and asked him what should be abolished next. 'The lottery, I think' was the grave reply. The state lottery, which the Government had introduced at the end of the eighteenth century to raise money for the war against the rebellious American colonies, and the numerous private sweepstakes that had grown up around it, reduced many working men to conditions of beggary and drove their families to the workhouse. For the Evangelicals almost worse than its social effect was the immorality involved in 'misleading the mind from those habits of continued industry which insure the acquisition of comforts and independence to delusive dreams of sudden and enormous wealth'.[9] While the Vice Society concentrated on stamping out illegal private sweepstakes, Wilberforce and his Saints organized a successful campaign in Parliament to persuade the Government to give up the national lottery. The budget of 1826 contained the last state lottery ever to be held in England. In the same year the Vice Society had struck a major blow against another kind of gambling by prosecuting thirty-nine fortune-tellers whom it claimed, not only 'delude their votaries by foretelling lucky numbers, and thus aggravate the evils attendant on lotteries and illegal insurances', but also 'promote improvident marriages among the lower classes'.[10]

Like many other people, the Evangelicals were disturbed at the prevalence of drunkenness in early nineteenth-century England. As we have seen, there was a general tightening-up of public house licensing by magistrates in the aftermath of the royal proclamation.

In Sheffield dram shops were outlawed, and in the dockland area of Plymouth the number of public houses was halved. Everywhere closing hours were rigidly enforced, and several county benches imposed a maximum period of an hour in which people could remain in a public house, drinking. The Vice Society stemmed a major cause of drunkenness when it persuaded employers to give up their custom of paying wages in public houses on Saturday evenings. In 1830 Evangelical peers in the House of Lords carried an amendment to the Beer Act, which ensured the closure of public houses during the times of Church services on Sundays. Unlike most Nonconformists, in the first half of the nineteenth century Anglican evangelicals were not generally teetotallers and did not believe in prohibiting the consumption of all alcoholic liquor. Several prominent Evangelicals were themselves brewers, among them T. F. Buxton and the Hanbury and Guinness families, and most Evangelicals in Parliament supported the freeing of the beer trade which took place in the 1820s and 1830s, hoping that this would help to cut down the consumption of spirits. In an effort to reduce spirit drinking, Evangelicals and Nonconformists came together in 1830 to form the British and Foreign Temperance Society, but it was not until the late 1850s that any Evangelicals showed enthusiasm for teetotalism. In 1857 the Revd Stopford J. Ram, the Vicar of Pavenham, compiled a list of total abstainers among the Anglican clergy, helped by Mrs Wightman, the wife of another Evangelical vicar, who was the author of an important teetotal tract, *Haste to the Rescue*. Five years later the Church of England Total Abstinence Society was founded. This society, which later became the Church of England Temperance Society, was an important pressure group in the Victorian teetotal movement, but was never as effective or powerful as the two great Nonconformist-dominated societies, the United Kingdom Alliance and the Band of Hope.

While the Evangelicals may have been reluctant to deny their countrymen the pleasures of moderate drinking, they showed considerable enthusiasm for attacking equally innocent pastimes. Evangelical clergy in Newmarket succeeded in getting Sunday race meetings cancelled; the Revd Henry Moule was able to get the Dorchester races stopped entirely. The Earl of Shaftesbury went through acute agonies of conscience when the Queen asked him to accompany her to Ascot in 1841. He eventually decided that he could not snub her by refusing to go and offered a prayer that his visit to the racecourse 'may not be productive of any mischief to the slight influence I may have in the world for carrying forward measures and designs of good to mankind'.[11] The London City Mission successfully campaigned for the closure of the street fairs at Camberwell, Greenwich and Fairlop and ended the famous Bartholomew fair on the grounds that they encouraged immorality and vice. Among the 'disorderly houses' which the Vice Society managed to close down were several dance halls and private theatres as well as other less savoury establishments. The Evangelicals had a profound dislike of the theatre, as was shown by the comments made during a discussion in the Eclectic Society in 1800 on why a Christian should denounce theatrical amusements. The Revd Josiah Pratt insisted, with rather dubious logic, 'a sermon is the essence of dullness after a play: this shows the evil of the play'; the Revd Basil Woodd was concerned that 'the theatre often exhibits false representations of Providence: things end well for the wicked', while the Revd John Venn declared that 'If Vice were to come in person to take up her residence in London, she would naturally visit the play-house.'[12] It was impossible for Evangelicals to close down public theatres, although a magistrate member of the Vice Society managed temporarily to shut the Royalty Theatre in the East End of London in 1803 on the grounds that it had become a rendezvous for prostitutes. What they were able to do, however, was to determine very largely what plays might be put on. The appointment of a Methodist as official reader of plays from 1802 to 1826 and constant Evangelical pressure on the Lord Chamberlain's office meant that British theatre-goers in the early nineteenth-century were subjected to an unrelieved diet of 'serious' plays.

The pastimes of bull- and bear-baiting and other cruel sports which were popular at the time incurred strong Evangelical disapproval. In a speech supporting one of several efforts by Evangelical M.P.s to get a measure through Parliament banning the sports, Wilberforce commented, 'wretched indeed must be the condition of the common people if we suppose that their whole happiness consists in the practice of such barbarity.'[13] So concerned were the Evangelicals about cruel sports that in 1824 they set up a special society to campaign for their abolition, The Royal Society for the Prevention of Cruelty to Animals, which had T. F. Buxton as its first chairman, and which still exists today. Although legislation was passed in 1835 outlawing bull- and bear-baiting, dog fights and cock-fighting, many of these practices continued, and by 1850 the R.S.P.C.A.'s inspectors were bringing offenders to the courts at the rate of over 200 a year.

One other vice was regarded by the Evangelicals as being serious enough to warrant being tackled by specialized agencies and not left to the general attentions of the Vice Society. This was failure to observe the Sabbath. No other aspect of the behaviour of their fellow countrymen was of more interest to nineteenth-century moral reformers than what they did on Sundays. The Evangelicals believed that, as Wilberforce put it, 'Sunday is intended for strengthening our impression of invisible and eternal things; and that as such, people can only innocently recreate themselves on that day by attending to their religious duties.'[14] They were determined that the rigid Sabbatarianism which they themselves practised, and which effectively reduced the day's activities to church-going and serious reading, should be extended to the whole country. England, they argued, had always been distinguished among the nations of the world for the strictness with which it had adhered to the fourth of the ten commandments. The notorious disregard for the Sabbath displayed in France, which had culminated in the revolutionaries' removal of Sunday from the calendar, had brought anarchy and confusion to the country. The same fate would befall Britain if it failed to observe the Sabbath more strictly. As Napoleon marshalled his troops in north-west France ready to invade England in the summer of 1806, Evangelical M.P.s were fighting desperately in Parliament to obstruct an emergency Government Bill for the nation's defence because it included the authorization of Sunday drilling by the militia. 'If the breach of the Sabbath was author-ised by law', John Newton had earlier written to Wilberforce, 'it would alarm me much more, than to hear that fifty or a hundred thousand French were landed or that our Grand Fleet was totally destroyed. I should consider it as a decided token that God had given us up.'[15]

From the outset, the promotion of a stricter observance of the Sabbath was a major feature of the Evangelicals' movement to reform English manners. George III's Proclamation prohibited 'all our loving subjects, of what degree or quality so ever from playing on the Lord's Day at dice, cards, or any other game whatsoever, either in public or private houses'. Within twelve months of its existence the Vice Society had brought convictions for Sabbath-breaking against 623 people and warned another 3,000 of the offence in London alone. The Society for Promoting the Observance of the Sabbath which was set up in 1809 to take over responsibility for this area of morality continued its work of bringing prosecutions under existing statutes, including the long-defunct Elizabethan Act of Uniformity which enforced compulsory attendance at church on Sundays on penalty of a one shilling fine. In 1831 another Sabbatarian organization was set up, the Lord's Day Observance Society, which still operates today from its Fleet Street headquarters. Meanwhile Evangelical M.P.s were eagerly promoting legislation to further the Sabbatarian cause. In 1780 they had secured an Act outlawing trading, professional entertainment and sport on Sunday, sections of which remain in force to this day. A Bill to outlaw Sunday newspapers in the early years of the nineteenth century received the support of Pitt until he was reminded that three of the four existing Sunday papers supported his Administration. Significantly, the first major issue which the earnest young hero of Disraeli's *Falconet* took up after his entry into Parliament was the Sabbatarian question.

In 1833 a measure was introduced into Parliament which, had it passed, would have gone far towards establishing the Evangelical Sabbath throughout the land. The Bill for promoting better observance of the Lord's Day was drawn up by the Lord's Day Observance Society and introduced by Sir Andrew Agnew, a dedicated Sabbatarian M.P. who had devoted most of his money to buying up sufficient shares in Scottish railway companies to be able to vote down their plans to run Sunday trains. Agnew's Bill prohibited all work, trade, public transport, public meetings and games on Sundays and gave vastly increased powers to magistrates and common informers to bring prosecutions against Sabbath-breakers. It would have deprived the poor of their one substantial meal in the week, the traditional Sunday joint of beef, which was cooked by bakers for those people who had no ovens, and would have denied working people the means of getting into the countryside on their one day of rest from the confined and noxious atmosphere of the factory or the mill. So appalled was Charles Dickens at the effects that Agnew's bill would have had on the poor if it was passed, that he took time off from writing the *Pickwick Papers* to publish a stinging attack on it. As it was, Agnew failed to carry his measure through its second reading by only six votes. He reintroduced the Bill in 1836, in an even stronger form which included the closure of markets on both Saturdays and Mondays to prevent the necessity for Sunday travel, and carried it as far as the committee stage. But George IV's death necessitated the calling of a new Parliament, to which Agnew was not elected, before the Bill's final reading.

Agnew's measure was not resurrected during Victoria's reign but the enthusiasms of the Earl of Shaftesbury and Archbishop Sumner for the Evangelical Sabbath ensured that many of its proposals were taken up. In 1849 Shaftesbury carried a measure ending the collection and delivery of mail on Sundays and two years later a deputation of leading Evangelicals to the Prime Minister ensured the Sunday closure of the Great Exhibition at the Crystal Palace. Legislation passed in 1854 closed all public houses on Sundays, but it had to be repealed the following year after angry riots in Hyde Park protesting against it. Undeterred by mounting opposition, Shaftesbury and Sumner prevailed on Lord Palmerston to order the Sunday closure of the National Gallery and the British Museum in 1856. In the same year Sumner stopped Sunday afternoon military band concerts in all London parks and the efforts of local Evangelicals achieved a cessation of public musical performances on Sundays in most other large towns. During the Sunday band concerts that they were unable to stop, members of the Lord's Day Observance Society were counselled to do what they could 'to make known the way of salvation by the distribution of a great number of tracts'. It is little wonder that in 1855 a National Sunday League was formed to counter the efforts of Sabbatarians, and that when Dickens came to write *Little Dorrit* in the same year he included a chapter on Sunday evening in London to show the effects which they had already had on life in the capital:

> Everything was bolted and barred that could by possibility furnish relief to an overworked people. No pictures, no natural or artificial wonders of the ancient world – all taboo ... Nothing to see but streets, streets, streets. Nothing to breathe but streets, streets, streets ... Nothing for the spent toiler to do but

to compare the monotony of his six days with the monotony of his seventh. (Chapter III)

The establishment throughout England of the drabness and dullness of the Victorian Sunday was the crowning achievement of the movement for the reformation of manners which the Evangelicals led during the first half of the nineteenth century. But it was by no means their only success. By the time of Victoria's accession, cruel sports had already been outlawed, the lottery abolished, many public fairs and wakes closed down and the theatre and the press effectively censored and gagged. There was still a lot of drinking, but the tightening of licensing regulations and the effects of the anti-spirits campaign had ended the excesses of the age of Gin Lane. Palmerston noted in 1844 that 'the greatest topers were those who take a half-dozen glasses,' a mere nothing by eighteenth-century standards. Scandalous sexual behaviour had not disappeared, but those who indulged in it were a good deal more discreet than they had been. On the eve of his accession to the throne in 1832, William IV was advised by the Marquess of Anglesey to keep quiet about his brood of illegitimate children: 'Looking at a picture of Charles II which was in the room, I observed that we were not living in times when that Monarch could be taken as a Model with impunity.'[16]

There is no doubt that a profound change took place in the morals and habits of English people in the first half of the nineteenth century. As Professor Harold Perkin states in his recent book on the period, 'between 1780 and 1850 the English ceased to be one of the most aggressive, brutal, rowdy, outspoken, riotous, cruel and bloodthirsty nations in the world and became one of the most inhibited, polite, orderly, tender-minded, prudish and hypo-critical.'[17] The evidence of this transition is clear throughout every level of society. Among the higher classes it is indicated by the marked decline in race-going, in attendance at theatres and other entertainments, and the closing down of several gaming clubs and pleasure gardens through lack of custom. The wild debauchery of the Regency bucks represented a final fling against the dull puritanism which they saw everywhere coming to prevail. Among the poorer classes, the signs of moral reformation are even more marked. The figures for crime and rioting showed a dramatic drop in the early part of the nineteenth century and the comments of contemporary social observers testify unanimously to the decline of the wild 'Irish temperament' generally attributed to the English poor in the eighteenth century and its replacement by a greater self-discipline and control. As public sports and diversions ceased, people forsook the streets and commons for the quieter pleasures of home. As early as 1825 Francis Place, the radical journalist, noted of London that 'the class of persons who used to be found at the waterside, and at the tea-gardens on Sunday now amuse themselves at home or walk in the parks', and in the same year a Lancashire man complained that 'the Athletic exercises of quoits, wrestling, football, prison bars and shooting with the long-bow are become obsolete – they are now pigeon fanciers, canary breeders and tulip growers.'[18] We are already in the dull domesticity of the Victorian drawing-room.

It would be wrong to suggest that the activities of the Evangelicals alone were responsibile for this major change in the habits and life-style of Englishmen in the early nineteenth century. The period was one in which a number of social and economic forces converged to produce a more sober and respectable population. The lack of colour and gaiety in clothes which many contemporaries noted may have had more to do with the development of cotton mills producing cheap plain garments than with the effects of tracts issued by the Evangelical Prayer Book and Homily Society against excess of apparel. Improvements in the water supply and reductions in the tax on tea and coffee probably did at least as much for the cause of sobriety as the activities of magistrates and temperance societies. Those in the higher classes who had enjoyed so much leisure in the eighteenth century found increasingly that their time was being taken up by the pressures of Parliamentary business or commercial ventures and that the money which they had formerly been able to fritter away at the races or the gaming clubs was now needed to finance improvements on their estates or to invest in manufacturing projects. The rising mercantile and professional classes had neither the time nor the taste for expensive and frivolous diversions. Above all, the lives of the poor were being disciplined and regularized by the pressures of the factory system far more effectively than they could ever be by the moral reformers. Those who had spent twelve or more hours a day throughout the week standing at a spinning machine, or working down a mine shaft, hardly needed the

Sabbatarians to tell them that Sunday should be a day of rest. The Government Commission investigating conditions in mines reported in 1842 that many women and girls were so exhausted by their week's labours that they slept through the whole of Sunday.

The Evangelicals were not the only people to promote the cause of moral reform in the early nineteenth century. As we have seen, many non-Evangelical magistrates keenly enforced the Royal Proclamation against Vice in the hope that it would cut down crime and disorder. Manufacturers and employers were naturally interested in encouraging regularity and sobriety among their workers. Campaigning for the closure of public fairs and wakes in the late 1780s, the *Leeds Intelligencer* commented that such junketings served only to make people 'waste their time to the great loss of their employers', and the *Bristol Journal* declared it to be 'the business of magistrates to lessen the number of diversions calculated to slacken the industry of useful hands'.[19] Nor was it only the forces of law and order and manufacturers who had an interest in suppressing vice and immorality in the country. No group of people were more determined to turn the British working classes into sober and serious-minded citizens in the early nineteenth century than the Radicals. There could, after all, be no revolution while people were more interested in drinking and fornicating than in reading the works of Thomas Paine. The 'sermons' which William Cobbett, the celebrated radical journalist, brought out in 1822, and which were aimed at a mass readership, fulminated against the sins of idleness, drunkenness and gambling just as strongly as any Evangelical tract ever did.

Most contemporaries agreed, however, in seeing the activities of the Evangelical moral reformers as a major contributory factor in producing the transformation in English manners which they witnessed in the early nineteenth century. Critics of the aims and the approach of the movement for the reformation of manners regarded it as a powerful force of repression which had deprived the people of their innocent pastimes and seriously eroded the freedom of individuals to do what they wanted rather than what was good for them. 'The doctrines called Evangelical make all the noise now,' Lucy Aikin told her American correspondent in 1828 'with much Puritanical rigour, in such points as the observance of the Sabbath and the avoidance of public amusements ... they make religion

exceedingly repugnant to the young and cheerful, by setting themselves against all the sports and diversions of the people.' In the same
year John Keble, the great Victorian divine, noted his alarm 'at the
amazing rate at which Puritanism seems to be getting on all over the
Kingdom'.[20]

The most common complaint of detractors of the Evangelical
moral reformers was that they showed a distinct class bias in the
vices which they chose to attack. Sydney Smith, a Whig clergyman,
who was the strongest and most perceptive critic of the movement
for the reformation of manners in the early years of the nineteenth
century, pointed out that the Vice Society concentrated entirely on
the activities of the poor and turned a blind eye to the vices of the
rich. On bull-baiting and bear-baiting it waged full-scale war, yet
did it once turn its attentions to hunting or shooting? 'Is there one
single instance', he asked, 'where they have directed the attention of
the Society to this higher species of suppression, and sacrificed men
of consideration to that zeal for virtue which watches so acutely over
the vices of the poor? ... At present they should denominate
themselves a Society for Suppressing the Vices of persons whose
income does not exceed £500 per annum.'[21] Charles Dickens made
exactly the same complaint about the Sabbatarians in the 1830s.
He said of Agnew's Bill, 'It is directed exclusively, and without
exception of a solitary instance, against the amusements and
recreations of the poor.'[22] In the eyes of its critics, the Evangelical
crusade to reform morals was a class-based movement designed to
discipline and control the poor while leaving the upper classes
untouched.

It is certainly true that the activities of the Vice Society and the
other Evangelical agencies of moral reform were directed almost
exclusively at the pastimes of the poor. This was not, however,
because the Evangelicals were indifferent to the vices of the upper
classes; it was simply that they believed different weapons to be
appropriate for promoting moral reform among the well-to-do. The
Evangelicals themselves were well aware of the manifest unfairness
inherent in attacking only working-class vices. Hannah More asked
in her *Thoughts On the Importance of the Manners of the Great*:
'Will not the common people think it a little inequitable that they
are abridged of the diversions of the public-house and the gaming
yard on Sunday evening, when they shall hear that many houses of

the first nobility are on that evening crowded with company, and such amusements carried on as are prohibited by human laws even on common days?'[23] But while they felt prohibition and prosecution to be the most effective way of attacking the vices of the poor, the moral reformers felt the upper classes would be more susceptible to exhortation and persuasion. The working classes could be reformed only by prohibitory legislation and punishment, but aristocratic sinners merely needed a well-aimed tract to be redeemed. It was a nice social distinction summed up by Hannah More: 'If the Rich and Great will not, from a liberal spirit of doing right and from a Christian spirit of fearing God, abstain from those offences, for which the poor are to suffer fines and imprisonment, effectual good cannot be done!'[24]

There is no doubt that the movement for the reformation of manners was to a certain extent class-based. Among its keenest supporters and promoters were middle- and upper-class magistrates and manufacturers who had an obvious interest in disciplining and controlling the behaviour of the working population. However, it is wrong to see the campaign against vice simply as a device dreamed up by manufacturers and by the forces of law and order to produce a disciplined and sober working class. Working people were them-selves active in it. The Sabbatarian cause, for example, received considerable popular support. In 1857 the National Lord's Day Rest Association was established by working men to promote Sunday observance among their colleagues. It distributed pamphlets on such subjects as 'Sunday Gas Work. Carbonising on the Lord's Day – can it be diminished?' and 'Why are you working today? A Question for Omnibus, Tramway-Car, Cab and Railway Servants'. There was strong working-class support for the Evangelicals' campaign to ban Sunday work in mines and factories and establish the right of every worker to have at least one clear day of rest every week.

Several critics of the Evangelicals accused them not only of showing a distinct class bias in their crusade against vice but also of being politically motivated. In the eyes of radicals and liberals, the Evangelical moral reformers were propagandists for authoritarian and repressive government who preached resignation and submis-siveness to the masses in their sermons and tracts, brought to the courts the disseminators of radical and revolutionary doctrines, and eagerly supported through Parliament measures which curbed free speech and free political association and allowed imprisonment without trial. Left-wing historians have taken up these contemporary criticisms and have portrayed the Evangelicals' campaign against vice as a counter-revolutionary crusade inspired by political and social considerations. They have generally echoed the verdict of William Cobbett that it was the Evangelicals' mission, at a time of acute poverty and suffering and therefore of potential social upheaval in Britain, to 'teach the people to starve without making a noise, and to keep the poor from cutting the throats of the rich'.[25]

The behaviour of the Evangelical moral reformers certainly suggested that they were at least partially motivated by political considerations. In Parliament, Wilberforce and his Saints, not content merely with supporting the emergency laws curbing political meetings and discussion and the frequent suspensions of *habeas corpus* which were imposed by successive Tory governments in the troubled years between the French Revolution and the Peterloo Massacre, actively assisted the passage of these savagely repressive measures with speeches linking them to the cause of morality and calling loudly for their enlargement and extension. Legislation banning associations of workers proposed by Wilberforce in 1799 formed the basis of the Combination Act introduced by William Pitt two years later, which effectively outlawed all trade union activity. Some of the prosecutions initiated by the Vice Society were distinctly political in character. During the 1820s, in conjunction with the Constitutional Association for Suppressing the Progress of Disloyal and Seditious Principles, which was predominantly Evangelical in membership, it regularly brought sellers of radical literature to the courts. Hannah More's *Cheap Repository Tracts* championed the virtues of absolute submission to authority and of resignation in the face of want and adversity quite as much as they called for moral and spiritual regeneration. So strongly political was their theme, indeed, that it was rumoured that they had been written at the behest of the Prime Minister, Pitt. In fact, in 1817 Miss More was approached by the Government and asked to help counteract the spread of radical opinions among the populace in the aftermath of the Napoleonic wars. She responded by starting a new series of cheap tracts, the *Stories for the Middle Ranks of Society and Tales for the Common People*.

In the advertisement to her new tracts in 1818, Hannah More

declared that her object was 'to improve the habits and raise the principles of the mass of the people at a time when their dangers and temptations, moral and political, were multiplied beyond the example of any other period in our history'. The Evangelicals felt that political radicalism, just as much as immorality, was a vice on which they were called to wage full-scale war. The doctrines of the European Enlightenment which spread through Britain in the aftermath of the French Revolution threatened to destroy conventional notions both of religion and morality and of property and authority. The two aspects of this dangerous new-fangled philosophy were indistinguishable and were equally to be resisted. It was no coincidence that Thomas Paine should be the author both of the freethinkers' Bible, *The Age of Reason*, and of the revolutionaries' textbook, *The Rights of Man*, nor that Mrs Carlile was well known as a publisher of a radical newspaper as well as being an atheist. 'The enemies of our political constitution are also enemies to our religion,' Wilberforce told Lord Milton after sitting on the Secret Committee which was set up to look into disturbances in the country in 1817.[26] Hannah More expanded on this point the following year in one of her *Stories for the Middle Ranks* which consisted of a dialogue between Mr Fantom, a vain and shallow man who had been corrupted by reading 'a famous little book written by the new philosopher, Thomas Paine', and Mr Trueman, a simple, honest tradesman who went to Church twice every Sunday, read his Bible without doubting, paid his taxes without disputing, and didn't meddle with things above his station. During their discussion, Trueman observed to Fantom:

> The connection of Jacobinism with impiety is inseparable. I generally find in gentlemen of your fraternity an equal abhorrence of Christianity and good government. The reason is obvious. There are restraints in both. There is subordination in both. In both cases the hatred arises from aversion to a superior. In politics you dislike an earthly king. The Scriptures also set up another king, one Jesus. In both instances, 'we will not have this man to reign over us' is your motto.[27]

Trueman's statement pinpoints the Evangelicals' overriding objection to radical politics. They detested it not just because its exponents were also those who attacked sound morality and revealed religion, but also because they believed that its practice was directly contrary to the teachings of the Bible. The opening verse of Chapter XIII of St Paul's Epistle to the Romans was a favourite text of the Evangelicals: 'Let every soul be subject unto the higher powers: for there is no power but of God. The powers that be are ordained of God.' Numerous sermons on this text were preached by Evangelical clergymen during periods of particular distress and unrest in the late eighteenth and early nineteenth centuries. The Revd Thomas Robinson, Vicar of St Mary's Leicester, and a strong believer in preaching to the people 'the duty of subordination', wrote to Wilberforce to applaud him for supporting Pitt's counter-revolution-ary measures in the 1790s and to assure him of 'the unanimity and firmness of the serious and evangelical clergy of the Church in their attachment to the present government'.[28] Arthur Young counselled all true Christians to support the continuation of the suspension of *habeas corpus* in 1798 as being fully consistent with the principles of 'that truly excellent religion which exhorts to content and to sub-mission to the higher powers.'[29] More than thirty years later, when T. B. Macaulay was rash enough to quote from the Bible in a House of Commons speech supporting Parliamentary reform, Colonel Sibthorp, an Evangelical M.P., immediately rose to correct him and to point out that 'he alluded to Scripture, but the tenor of the observations which he made was in direct contradiction of the precepts which the Scriptures inculcated – namely obedience to superiors, and a proper respect for all orders of society.'[30]

The intensity of the Evangelicals' dislike of radicalism and the vigour with which they campaigned against it often made them look as though they were motivated more by political sentiments than by considerations of religion and morality. Many of Hannah More's tracts concentrated far more on stressing the importance of obeying superiors and of facing economic hardship without protest than on chastising drunkenness and fornication. Her best-selling *Shepherd of Salisbury Plain* was simply a long panegyric to the virtues of contentment and resignation in the face of grinding poverty and want. Her *Village Politics*, which was written in 1793 'to counteract the pernicious doctrines which, owing to the French Revolution, were then becoming seriously alarming to the friends of religion and government in every part of Europe', and addressed to 'all the Mechanics, Journeymen, and Labourers in Great Britain', concentrated on ramming home the message of obedience to the superior powers. Like the story of Mr Fantom and Mr Trueman, it took the form of a dialogue, this time between Jack Anvil, an honest blacksmith and Tom Hod, a mason who wanted 'a new constitution, liberty and equality', having been seduced by reading the works of Thomas Paine. During the course of their discussion Jack quotes extensively from Paul's Epistles to the Romans and persuades Tom, with no apparent difficulty, that England has the best king, the best laws and the most liberty of any country in the world. The story ends with Tom singing 'the Roast Beef of England' and agreeing not to carry out the rather flamboyant gesture of burning his copies of Paine's work to show his conversion from revolutionary principles but rather to 'study to be quiet, work with his own hands, and mind his own business'.[31]

A similar impression of political considerations overriding concern with morality is given by Wilberforce's behaviour in Parliament during the period of acute social and economic unrest between 1817 and 1819. The leader of the Saints was one of the chief members of the Secret Committee on the disturbances in the country, whose alarmist report led directly to the passage of the notorious Six Acts which effectively gagged the press, banned public meetings and associations and allowed imprisonment without trial. He spoke enthusiastically in favour of nearly all of these repressive measures and vigorously opposed efforts to get inquiries into the Government's use of spies and informers and the continued suspension of *habeas corpus*. Worst of all, he spoke vehemently against all proposals to hold a Parliamentary inquiry into the conduct of the magistrates of Manchester over the notorious Peterloo Massacre in 1819, when a peaceful crowd attending a reform meeting had been charged by a troop of cavalry. As a result, eleven people had died and many hundreds had been injured. Wilberforce opposed an inquiry on the rather insubstantial grounds that Parliament 'would be obliged to examine men who professed the new system of morality, and who defied the laws of God and Man'.[32] Nothing that Wilberforce did rankled more with the radicals than his apparent condonation of the Peterloo massacre. Hearing of his speech in Parliament on the subject, Francis Place described him as 'an ugly epitome of the Devil', and in 1820 the *Black Dwarf* summed up his creed as follows:

The Holy Scriptures explicitly state it to be the indispensable duty of Christians to be subject to the higher powers (in Church and State) – to obey magistrates (though as bad as the Manchester ones!) – to render tribute, to whom tribute is due (that is to pay taxes!), and to submit themselves to every ordinance of man for the Lord's sake.[33]

Despite appearances to the contrary, however, the Evangelicals were not in fact politically motivated in their attacks on radicalism. They were convinced that the nature of the disease which afflicted Britain in the late eighteenth and early nineteenth centuries was essentially moral rather than economic or political. It is true that they supported repressive government and preached submission to higher powers; this was because they were terrified that the spread of radical propaganda would threaten religion and because they believed that the Bible taught the duty of subordination. But ultimately, they did not see radicalism as fundamentally vicious, but rather as completely wrong-headed. It was the individual moral regeneration of its inhabitants which they believed would save Britain, rather than any reform of its constitution. The natural response of the Evangelicals to the widespread popular disturbance which they saw in the country was to call for a reassertion of the principles of Christian morality. When Tom Hod asked Jack Anvil if he had read *The Rights of Man*, the latter replied 'No, not I; I had rather by half read "The Whole Duty of Man"'. Wilberforce's first reaction on hearing of radical meetings in Yorkshire in 1805 was to propose a day of fasting and humiliation in the county. Subsequently he reflected that 'a good national education, by training up the people in the principles of true religion, would do more even towards our political benefit than any other measure whatever.'[34]

The radical critics of the Evangelicals misread their call for closer adherence to Christian morality as a political commitment to the cause of repressive government. In fact the Evangelicals had a moral message for the rulers of the country which was just as stern as their message to the masses. If the people were at fault for allowing themselves to be swayed by the arguments of infidels and false prophets then so was the Government for not attending more closely to the very real poverty and distress from which the country was suffering. In 1800 Wilberforce noted: 'I have been using my utmost endeavours to impress the minds of ministers, and of my brother members, with a sense of the necessity of taking effectual steps for the relief of the lower orders ... much hurt by the coolness and dilatoriness of Government.'[35] After the Peterloo Massacre, the *Christian Observer* reminded the Government that it had a moral obligation not only to 'stem the tide of sedition, irreligion, and impiety which threatens to inundate us', but also to 'devise measures to abate the pressure of want upon the labouring classes, and to prevent, if possible, its recurrence'.[36]

Even if they were not politically motivated, the activities of the Evangelical reformers inevitably had the effect of diminishing personal liberty and encouraging the forces of authority and repression in society. The prosecutions which they brought against the sellers of obscene and blasphemous literature naturally encouraged others to bring to the courts those who distributed works advocating social and political revolution, while the Vice Society's use of spies and informers made it considerably easier for the Government to use the same techniques. It was no coincidence that the Evangelicals' campaign against vice occurred at the same time as the passage on to the statute book of the most repressive legislation ever in British history. Both inside and outside Parliament, Evangelicals campaigned vigorously for the extension of the powers of magistracy and police. The Vice Society constantly called for firmer action and severer sentences from local benches and Wilberforce always lent his support to measures designed to strengthen the forces of law and order in the land. In 1792 he intervened at a critical stage of the debate on the Middlesex Justice Bill to ensure that it included a clause facilitating the arrest of suspected persons and in 1804 he spoke warmly in favour of the Misdemeanours Prosecution Bill, which aimed at stimulating criminal prosecutions by allowing the expenses involved in bringing them to be paid out of the rates.

It was this general threat to the liberties of the individual posed by the Evangelicals' efforts to inflict their own concept of good behaviour on their fellow men through private prosecutions and legislation that ultimately alarmed their critics more than their possible class bias or political motivation. Sydney Smith found something particularly repulsive about the way the moral reformers used a spy or informer, 'who gets access to my house and family, worms my secret out of me and then betrays me to the magistrate', and about the way they set themselves up as self-appointed moral censors when 'there are in England about 12,000 clergy, not un-handsomely paid for persuading the people, and about 4,000 justices, thirty grand juries and 40,000 constables, whose duties and whose inclination is to compel them to do right.'[37] Similar comments were made in the House of Commons when Evangelicals introduced bills which sought to impose their own strict morality on the country at large. When they brought forward a measure to outlaw bull-baiting in 1802, William Wyndham, a Tory M.P., commented that 'this petty meddling legislative spirit cannot be productive of good: it serves only to multiply the laws, which are already too numerous, and to furnish mankind with additional means of vexing and harassing one another'; and in the course of a debate on a similar Bill two years later General Gascoyne, another Tory, observed with some concern 'a disposition in many of the members to deprive the poor of their recreations and force them to pass their time in chanting at conventicles'.[38]

Occasionally the Evangelicals themselves betrayed doubts about the rightness of what they were doing. Explaining in his diary why he had not opposed a bill authorizing Sunday posts in 1795, Henry Thornton wrote 'it seems a difficult question to say how far we who know ourselves to be a minority and differ as such should press our own systems on the Legislature.'[39] This was a rare moment of hesitation, however. In general, the Evangelicals do not seem to have felt any qualms about using prosecution and legislation to impose their own moral code on the rest of the country. When John Stuart Mill wrote his great treatise *On Liberty* in 1855 it was significant that he saw the greatest threat to personal freedom coming not from the interference of Government but from the activities of moral re-formers (he instanced especially the Sabbatarians in England and the Prohibitionists in America):

> Wherever the Puritans have been sufficiently powerful ... they have endeavoured, with considerable success, to put down all public, and nearly all private, amusements ... There are still in this country large bodies of persons by whose notions of morality and religion these recreations are condemned; and those persons belonging chiefly to the middle class, who are the

ascendant power in the present social and political condition of of the kingdom, it is by no means impossible that persons of these sentiments may at some time or other command a majority in parliament. How will the remaining portion of the community like to have the amusements that shall be permitted to them regulated by the religious and moral sentiments of the stricter Calvinists or Methodists? Would they not with considerable peremptoriness, desire these intrusively pious members of society to mind their own business? This is precisely what should be said. (Chapter IV)

6

Philanthropy and Paternalism

In the last year of his life the Earl of Shaftesbury told his biographer, Edwin Hodder, 'I am essentially and from deep-rooted conviction an Evangelical of the Evangelicals. I have worked with them constantly, and I am satisfied that most of the great philanthropic movements of the century have sprung from them.'[1] It was a reasonable claim. Most of the famous humanitarian ventures of the nineteenth century had Evangelical inspiration and leadership: Elizabeth Fry's work in prisons; Josephine Butler's crusade on behalf of prostitutes; Dr Barnardo's mission to deprived children; Edward Rudolf's establishment of the Church of England's Children's Society for Waifs and Strays; and the movements which Shaftesbury himself led to reform the factory system, humanize the laws relating to lunatics and establish decent housing for the working classes. The work of these and other Evangelical pioneers helped to make philanthropy a major 'industry' in Victorian England and established a tradition of voluntary charitable activity which remains in the country to this day. It also pointed the way for Government action and so laid the foundations of the Welfare State.

The Evangelicals were drawn to philanthropic work by a variety of motives. In part they were simply obeying Christ's command to clothe the naked and feed the hungry and remembering his words: 'Inasmuch as ye have done it unto one of the least of these my brethren, ye have done it unto me.' In part, they also undertook it as a preliminary to attempts at conversion. Just as the slaves had to be freed before they would be in a position to receive the Gospel, so the poor must be raised from the depths of misery and deprivation if they were to heed the call to vital religion. But above all, the Evangelicals devoted themselves to 'good works' because they were profoundly moved by human want and suffering. Their evangelizing interests took them naturally into those places where humanity was at its least regenerate, into the prisons and brothels, the factories and slums. The cruelty and misery which they saw there angered and appalled them and resolved them to devote themselves to fighting for reforms and improvements.

The basis of the Evangelicals' response to poverty and suffering was emotional rather than ideological. The sight of a half-starved child brought tears of compassion and led them to dig deep in their pockets, not to ponder on the economic and social order which had brought it to that state. Many Evangelicals were deeply conservative in their social attitudes and held that since poverty was ordained by Providence to be the inevitable lot of the masses, it could never therefore be eliminated. All of them agreed that sin was at the root of human misery and that religion alone offered a lasting remedy to it. The Evangelicals did not believe that poverty should be tackled by reconstructing the social and economic order, as the Christian Socialists advocated. They certainly did not agree with the radicals that the poor should organize themselves to agitate for a change in their condition. They did, however, feel an overwhelming responsibility to relieve human suffering wherever they found it and a keen determination to call those with wealth and influence to do the same. Their attitude is nicely summed up by a prayer of Henry Thornton's: 'Give to the poor contentment with their lot, and to the rich a spirit of compassion and benevolence.'[2]

Much Evangelical philanthropy followed directly from missionary work among the poor and went hand in hand with efforts at conversion. Hannah More and her sisters attended to the temporal as well as the spiritual needs of the inhabitants of the Mendips and established clothing schemes and mutual benefit societies in each of the villages. W. J. Orsman began his evangelizing activities among the East London costermongers by setting up a fund for the purchase of new barrows and donkeys. Dr Barnardo first saw the plight of destitute children in the 1860s when he was a ragged school teacher. The comprehensive booklets of instructions given to the London Bible Women included recipes for cheap soup and details of how to make beds which could be sold to the poor for six shillings each.

Marion, the first Bible woman, established a dormitory in Clerken-
well for watercress girls. As the only people prepared to venture into
the slums and alleys of the metropolis, the Bible Women and the
London City missionaries inevitably found themselves combining
the functions of social worker and health visitor. Many Evangelical
clergymen set up relief agencies attached to their churches. John
Venn divided the parish of Clapham into eight districts, each of
which had a visitor who regularly went round visiting the sick and
needy. His son, also John, who was vicar of St Peter's, Hereford,
set up the Hereford Society for aiding the industrious, which
enabled the poor to rent allotments cheaply and to buy coal at
sixpence a hundredweight. Rowland Hill established a society
to provide decent clothes for the poor of Blackfriars because he
felt it was want of them that kept people away from church on
Sundays. His Surry Chapel also had a school of industry, a society
for the relief of poor women and a number of almshouses attached
to it.

The intermingling of evangelistic and philanthropic motives was
especially apparent in the Evangelicals' work among prostitutes.
The chance of being able to redeem both the bodies and souls of a
particularly wretched and unregenerate section of humanity made
this a favourite area of activity for them. As chaplain to the Lock
Hospital, which annually treated over 500 girls for venereal disease,
the Revd Thomas Scott was the first to see the importance of
providing residential care for ex-prostitutes and he raised money to
erect a hostel where they could stay until they found employment.
While it was being built, he had several girls lodging in his own
house free of charge. Another Evangelical clergyman, the Revd
Baptist Noel, continued Scott's work in the 1830s and set up the
Female Aid Society which opened its first hostel for ex-prostitutes in
Islington. In the following decade two teachers from ragged schools
started the London by Moonlight Mission, a venture which involved
missionaries going into the streets and pleading with prostitutes to
change their ways. Those who could be persuaded were taken into
hostels and homes. Subsequently the Midnight Meeting Movement
and the Female Mission to the Fallen issued invitations to prostitutes
to come to midnight gatherings with refreshments provided, where
attempts to redeem them were made by Evangelical ladies stationed
at strategic points in the meeting-halls. Evangelical activity among

prostitutes continued through the 1850s with the foundation of the Rescue Society in 1853, the London Female Preventive and Reformative Institute four years later and the establishment of Homes of Hope at the end of the decade. In 1866 Josephine Butler began the work among Liverpool prostitutes that was to lead her later to campaign for the repeal of the Contagious Diseases Acts, which regulated and so effectively legalized prostitution in England.

Not surprisingly, it was particularly in the specialized agencies that the Evangelicals set up in an effort to convert the urban working classes that philanthropic work was undertaken. Ragged schools generally provided washing facilities and basic clothing for their pupils. In 1851 three London schools had the bright idea of putting twenty-five of their boys to work as shoeblacks at the Great Exhibition. Other boys were sent out as 'broomers' to sweep the city's pavements or found jobs as messengers. Soon most ragged schools were providing employment for their pupils. In 1867 the Destitute Children's Dinner Society was set up to provide free food for all ragged school pupils. The London City Mission concentrated particularly on the problem of the homeless in the metropolis. In 1850 it carried out a survey of cheap accommodation in London which revealed that there was virtually nothing available for the poor other than the few thousand beds available in night shelters and refuges which had been set up by Evangelicals around the city, and the ill-regulated and often insanitary common lodging houses. On the basis of the survey Shaftesbury introduced legislation in 1850 which laid down minimum standards for lodging houses. Three years later the London City Mission established its own housing society to provide cheap homes for the working classes.

To further their philanthropic activities the Evangelicals set up voluntary societies. Ever since the Clapham Sect had founded the Society for Bettering the Condition and Increasing the Comforts of the Poor (the Bettering Society) in 1798, new charitable organizations had been started at an average rate of six a year, until by the middle of the nineteenth century there were nearly 500 of them, ranging from the Society for the Reception of Penitent Prostitutes and the Friendly Female Society for the Relief of Single Women of Good Character, to the City of London Truss Society, and the Institution for the Cure of Various Diseases by Bandages and Compression. So numerous were these philanthropic ventures that in 1853 the Government appointed the Charity Commissioners to oversee their activities. Co-ordinating societies like the Ragged School Union and the Reformatory and Refuge Union were set up to bring together those organizations which were active in the same field. In 1856 a London Evangelical clergyman, William Pennefather, initiated an annual conference for all those involved in philanthropic work and six years later his wife established an Association of Female workers which brought together representatives of most of the main charitable societies. In 1869 the Charity Organization Society was founded to co-ordinate the efforts of all the voluntary societies.

The Evangelicals established the voluntary charitable society as the characteristic vehicle for philanthropic activity in Victorian England. It is principally to them that the country owes its tradition, still strong today, of voluntary social service undertaken by unpaid workers and supported by the subscriptions and donations of private individuals. Of course, not all the charitable organizations which grew up in the early nineteenth century were started by Evangelicals, but the great majority were; it has been calculated that three-quarters of all the voluntary charitable organizations in existence in England in 1850 were Evangelical in character and control. The Evangelicals taught their countrymen the principle of generous giving to charity. Wilberforce devoted a quarter of his income to philanthropic objects before he was married and Henry Thornton gave away a third of his wealth even after marriage. On a visit to England towards the end of Victoria's reign, Hugo Munsterberg, the German psychologist, commented 'There is no country in the world in which so large an amount is given in charity.'[3] The Evangelicals also provided a large and eager voluntary labour force for charitable activity in England by persuading middle-class ladies that they had a particular responsibility to attend to the welfare of the poor.

In 1798 Sarah Trimmer published a small work entitled *The Economy of Charity*. The book, which achieved considerable sales, was addressed to 'ladies of rank and fortune to encourage them to take up Sunday School work and voluntary benefactions'. Its message, that in the performance of good works among the poor and needy lay the special duty of the female sex, was taken up and repeated in nearly every Evangelical tract written specifically for women in the early nineteenth century. It was the theme of the numerous accounts of the activities of famous female philanthropists like Elizabeth Fry and Catharine Marsh that appeared during the period and of many of the books written by Hannah More. In one of her most popular and influential works, *Coelebs*, Miss More made her heroine devote two evenings a week to visiting the homes of the poor in her village, while in her *Strictures on Female Education*, she summed up the Evangelical call to the ladies of England:

> It would be a noble employment, and well becoming the tenderness of their sex, if ladies were to consider the superintendence of the poor as their immediate office and set apart a fixed portion of their time as sacred to the poor, whether in relieving, instructing or working for them.[4]

In extolling the virtues of female philanthropy, the Evangelicals were not advocating a completely new role for women. It had always been the practice among well-off ladies in the country to visit the homes of the poor and distribute food and clothes among the sick and needy. The effect of Evangelical propaganda was greatly to extend this practice and to give a new purpose and direction to the lives of many middle-class women at a time when they particularly needed it. Throughout the nineteenth century women outnumbered men in Britain. For those who failed to marry, or who were widowed early, there were virtually no careers or occupations open to follow. Even for many married women life was often inactive and monotonous. It is not hard to see why the Evangelicals' call on the female sex to minister to the poor and needy evoked such a strong response; it solved the problem of the 'surplus' women. 'There is no class of persons', Wilberforce commented in the 1830s, 'whose condition has been more improved in my experience than that of unmarried women. Formerly there seemed to be nothing useful in which they could naturally be busy, but now they may always find an object in attending the poor.'[5] Lucy Aikin wrote to Dr Channing in the same vein in 1841, attributing to the influence of Sarah Trimmer and Hannah More the fact that the practice of visiting the poor had now become 'a fashion and a rage' among English women:

> This philanthropic impulse acted at first chiefly within the Evangelical party; but that party became, at length, great

enough to give the tone to society at large; and the practice of superintending the poor has become so general, that I know no one circumstance by which the manners, studies and occupations of Englishwomen have been so extensively modified, or so strikingly contradistinguished from those of a former generation.[6]

Women responded to the Evangelical call to good works in large numbers. The lady bountiful became a familiar figure in the Victorian period. Not surprisingly, those who had already embraced vital religion were the most enthusiastic to devote themselves to the work. 'Serious' ladies from the aristocracy visited the homes of poor tenants on their estates and, when in London, helped to distribute tea at workhouses and mission rooms. Women of humbler origin became district visitors or enrolled in the Deaconess Institution, which the Revd William Pennefather and his wife had established at Mildmay in 1860 for 'females desirous of labouring in the Lord's Vineyard as Phoebe did of old'. Victorian fiction includes two memorable portrayals of Evangelical 'do-gooders': Miss Clack in *The Moonstone*, the stalwart supporter of the Mothers' Small Clothes Conversion Society which existed, 'as all serious people know, to rescue unredeemed fathers' trousers from the pawn-brokers and to prevent their resumption, on the part of the irreclaimable parents, by abridging them immediately to suit the proportions of the innocent son'; and Mrs Pardiggle in *Bleak House* who proudly listed her activities to all new acquaintances: 'I am a school lady, I am a visiting lady, I am a reading lady, I am a distributing lady, I am on the local linen box committee and many general committees, and my canvassing alone is very extensive.'

Miss Clack and Mrs Pardiggle exemplify a figure with which the Victorians were all too familiar, the 'professional philanthropist'. In the same year that Lucy Aikin commented that visiting the poor was now all the rage, Lord Shaftesbury noted after a particularly successful tea party at the Jurston Street Ragged School: 'these things are now becoming "fashionable". Humanity will soon be considered "elegant", "genteel", etc.'. He was right; philanthropy was fast becoming a cult. More and more ladies were taking up poor visiting as a socially desirable pastime, especially once it became known that the Queen herself undertook it. Affected sentimentalists were appearing on public platforms to plead the philanthropic cause, like Mr Godfrey Ablewhite in *The Moonstone*: 'a barrister by profession, a ladies' man by temperament and a good Samaritan by choice, female benevolence and female destitution could do nothing without him ... As a speaker at charitable meetings the like of him for drawing your tears and your money was not easy to find.' The Victorians may have overdone their philanthropy; but at least a society where do-gooding is fashionable is preferable to one where the want and suffering of the poor is ignored, as had at least partly been the case in England until the Evangelicals helped to awaken the consciences of their countrymen.

The Evangelicals believed that poverty and suffering were better dealt with by voluntary charitable effort than by compulsory action on the part of the state. They felt that Government action in this sphere by-passed the moral responsibilities of individuals to use their time and money to help those in need. As we have seen, the direct emotional nature of the Evangelicals' response to social and economic problems made them more likely to set up a relief society than to campaign for reforming legislation. None the less, there were certain areas where human suffering and misery were so acute that they believed state action was necessary to relieve it. Evangelicals were in the forefront of all the major campaigns for humanitarian legislation in the early nineteenth century. They had the great advantage over other groups pressing for state action of having direct knowledge of the conditions prevailing in factories and slums through the reports of missionaries working among the poor. Sometimes Evangelical missionaries themselves campaigned for government action to alleviate suffering and hardship. Evangelists of the London City Mission, for example, agitated successfully for the erection of drinking fountains in the slum areas of the City. More often, they backed up the efforts of Evangelical M.P.s to secure legislation.

Evangelical M.P.s were actively involved in the three main humanitarian movements of the early nineteenth century. They strongly supported the campaign to outlaw the employment of young boys as chimney sweeps' apprentices, which achieved success in 1834 when Shaftesbury secured legislation ending the scandal of the 'climbing boys' whose plight Charles Kingsley was to describe so graphically in *The Water Babies*. They were keen advocates of the cause of criminal law reform, and voted enthusiastically for the destruction of the savage eighteenth-century penal code which hanged a man for stealing sixpence, believing, as T. F. Buxton put it, that this was directly contrary 'to the temper and spirit of that mild and merciful religion, which desireth not the death of a sinner, but rather that he should turn from his wickedness and live'.[8] They were also in the forefront of the movement for prison reform, spurred on by reports brought back by missionaries and chaplains engaged in evangelistic work in gaols of the appalling conditions suffered by prisoners. In 1819, Buxton, who was the brother-in-law of the famous prison reformer, Elizabeth Fry, published *An Inquiry Whether Crime or Misery are Produced or Prevented by our Present System of Prison Discipline*. The book had a major influence on Robert Peel and helped to inspire the reforms which, as Home Secretary, he introduced in the English prison system in the 1820s. Evangelical agitation in Parliament was instrumental in securing the abolition in 1853 of the practice of transportation, and the gradual phasing out of the treadmill from English gaols in the latter part of the nineteenth century.

One major campaign for state action to alleviate human suffering particularly associated with the Evangelicals was, of course, the movement to humanize conditions in England's factories. In 1794 the Revd Thomas Gisborne first drew attention to the terrible conditions endured by children working in factories and commented, 'this case seems to call loudly for the interference of the Legislature.'[9] Six years later the Bettering Society called specifically for legislation to limit the number of hours worked by children in cotton mills, to regulate the age and conditions of apprenticeship and to provide for the regular inspection of factories. It was to take nearly fifty years of sustained agitation, much of it in the face of indifference and even hostility from manufacturers, to put these measures on to the statute book and to make the Government accept that it had a responsibility to intervene in the running of industry to protect those employed in it. The progress made by the factory reformers was pitifully slow. In 1802 Sir Robert Peel the elder carried through Parliament a Bill drafted by the Bettering Society which ended the forced apprenticeship of orphan children to the Lancashire cotton mills and abolished night work for children, but he failed to secure further reforms, despite strong support from

Wilberforce and Spencer Perceval. Successive attempts by Evangelical M.P.s to introduce measures regulating the employment of children in factories met with no success. In 1830 the Ten Hours Movement was launched by a group of Yorkshire Evangelicals headed by the Revd G. S. Bull, a Bradford curate, to campaign for legislation limiting the number of hours which could be worked in factories. The Parliamentary spokesman of the movement, Michael Sadler, M.P. for Leeds, carried a bill in 1833 restricting the number of hours which children could work to eight a day. It was not until 1847, however, that the Evangelicals were finally able to secure legislation limiting all factory workers to a ten-hour day and establishing a centralized factory inspectorate.

The Evangelicals pursued their campaign for factory reform so determinedly because they believed that the spiritual as well as the temporal interests of the workers depended on it. Side by side with their call for a limitation in the number of hours worked by factory operatives went a demand that the leisure thus provided should be used for religious instruction. Sir Robert Peel told M.P.s in 1802 that the first main object of his Bill was to promote the religious and moral education of the factory children. It was the Sabbatarian enthusiasms of its promoters, rather than any humanitarian considerations, that were responsible for the inclusion in the 1847 Act of the provision that there should be no work in factories on Saturday afternoons or Sundays. When the great battle to secure a ten-hour working day had finally been won, the Earl of Shaftesbury, who had taken over leadership of the movement from Sadler in 1833 and carried the 1847 Factory Act through Parliament, told a gathering of those who had been active in the campaign: 'You will remember the principal motive that stimulated your own activity, and the energetic aid of your supporters in parliament, was the use that might be made of this leisure for the moral improvement of the factory people.'[10]

Shaftesbury is traditionally thought of as the champion of factory children, just as Wilberforce is regarded as the liberator of slaves. Both men suffer from being remembered primarily for only one of many achievements in their lives. Shaftesbury was at the head of virtually every campaign to get humanitarian legislation in the middle of the nineteenth century. In 1842 he had carried through Parliament a measure outlawing the employment of women and boys under ten in coal mines and so ended one of the greatest scandals of the Industrial Revolution. Three years later he was responsible for legislation regulating madhouses and lunatic asylums, which brought to a culmination years of agitation on behalf of the mentally ill. Within twelve months of steering the Ten Hours Act through Parliament, Shaftesbury secured a Government grant to enable a thousand ragged school children every year to emigrate and start a new life in the colonies. In 1853 he promoted the first piece of legislation designed to secure decent housing for the working classes, the Common Lodging Houses Act. He served as Chairman of the permanent Commission on Lunacy set up by the Government in 1845 and of the Board of Health, established in 1848. In 1855 he was responsible for organizing the Sanitary Commission which went out to the Crimea in 1855 and, according to Florence Nightingale, saved the British Army there.

Shaftesbury was indeed the 'professional philanthropist' *par excellence*. Almost all his waking hours were given up to philanthropic ventures. When he was out of Parliament in 1846, he spent his days touring the slums of London in the company of a doctor and an evangelist from the London City Mission. Shaftesbury did as much for humanitarian causes outside Parliament as he did within it. He regularly chaired the public meetings of the major philanthropic societies and was an active committee member of most of them. In 1866 he obtained from the Admiralty a disused frigate and set it up in the Thames as a national refuge and school of industry for homeless and destitute children. This was the first of the many Shaftesbury homes which he established around the country and which still exist today, serving the purpose for which he created them. In 1873, when his wife died, he set up in her memory a fund for watercress and flower girls. Shaftesbury's approach to poverty and suffering was unashamedly sentimental — he was often moved to tears by what he saw on his tours round slums and factories — but it was also eminently practical. When on one of his perambulations through East London he came across a ragged school struggling to exist in a broken-down and filthy stable, he went back immediately to the Houses of Parliament, stationed himself at the members' entrance and asked everyone who came in to give him a sovereign. He returned to the school later in the day with £28 and ordered its immediate repair.

Every humanitarian cause with which Shaftesbury's name was associated he had initially taken up because he felt that in doing so he was obeying the commandment of God. When in 1833 the Revd G. S. Bull asked him if he would take over the Parliamentary leadership of the Ten Hours Movement made vacant by Michael Sadler's departure from the House of Commons, Shaftesbury replied: 'I dare not refuse the request you have so earnestly pressed. I believe it is my duty to God and the poor . . . to me, it appears less a matter of policy than of religion.'[11] It was not simply the rightness of the cause itself that made Evangelicals campaign for humanitarian legislation; it was also that they felt a direct commission from the Lord to do so. The sense that they were called to the task by God fortified and hardened their determination as they struggled to awaken their fellow men to the need for action to alleviate the appalling suffering and cruelty in the land. Often it was the very strength of the Evangelicals' convictions which did most to dispel the indifference and hostility with which contemporaries regarded their campaigns and to evoke a warm and sympathetic response. After he had introduced the report of his commission on the employment of children in mines in June 1842, Shaftesbury noted in his diary:

> As I stood at the table, and just before I opened my mouth, the words of God came forcibly to my mind, "Only be strong and of good courage" — praised be His Holy Name, I was as easy from that moment as though I had been sitting in an arm-chair. Many men, I hear, shed tears ... Members took me aside, and spoke in a *very serious* tone of thanks and admiration.[12]

Shaftesbury's great achievement was to establish it as the right and duty of the state to interfere in the organization of industry and commerce to protect the interests of the workers. More than any other single individual, he championed the doctrine of benevolent state intervention which was the Evangelicals' distinctive contribution to the development of the Welfare State in Britain. Of all the groups who campaigned for legislative action to deal with social and economic problems in the early nineteenth century, the Evangelicals alone formulated a coherent argument on which to base Government interference. In place of the prevailing notion of laissez faire they offered the philosophy of paternalism. During a debate on the plight of workers in the silk trade in 1827, Michael Sadler deplored the fact that manufacturers had unlimited opportunities to pursue wealth and gain while their employees had not even the means to ensure a living wage. He called for the Government to intervene and 'to exhibit itself in the attitude of a kind parent who, while exulting in the strength and vigour of his elder born, still extends his fostering care to the young and helpless branches of his family'.[13] Five years later, in a speech moving the second reading of his Bill to regulate the employment of children in factories, he called on the Legislature to act 'as we could wish others (had done) regarding our own children under like circumstances, or as we shall wish we had done when the Universal Parent shall call us to a strict account for the conduct of the least of these little ones.'[14] Here was a clear statement of the doctrine of paternalism which Shaftesbury was to establish as the basis of Government policy on social and economic issues, and which was to inspire most of the social welfare legislation passed in the Victorian age.

It is not surprising that the Evangelicals' great contribution to Victorian social reform was the theory of paternalist government. Their whole attitude to the poor and the suffering was intensely and unashamedly paternalistie. This was what critics objected to about Evangelical philanthropy. One might think that the work of the ragged schools would have won the approval of those two great champions of the poor and destitute in mid-nineteenth century England, Henry Mayhew and Charles Dickens. In fact, both men had a strong antipathy towards the ragged school movement and violently attacked it in the press. What they disliked was the Evangelicals' desire not just to relieve the temporal wants of the poor but to convert and improve them as well. Evangelicals were strongly criticized for patronizing the objects of their philanthropy and treating them as children rather than assisting them to stand on their own feet and help themselves. This, it was argued, only encouraged the poor to remain weak and helpless. Writing to Dr Channing in 1831 about the popularity among middle-class ladies of visiting the poor which the Evangelicals had fostered, Lucy Aikin commented: 'A positive demand for misery was created by the incessant eagerness manifested to relieve it. In many places the poor, those amongst them especially who have known how to put on a little saintliness, have been actually pampered and rendered like the indoor menials of the wealthy – lazy, luxurious, discontented, lying and worthless.'[15]

It is true that the Evangelicals were more interested in 'improving' the poor than encouraging them to help themselves and that their attitude does often seem patronizing. Mrs Trimmer advised the readers of her *Economy of Charity* to 'devote their personal attention only towards those of the poor who distinguish themselves by their cleanliness: in the meantime, ladies may perhaps depute those by whom they send their benefactions to give the others hopes of future kindnesses, on no other condition than that of their cleaning themselves, their children and apartments'.[16] Ragged schools refused to admit those children who would not wash themselves in the baths which they provided. There was a certain inevitable condescension in the Evangelicals' dealings with the poor, occasioned as much by their strong urge to redeem and convert them as by a sense of social superiority. It is well brought out in the reflections with which Hannah More closed her account of her work in the Mendips:

> I have devoted the remnant of my life to the poor, and to those that have no helper; and if I can do them little good, I can at least sympathize with them; and I know it is some comfort for a forlorn creature to be able to say, 'There is somebody that cares for me'. That simple idea of being cared for has always appeared to me to be a very cheering one. Besides this, the affection they have for me is a strong engine with which to lift them to the love of higher things; and though I believe others work successfully by terror, yet kindness is the instrument with which God has enabled *me* to work.[17]

There was, however, another side to paternalism. The Evangelicals' conception of the poor as helpless children may have led them to be condescending and patronizing but it also led to a more direct and more compassionate response to their plight than was forthcoming from those who regarded them simply as victims of a particular economic or social system. Their concern to improve and convert the poor may have smacked of self-righteousness, but at least it betokened an interest in them as individuals, each with an immortal and infinitely important soul to be redeemed, rather than merely as units in the annual statistics on the incidence of poverty. Shaftesbury summed up the positive side of Evangelical paternalism when he said in 1846, 'my desire has been to raise up the moral character and feelings of the working classes; and this end can be effected only by instructing them of their real dignity as immortal beings and treating them as such.'[18] No Benthamite social reformer could claim as much.

After officiating at the annual prize giving of the Ragged School Union in 1870, Shaftesbury noted in his diary:

> Never was I more touched, never more sorrowful. It is probably, the close of these Christian and heart-moving spectacles. The godless, non-Bible system is at hand; and the Ragged Schools, with all their Divine polity, with all their burning and fruitful love for the poor, with all their prayers and harvests for the temporal and eternal welfare of forsaken, heathenish, destitute, sorrowful, and yet innocent children, must perish under the all-conquering march of intellectual power.[19]

The Evangelicals watched with increasing concern as, at the end of the nineteenth century, the initiative in policy making passed to the Utilitarians and the social scientists. They witnessed the gradual acceptance by the Government and the public of a doctrine of social reform very different from their own, which sought to eliminate want and suffering by massive programmes of social and economic reconstruction rather than by redeeming the individual sinner, and which relied on secular rather than religious agencies for its implementation. They saw their own beloved ragged schools give way to the more efficient and better-regulated institutions set up by the National Education Board. It was, of course, an inevitable development for which the Evangelicals had themselves paved the way, by insisting that the state had a duty to look after the welfare of its members. But this did not make it any less painful for them to behold. Bureaucratic schemes of social reform, however scientific and comprehensive they might be, could never achieve the same depth of sympathy with the poor as Evangelical paternalism had. As the hearse containing the Earl of Shaftesbury's coffin made its way to Westminster Abbey on October 8th, 1885, it passed through streets lined with deputations from ragged schools, costermongers' and flower girls' relief societies, missions, refuges, and training ships. Many of them held banners on which they had painstakingly woven such texts as 'I was naked and ye clothed me' and 'I was a stranger and ye took me in'. While the coffin was being carried up the steps into the Abbey, with the Costermongers' Temperance Society Band playing 'Safe in the Arms of Jesus', a poor labourer turned to his companion and said in a choking voice 'Our Earl's gone! God A'mighty knows he loved us, and we loved him. We shan't see his likes again.'[20]

7

The Age of Societies

Shaftesbury's funeral service in Westminster Abbey was attended by representatives of nearly 500 different societies, most of which had been established by Evangelicals during his lifetime. The enthusiasm which the Evangelicals showed for setting up societies to convert and reform their contemporaries was one of their most important and enduring legacies to the Victorians. From it developed that passion for doing and organizing which still characterizes the English today. In his celebrated essay on the Clapham Sect written in 1849, Sir James Stephen concluded that the proliferation of societies was one of the most striking consequences of the Evangelical Revival. He noted that whereas the effect of religious enthusiasm on the continental mind was to turn it to speculation and mysticism, in the case of the practical Englishman it was more likely to lead to the formation of a voluntary organization. 'Ours is the age of societies,' he continued; 'For the redress of every oppression there is a public meeting. For the cure of every sorrow there are patrons, vice-presidents and secretaries. For the diffusion of every blessing of which mankind can partake in common, there is a committee.'[1]

Of the many groups and interests with a cause to promote in the early nineteenth century, none organized themselves so systematically or on so large a scale as the Evangelicals. The level and variety of their activity was phenomenal: in one week in May 1829 fifty public meetings of different Evangelical societies were advertised in the *Record* as taking place in London alone. They ranged from a sale of useful work for the Metropolitan City Mission to a breakfast-time gathering of the Sunday School Union. Every conceivable evangelistic and philanthropic object had a society devoted to it, however obscure and trivial it might seem. There probably was somewhere a real organization dedicated to the same aim as the British Ladies' Servants' Sunday Sweethearts Supervision Society patronized by Miss Clack in *The Moonstone*. At the other end of the scale there were the huge societies devoted to mainstream evangelistic work like the British and Foreign Bible Society (the Bible Society for short) which, by the middle of the nineteenth century, had 460 auxiliaries, 373 branches and nearly 2,500 local associations, and an annual income of well over £100,000.

The Bible Society was by far the largest and most important of the voluntary organizations which the Evangelicals set up. Tradition has it that it owed its origin to the initiative of the Revd Thomas Charles. One day in 1802, while walking in the Welsh parish to which he had been exiled because of his seriousness, Charles met a young girl whom he recognized as an attender at his church and whom he asked to repeat to him the previous Sunday's lesson. The girl replied that she was unable to do this as bad weather during the week had prevented her from making her usual seven-mile walk over the hills from home to the church to read the Bible. Moved by this encounter, Charles asked the committee of the Religious Tract Society if there was any way in which Bibles could be distributed to the people of Wales. 'Surely a society might be formed for the purpose,' one of the committee suggested, 'and if for Wales, why not for the Kingdom? and if for the kingdom, why not for the world?' A public meeting was called in Bishopsgate on March 7th, 1804 and there the Bible Society was founded 'to undertake the circulation of the Scriptures, and of the Scriptures only, without note or comment'. This latter aim provoked strong criticism from orthodox Anglicans who felt that the Society was seeking to supplant the Church's traditional role as interpreter of the Bible.

Despite the hostility with which it was regarded by many Anglicans, the Bible Society rapidly developed to become the largest evangelistic organization in England. Within twenty years of its foundation it had spent very nearly £1,000,000 on printing and distributing the Scriptures in 130 languages including eighty in which the Bible had not previously been available. To finance this gigantic operation, and to handle its work on the home front, the Society had a carefully graduated network of auxiliaries, which operated at county and city level and whose primary aim was 'to interest the higher and more wealthy classes of the community and to procure their contributions', branches covering towns and districts of cities which were intended 'to excite a similar feeling in the labouring classes', and local associations which allocated individual villages and areas of towns to sub-committees who undertook regular door-to-door canvasses of the houses in their district to ascertain 'Bible wants'.[2] Like so many other Evangelical ventures, the Bible Society got particularly active support from women. By 1820 there were thriving Ladies' Bible Associations in London, Bristol, Southampton, Brighton, Reading, Weymouth, Henley, Abingdon, Maidenhead and Farnham, while in Liverpool, which was divided into 332 sub-districts for Bible Society purposes, there were 600 women at work, who in one period of three months had raised £972 and found over 7,000 new subscribers for the Society. As a contemporary critic observed in 1822, the Bible Society met you everywhere you went – 'in the Anniversary and the committee meeting – in the city and village – in advertisements in the newspapers, and in placards on the walls. It crosses you in your walks, with troops of female associates; it is the theme of your social parties, and of your domestic circles. It ascends your pulpits, and canvasses for charity at your doors.'[3]

Several other Evangelical societies were sufficiently large to follow the Bible Society's practice of having auxiliaries and branches throughout the country. The Church Missionary Society, the Religious Tract Society, the Jew Society, the Vice Society and the Bettering Society all had a membership of several thousand, including, except in the case of the C.M.S., many Nonconformist evangelicals as well as Anglicans. The Vice Society and the Bettering Society had a large number of members who were not evangelicals at all, as did most of the societies set up by Evangelicals in the early nineteenth century for general philanthropic purposes. Only the organizations with distinctly religious objects, like the Lord's Day Observance Society and the Church Pastoral Aid Society, had exclusively evangelical membership. In those which were devoted to popular humanitarian causes, like the Anti-Slavery Society and the R.S.P.C.A., non evangelicals often attained high office and played a leading role.

All the Evangelical societies were organized and financed in the same way. They were run by a committee of leading Evangelical laymen with a full-time secretary and supporting staff working from a central London headquarters. To raise funds, local branches held sales of work and tea parties and organized house-to-house collections to supplement the money obtained from subscriptions and donations. The Evangelical societies invented many of the fund-raising devices used by voluntary charities today. We have already seen that the Church Missionary Society invented the system of weekly pledged gifts which is now operated so successfully by Oxfam. The ladies of the Bible Society similarly pioneered the technique of house-to-house collection and added the word 'canvass' to the English language. The origins of the innumerable summer fêtes held on vicarage lawns to raise money for charity are to be found in such Evangelically inspired events as the 'serious fancy fair' held in the Vicar of Wrexhill's garden in 1834 'for the promotion of an object most precious in the eyes of all professing Christians, namely, the fitting out of a mission to Fababo'.

To add respectability to their cause, and to swell their funds, the Evangelical societies eagerly sought aristocratic and even royal patronage. In the early decades of the nineteenth century this was difficult to obtain—Evangelicalism was not well enough established and to many it still smacked dangerously of enthusiasm. But as the upper classes themselves came under the influence of vital religion and seriousness became fashionable, members of the aristocracy were only too keen to lend their support to Evangelical societies. By 1834, when Lord Bexley, a former Chancellor of the Exchequer, became President of the parent Society, most of the Bible Society's Auxiliaries had local bigwigs as their Vice-Presidents, and two members of the Royal family had agreed to be patrons of the Society. They were the Duke of Gloucester, who was also President of the Anti-Slavery Society and the Bettering Society, and the Duke of Kent, who was also President of the R.S.P.C.A. and a Vice-President of the Jew Society.

The aristocratic patrons were publicly paraded at the large anniversary meetings which the Evangelical societies held once a year. At these gatherings, members from all over the country met together to hear a report of the Society's activities over the past year, vote on future policy, contribute to a collection and receive general uplift and encouragement from speeches by noted Evangelical leaders. It was particularly important for societies to secure well-known speakers, since the speeches made at Anniversary meetings were widely reported in the press. Wilberforce and Shaftesbury were the most popular and sought-after speakers but occasionally societies managed to attract even bigger names. Prince Albert made his public debut in England at the 1840 meeting of the Society for the Extinction of the Slave Trade and he spoke at several subsequent anniversaries of Evangelical Societies.

Early on in the nineteenth century the main Evangelical societies established the practice of holding their anniversary meetings during the same week in May. This obviously made it very much easier for those who lived some distance from London and who were members of more than one society to get to the meetings. It also established an annual Evangelical jamboree in the capital with meetings and other activities from early morning to late at night throughout the week. 'Every year the meetings increase in seriousness and talent' wrote Henry Thornton's daughter Marianne, who was a regular attender at the May meetings during the 1820s and reported on them to Hannah More.[4] By 1830 the week had become so crowded that the whole month of May was given over to anniversary meetings and other Evangelical activities. Large numbers of Evangelicals came up from the country to stay in the capital for the month in what soon became a major social event. When, in *The Vicar of Wrexhill*, Mrs Mowbray expressed disapproval at the apparent worldliness shown in Mr Corbold's remark that he regretted his daughter missing the London season, the regenerate attorney quickly put her right by telling her:

> The London season of which I speak is that when, during about six blessed weeks in the spring, the chosen vessels resort in countless numbers to London, for the purpose of being present at all the meetings which take place during that time, with as much ardour and holy zeal as the worldly-minded show in arranging their fêtes and their fooleries.[5]

Predictably, the keenest patrons of this 'serious' London season were women. A late nineteenth-century observer suggested a possible explanation for this when he commented on the May meetings that: 'a large number of those present are ladies in the middle class in easy circumstances, who by reason of their religious opinions are shut out from many of the ordinary sources of emotion. At these meetings their feelings and sympathies are powerfully aroused and their imagination largely worked upon'.[6] High emotion was certainly a common ingredient of the May meetings. Marianne Thornton recalled that during the 1825 anniversary of the Anti-Slavery Society, where for the first time Wilberforce was not present because of illness, Daniel Sykes, an Evangelical M.P. and close friend of the abolitionist, wept so much that he had to leave the platform; James Stephen collapsed with emotion; and Wilberforce's son William broke down in tears when he was asked to say a few words on behalf of his father. Many a female heart must have thrilled to the oratory of May speakers like Mr Godfrey Ablewhite, whom Miss Clack sent her maid to hear as a special treat when she was in London and who needed only 'a handkerchief and a glass of water' to reduce his audience to tears.[7]

From 1831 most of the May meetings of the Evangelical societies took place in the same building. In 1824 a group of Evangelicals had set up an association to provide a central hall where societies could hold their anniversaries and seven years later Exeter Hall in the Strand was opened for the purpose. It contained a large hall seating 3,500, a smaller one with room for 600, and twenty-one committee rooms. Exeter Hall rapidly became a centre for all Evangelical activities. Its halls were regularly filled to capacity for Society meetings and anniversaries. In 1843 3,000 people had to be turned away when Prince Albert addressed a meeting for the promotion of Christian Unity. The Y.M.C.A. held its popular lectures for young men there and several Evangelical societies, including the R.S.P.C.A. and the Ragged School Union, set up their headquarters in the building. The Sacred Harmonic Society, founded in 1832, was based there and regularly performed Handel's oratorios and other large scale choral works using up to 500 voices in the larger of the two halls, which in 1837 was equipped with an organ. Exeter Hall was, indeed, the centre of London's musical life until the opening of the Albert Hall in 1871, and in 1847 Mendelssohn conducted a perform-ance of *Elijah* there. But it was as the venue of the great May meet-ings of the Evangelical societies that it was most famous. Within its massive walls, wrote Sir James Stephen in 1843, 'the changeful strain rises with the civilisation of Africa, or becomes plaintive over the wrongs of chimney-boys, or peals anathemas against the successors of Peter, or in rich diapason calls on the Protestant churches to wake and evangelise the world.'[8]

At the Exeter Hall meetings Evangelicalism went on parade as a highly organized and militant national movement. Already the Evangelicals had a comprehensive network of societies covering the entire country and involving hundreds of thousands of people. After 1831 they had also a national headquarters and a major public platform. The power which this gave to Wilberforce and later to Shaftesbury as acknowledged leaders of the Evangelical world was considerable. In a highly perceptive article in 1824 a correspondent to *Blackwood's Edinburgh Magazine* had pointed to the growth of Evangelical societies in England, which he claimed now reckoned their following in millions, and likened their members to the troops of a great private army, 'divided for its more easy management into an infinity of regiments, profusely officered, in the very highest state of discipline and appointment, and all times ready to take the field at a moment's notice,' at the command of General Wilberforce. Had the societies restricted themselves simply to religious and philanthropic objects, he argued, there would be no danger in this situation but, as it was, 'the Wilberforce party have led them in a path which they can only follow either to their own ruin or to that of the nation ... they have converted these societies into a tremendous political faction.'[9] He was, of course, absolutely right: the Evangelical societies were massive pressure groups used by Wilberforce and other Evangelical politicians to back up their campaigns in Parliament.

Blackwood's correspondent was not the first contemporary to see the potential political power of the Evangelical societies. As early as 1803 an Irish theologian, writing to Lord Castlereagh to persuade him to revoke a law banning evangelists from preaching to the Negroes in Jamaica, told him that if he did not act there was a strong chance that the Government would lose the support of the large group of people in the country, whom he estimated at a million in number, who supported religious societies. Fourteen years later the *Anti-Jacobin* magazine carried an article on Wilberforce and his party of Saints in Parliament which concluded that:

Formidable as they are, in a political point of view, from their numbers, they have become infinitely more so, from the superior manner in which, like the Jesuits, they have organised a regular system of communication, throughout the kingdom; which enables their followers to receive their impulse, and support their measures, on every political question in which they take a part. On such occasions, they have literally so covered the floors of the Houses of the Lords and Commons with petitions, as almost to awe the Legislature into an acquiescence with their wishes.[10]

The author almost certainly had in mind the campaign mounted by the Evangelicals to get the religious clauses inserted into the East India Company Charter in 1813. Wilberforce had commented at the outset of this campaign that it would be necessary 'to call into action the whole force of the religious world' and the C.M.S. had responded by organizing a huge canvass of support for the religious clauses which resulted in the arrival of well over 800 petitions, bearing more than half a million signatures, on the floor of the House of Commons. When the Charter Bill was passed with the religious clauses included, Wilberforce noted in his diary, 'the petitions, of which a greater number than were ever known, have carried our question instrumentally, the good providence of God really.'[11]

On several other major issues in the early nineteenth century Evangelical societies succeeded in bringing pressure to bear on the Legislature to secure implementation of their views. As we have already seen, it was in response to agitation by the Bettering Society that Robert Peel introduced his bill to improve the condition of factory children in 1802, and it was as a result of vigorous campaigning by the R.S.P.C.A. that several cruel sports were outlawed in the 1830s. The successful passage through Parliament of Buxton's Bill to abolish slavery in 1833 owed a good deal to the lobbying and canvassing activities of the Anti-Slavery Society. By means of propaganda the Society created strong anti-slavery feeling among the public and then encouraged people to impress their views on the Legislature by voting in the General Election of 1832 only for those candidates who pledged themselves to support abolition. Sir George Stephen, brother of Sir James, and like him actively involved in the campaign to emancipate the Negro slaves, later wrote a book, *Anti-Slavery Recollections*, to show how abolition had been 'the result of popular feeling excited by religious pressure'. 'It was self-evident', he wrote, 'that if the religious world could be induced to enter upon the subject, severing it from all its political relations and viewing it simply as a question between God and man, the battle was won.'[12]

In campaigning for new legislation, and especially in their agitation for the abolition of slavery, Evangelical societies had pioneered the techniques of pressure group politics. They had shown how public feeling could be aroused on a particular issue by lectures, leaflets, posters and public meetings and then brought to bear on the Legislature by means of petitions and electoral pledges. They had also demonstrated the importance for those groups and interests seeking to apply 'pressure from without' on Government and Parliament of expressing their demands in terms of a great moral cause calculated to win the support of the respectable and religious middle classes. It was not surprising, in view of their success, that the Evangelical societies should have been taken as models by pressure groups in the later nineteenth century. Their achievements probably go a long way towards explaining the Victorians' optimism about the ease with which the world could be changed and their tendency to feel that once a society was established to attack a particular problem, that problem was already as good as solved. It was a strange legacy to have been left by those who believed in man's utter depravity, but the fact was that the Evangelicals did feel that the world could be made a better place and they had an almost unbounded optimism about their own ability, with God's grace, to effect this. The corollary of their insistence on man's helplessness and worthlessness when in an unregenerate state was an unlimited confidence in his potential and power to do good when charged with the animating force of vital Christianity. When, at the 1820 Anniversary Meeting of the C.M.S., a platform speaker who had been in India for many years warned the audience not to expect too much from missionary efforts there, Wilberforce immediately rose to protest: 'We know nothing of despondency here. We proceed as the word of God directs us; we must, we can, we will, we ought, we shall prosper.'[13]

Hundreds of thousands of people joined the Evangelical societies in the first half of the nineteenth century and many more took part in the great campaigns which they had organized for religious and humanitarian reforms. They were not for the most part cranks or fanatics – they were sober, honest, well-meaning men and women, respectable rather than pious, and coming predominantly from the middle class. They were perhaps rather dull, leading the 'life of disputes, tea meetings, openings of chapels and sermons' for which Matthew Arnold lambasted the English middle classes in his *Culture and Anarchy*.[14] They were probably rather self-righteous, feeling about themselves as Mrs Pardiggle felt about her children: 'they are not frivolous; they expend the entire amount of their allowance in subscriptions, under my direction; and they have attended as many public meetings, and listened to as many lectures, orations and discussions as generally fall to the lot of few grown people.'[15] But they were determined to fight for what they believed to be right and not to be bought off by bribes, or blandishments or compromises. It was the achievement of the Evangelical societies to have created this 'serious' public in England and organized it into a coherent and active political force.

8

The Cult of Conduct

If they could not convert the entire population of England to vital Christianity, the Evangelicals hoped at least to make sure that all should act as though they had been. However much they might denigrate mere morality and claim that only man's inner state was of any ultimate significance, they were extremely interested also in his outward conduct. In an effort to get their unregenerate contemporaries to conform to their own particular notion of what constituted good behaviour, the Evangelicals consciously lived out their own lives as examples to be followed, did all they could to introduce 'serious' influences into society, and bombarded their countrymen with treatises and manuals on the proper conduct for 'serious' men and women to adopt. Because it provided a useful and timely ethic for the emerging middle class, the model of behaviour which the Evangelicals sought to put across was widely taken up and followed in nineteenth-century England. Its adoption was very largely responsible for creating the cult of respectability and conformity which characterized the Victorian middle classes and which so annoyed their critics.

The Evangelicals had a very high view of the part that the influence and example of others could play in affecting a man's behaviour both for good and ill. They went to considerable lengths to ensure that their contemporaries were spared those influences which were not conducive to sound morality. The Revd J. W. Cunningham refused to erect a headstone on the grave of Allegra, the illegitimate daughter of Lord Byron, when he buried her in his churchyard in 1822 because he felt that the commemoration of her existence might have a corrupting effect on the boys of Harrow School. As we have already seen, many Evangelicals were careful to ensure that their own children were not tainted by coming into contact with the offspring of unregenerate parents. They regarded the influence which they themselves had over friends and associates as one of the most important 'talents' committed to their care and constantly encouraged their children to set an example to their contemporaries. When Henry Thornton's son, also called Henry, went up to Cambridge in 1818, Hannah More reminded his mother that:

> Much will be expected of him, his example must give the tone to the young men who have not had the advantage of such parents ... it behoves such youths as Henry Thornton and Tom Macaulay to raise the depressed standard of religion and morals by their exalted principles and exemplary conduct![1]

One of the most powerful ways in which the Evangelicals believed that they could influence people's behaviour was by making available in cheap and popular form accounts of heroic lives devoted to noble ideals and ends. An Evangelical clergyman complained in 1802 that 'men of honour are the respected personages of the day, and what are these? compounds of the duellist, the gambler, the debauchee, the seducer, the adulterer, and not unfrequently, the intentional suicide. Such are the persons who are idolized in many circles.'[2] The origins of those innumerable series of Great Lives which appeared throughout the nineteenth century and which encouraged the Victorian cult of hero worship lie in the Evangelicals' attempts to provide their countrymen with rather more 'serious' types on which to model their lives. Apart from the numerous missionary biographies published by the C.M.S., these included *The Splendid Lives* series produced by the Sunday School Union and, later, the stories of manly heroes featured in the *Boy's Own Paper* which was started by the Religious Tract Society in 1878. In 1858 the Revd J. H. Gurney produced a work pointedly entitled *God's Heroes and the World's Heroes* and some years later another Evangelical clergyman, the Revd S. F. Harris, published a series of portraits of *Earnest Young Heroes* to illustrate 'lives short in duration but great in purpose'. Many of these publications achieved substantial sales, particularly among the young, with whom biographies of military heroes were especially popular. The most successful of the many Evangelical lives of 'serious' soldiers was Catharine Marsh's

Memorials of Captain Hedley Vicars which sold 70,000 copies within a year of its publication in 1856, so fully answering the prayer of its author that 'these pages may meet the eye of some of the many Englishmen who have more of Christ's religion in their hearts than they have ever avowed in their lives ... and inspire their manly hearts to emulate the noble example of a Christian soldier.'[3]

Direct exhortation and propaganda played a major part in the Evangelicals' campaign to propagate 'serious' behaviour among the people of England. The Cheap Repository Tracts and the publications of the Religious Tract Society constantly urged their readers to lead regular, disciplined, sober lives and warned of the dangers of loose and immoral conduct. The agencies which the Evangelicals established to convert the working classes also set out to change their behaviour by a combination of direct exhortation and a system of rewards and punishments. Hannah More explained to Wilberforce that every year in each of her Mendip villages, 'we collect all the facts we can as to the conduct of the villagers: whether the church has been more attended, fewer or more frauds, less or more swearing, scolding or Sabbath-breaking. All this is produced for or against them, in battle array, in a little sort of sermon made up of praise, censure, and exhortation, as they may be found to have merited.'[4] Girls who had regularly attended the Mendip schools and been exemplary in their conduct were, on marriage, presented with five shillings, a Bible, and a pair of white socks knitted by the More sisters. Most Sunday schools rewarded good behaviour by issuing tickets, a certain number of which entitled the holder to a free book or tract. Ragged schools encouraged city slum dwellers to cultivate flowers and held regular flower shows to teach the virtues of forethought and prudence, 'for if they would win the prizes, they must purchase their plants long beforehand, and expend money on what might only be a probability of success'.[5]

The ideal of behaviour which the Evangelicals sought to put across to the working classes was an extremely simple one. It was summed up by Robert Raikes' remark that the aim of the Sunday school was to 'establish notions of discipline and duty'.[6] The Evangelicals exhorted the poor to cultivate the virtues of frugality, sobriety, cleanliness and regularity, to accept with gratitude the lot which Providence had ordained for them, and to honour and obey their social superiors. 'Principles, not opinions, are what I labour to give them', wrote Hannah More of her Mendip system. It is difficult to avoid the feeling that, albeit perhaps unconsciously, middle-class Evangelicals were trying to get the poor to adopt a style of behaviour which by increasing their productivity in the fields and factories and by steering them away from revolutionary sentiments and aspirations would make their own lives more comfortable and secure. This is certainly the way most recent historians have interpreted the motivation of Hannah More and her fellow tract-writers. She herself put it more simply; she told the members of a friendly society which she had established in the Mendips, 'we wish to recommend you to do your duty in that state of life where God has placed and called you.'[7]

By far the greatest part of the Evangelicals' effort to extend their own concept of proper behaviour to others was directed not at the poor, but at the middle and upper classes. They believed that the morals of the lower classes could best be reformed by prohibitory legislation and prosecution as advocated and undertaken by the Vice Society and other agencies in the campaign for the reformation of manners. 'By them argumentative and bulky treatises on morality will not be read,' the Revd Thomas Gisborne explained when he was asked why the manuals on conduct which he wrote were not addressed to the mass of the people; 'the careful perusal of their Bible ... aided by the public and private admonitions of their pastors, are to them the principal sources of instruction.'[8] With the higher classes, on the other hand, detailed instruction and exhortation was thought to be a more effective and appropriate way of securing good behaviour. Furthermore, as Hannah More pointed out in the foreword to one of her many treatises on how the upper classes should conduct themselves, 'their lives are naturally regarded as patterns, by which the manners of the rest of the world are to be fashioned.'[9] Once get the high-born to behave seriously, the Evangelicals believed, and the people would follow.

The titles of the major manuals on conduct which were written by Evangelicals in the late eighteenth and early nineteenth centuries show clearly the social class which they were trying to reach. The earliest work was Henry Venn's *Complete Duty of Man*, published in 1763 and written to supersede the classic eighteenth-century treatise on behaviour, the *Whole Duty of Man*. Twelve years later Thomas Gisborne brought out his two-volume *Enquiry Into the Duties of Men in the Higher and Middle Classes of Society*, to which he added a sequel, *An Enquiry Into the Duties of the Female Sex*, in 1797. Hannah More published her first treatise on behaviour, *Thoughts On the Importance of the Manners of the Great to General Society*, in 1787 and subsequently produced two important books on the conduct proper for females, *Strictures on Female Education with a view of the principles and conduct prevalent among women of rank and fortune* (1799) and *Hints toward forming the character of a young princess, addressed to Princess Charlotte* (1805), and a two-volume work on *Christian Morals* in 1813. The last of the major Evangelical manuals on conduct was William Roberts' *Portraiture of a Christian Gentleman*, published in 1829, and dedicated, appropriately, to Miss More.

These eight works, all of which achieved large circulations and ran to several editions, were the forerunners of those innumerable books on how to behave which the Victorians found so necessary for their edification and improvement. Their aim, as put forward by Gisborne, was 'to apply moral truths to practical purposes; to point out their bearings on modern opinions and modern manners; and to deduce from them rules of conduct by which the inhabitants of this country, each in his particular station, may be aided in acquiring the knowledge and encouraged in the performance of their several duties'.[10] Every conceivable occupation and aspect of life was covered in the Evangelical manuals. Gisborne's *Enquiry* began with a chapter on the duties of a sovereign and ended with the duties of private gentlemen, taking in the duties of those engaged in virtually every other middle- and upper-class occupation on the way. He had a chapter on the duty of husbands and wives which called on them to be 'kind and tender-hearted inspectors of each other's conduct, meekly pointing out errors, and with love admonishing for faults', and he even had a chapter on the duties of domestic management which condemned 'the practice of allowing large quantities of wholesome food to be destroyed by being stewed down into stimulating sauces ... instead of being distributed to relieve the wants of the necessitous'.[11] Roberts' book had individual chapters devoted to the politics, exterior intercourse and familiar talk proper for a Christian Gentleman to indulge in and ended with one on 'Deportment in the Worship of God on the Lord's Day' which contained a section on postures appropriate to the several parts of the church service.

Predictably, the model of good behaviour put across in the Evangelicals' treatises was a fiercely puritanical one. The stress in all of them was on self-denial and restraint rather than on liberty and self-fufilment. 'Patience, diligence, quiet and unfatigued perseverance, industry, regularity and economy of time – these are the dispositions I would labour to excite', wrote Hannah More in her book on female education.[12] Servants and children fared particularly badly at the hands of the Evangelical moralists. They were enjoined simply to honour and obey their elders and betters and do very little else besides. The sentence which was to spell doom for many a child in the nineteenth century was first pronounced by Hannah More when she declared that young people should be trained 'to an habitual interior restraint, an early government of the affections, and a course of self-control over those tyrannising inclinations which have so natural a tendency to enslave the human heart'.[13] It was from the Evangelical manuals, more than from any other source, that the Victorians derived their notion that children should be seen and not heard.

In their manuals addressed specifically to women, the Evangelicals launched a fierce attack on the triviality and sinfulness of the pastimes which traditionally occupied females in the English upper classes. Attendance at theatrical and operatic performances and at social gatherings and parties was severely condemned. Dancing was regarded as particularly sinful; Sir Richard Hill, a leading Evangelical M.P. of the late eighteenth century, was so scandalized at hearing a young lady say that she could see nothing wrong with going to dances that he published a lengthy Address to persons of fashion 'to demonstrate with the clearest evidence that BALLS are entirely inconsistent with the spirit of Christianity, and that it is not possible to be present at them without incurring great guilt.'[14] At home, women were not to play cards or read novels and other light literature, nor, decreed Hannah More, were they to indulge in the dishonest and deceitful practice of instructing their servants to tell unwelcome visitors that they were 'not at home'. There was some doubt among Evangelicals as to whether women should be allowed to sing; Hannah More said definitely not, but when Lady Catherine Graham asked Wilberforce about the propriety of her daughters singing, he replied that he had no objection provided the songs were carefully selected and 'contained no sentiments improper for a

Christian to utter — I allude to such as love songs and jovial or festive songs.'[15]

What did the Evangelicals say that women were to do, having deprived them of most of the occupations that they traditionally engaged in? For married women they suggested three major occupations: promoting the general comfort and well-being of their family, moulding the minds of the young, and improving the general level of manners in society by their influence and example. Unmarried women, said Gisborne, should devote their time to four main pursuits: cultivating the art of serious conversation and letter-writing; reading *improving* literature, i.e. 'whatever writings may contribute to her virtue, her usefulness, and her innocent satisfaction, to her happiness in this world and in the next'; taking moderate exercise in the open air; and engaging in works of practical charity.[16] This last occupation, as we have already seen, was urged on women in numerous Evangelical tracts and pamphlets apart from the specific manuals on conduct.

There was a sense in which the Evangelicals liberated women by giving them a positive role to play in their families and in society. This may help to explain why it was that the model of female behaviour exhibited in their treatises was so widely taken up by women in the nineteenth century. But the Evangelicals' notion of what conduct was proper for females was also severely restrictive. In concentrating entirely on a practical role for women, it denied them an alternative intellectual life. Hannah More stated that the end to be aimed at in educating females 'is to qualify them for the practical purposes of life. Their knowledge is not often, like the learning of men, to be reproduced in some literary composition, nor even in any learned profession; but it is to come out in conduct.'[17] Lucy Aikin indicated some of the effects that the general adoption of the Evangelical ideal of female behaviour had when she complained that the practice of visiting the poor 'has diverted the minds of numbers (of women), not from dissipation only, but from literature, from the arts, from all the graces and amenities of polished life, and rendered many a home intolerable to husbands, fathers and brothers, thereby causing more moral mischief than all their exertions could eradicate among the poor.'[18] It was very largely from the Evangelicals that the Victorians developed their view of women as 'Angels in the Home', pure and virtuous, but utterly submissive and inclined to be stupid.

The message for men in the Evangelicals' manuals on conduct was simple: 'Let them instantly quit the dice box, the turf, and the tavern; every wicked and trifling employment, and repair each to his proper station.'[19] It was a call to a quieter and more serious style of life than that traditionally practised by the upper classes, which would centre around the duties of work and business and find its recreations in the solid homely comforts of good food, healthy exercise and family activities, rather than in the coarse amusements of the gaming table and the hunt or the refined pleasures of art and literature. To indicate the kind of behaviour which they regarded as proper for 'serious' men and which they wished to see generally adopted, the Evangelical moralists often cited the example of King George III, who, as William Roberts observed in his description of him as the perfect Christian Gentleman, 'rose early, visited first the house of God, and after the regular and punctual dispatch of business divided the day between manly amusements, frugal repasts, and peaceable, pure and homely delights'.[20]

In their treatises, the Evangelicals challenged the traditional basis of English upper-class behaviour. This was the principle of honour which held that the maintenance of personal reputation should be the great determinant of a man's conduct. The code of honour was displayed most clearly in the practice of duelling so common in late eighteenth- and early nineteenth-century England and it was significant that the Evangelicals launched a particularly fierce attack on the contemporary custom of settling quarrels by duels which they regarded as directly contrary to Christian principles of humility and forgiveness. The duel fought between William Pitt and the Whig M.P. George Tierney in 1798 aroused strong Evangelical anger. Hannah More protested: 'What a dreadful thing, that a life of such importance should be risked (or indeed any life at all) on the miserable notion of false honour! To complete the horror, too, they chose a Sunday!' Wilberforce was only stopped from introducing in Parliament a Bill outlawing duelling by the realization that it would be interpreted as a call for Pitt's dismissal.[21] The Evangelicals gradually convinced their contemporaries that the gentlemanly way to behave when personally slighted or attacked was not to challenge one's adversary to a duel but to forgive him. Their hand is clearly visible in the 1844 amendment to the Articles of War which declared it 'suitable to the character of honourable men to apologise and offer redress for wrong or insult committed, and equally so for the party aggrieved to accept frankly and cordially, explanation and apologies for the same'.[22] Eight years later the last duel was fought in England.

After a visit to Eton College in 1844 Lord Shaftesbury noted in his diary about the education offered there:

> it fits a man, beyond all competition, for the drawing room, the Club, St. James' Street, and all the mysteries of social elegance; but it does not make the man required for the coming generation. We must have nobler, deeper and sterner stuff; less of refinement and more of truth; more of the inward, not so much of the outward, gentleman; a rigid sense of duty, not a 'delicate sense of honour'.[23]

His words indicate very clearly the new principle which the Evangelicals wished to see determine men's behaviour. In place of honour, they substituted the concept of duty. No word occurs more often in their manuals and treatises on conduct. The ideal pattern of behaviour which they sought to put across to the middle and upper classes was one in which pride and regard for personal gratification and reputation had been replaced by a serious consideration of the obligations and responsibilities which attached to their wealth and station. It was, in short, the call of duty.

There is one very striking feature about the Evangelicals' pronouncements on how their contemporaries ought to behave. The concepts which they attacked were essentially aristocratic and the values which they exalted were predominantly bourgeois. The Evangelicals' most persistent complaint was about the dominance throughout society of the views and habits of the aristocracy—they cited particularly the principle of honour, the cult of fashion, and a penchant for ostentatious and frivolous diversions. Their great aim was to secure the triumph of the virtues of hard work, plain living and moral propriety which characterized the middle classes. 'Domestic restraints and family economy are voted bores,' Wilberforce complained in 1800, 'while whatever ways of thinking, speaking and acting become popular in the higher classes, soon spread through every other.'[24] Eight years later the Revd James Bean expressed the hope that one of the main effects of the Evangelical Revival on the English middle classes would be that 'frivolous imitation of the higher circles would not so frequently meet us in their houses'.[25] His prediction proved correct: the middle classes did not just cease to emulate the behaviour of the aristocracy in the early nineteenth century; they came positively to despise it. John Stuart Mill noted in 1840 that: 'the daily actions of every peer and peeress are falling more and more under the yoke of bourgeois opinion; they feel every day a stronger necessity of showing an immaculate front to the world.'[26]

The first half of the nineteenth century saw the emergence of the professional middle classes in English society. It was during this period that lawyers, bankers, businessmen, civil servants, doctors, engineers and others organized themselves into professional bodies and associations. The model of behaviour put forward by the Evangelicals exactly fitted the needs and aspirations of these people. It extolled many of the values and disciplines which they themselves needed if they were to make successful careers, and it also provided them with a means of showing their equality with, and ultimately their superiority to the aristocracy from whom they sought to take over the leadership of many key areas of national life. To a large extent, the Evangelicals' treatises on behaviour were aimed specifically at this particular group. The whole purpose of Gisborne's *Enquiry into the duties of men*, which had separate chapters on politics, the civil service, the armed forces, the law, medicine, the Church, trade and business, was to show the deep and serious importance of these professions and of the responsibilities which attached to them. The book reads almost like a recruitment manual for the professions. It is not surprising that the early Victorian middle classes, seeking a code of behaviour which would suit their professional needs and ambitions, eagerly espoused the model provided by the Evangelicals.

The Evangelicals played a major part in creating Victorian middle-class morality. Many of its most characteristic features are to be found in their manuals on the proper conduct for 'serious' men and women – the primacy of duty, the gospel of work, the sinfulness of enjoyment, the sanctity of home and family. By dwelling so much on how people should behave and making proper conduct seem all-important, the Evangelicals gave the Victorian middle classes that obsession with doing what they felt they ought rather than what they wanted which often led them to seem hypocritical. In stressing the importance of absolute conformity to their own notions of right and wrong, they established the cult of respectability which critics blamed for making the Victorians dull and unoriginal. Matthew Arnold accused the Evangelicals of turning the English middle classes into puritan philistines 'drugged with business ... and their senses blurred for any stimulus beside, except religion'. John Stuart Mill blamed them for crushing individuality and originality and teaching 'whatever is not a duty is a sin'.[27] Their accusations were fair; there was undoubtedly a very repressive side to the legacy which the Evangelicals left to the Victorian middle classes. But there was also a sense in which the model of behaviour put forward in their treatises and manuals liberated them.

9

Serious Callings

Four careers seem to have appealed particularly to lay Evangelicals in the early nineteenth century: commerce, the civil service, the armed forces and politics. Significantly, all of them demanded a style of life and a scale of values similar to those prescribed in the Evangelical manuals on conduct. By establishing these careers as responsible and important occupations fit for serious men, and by endowing them with distinct ideals and status, the Evangelicals helped to effect the crucial change that occurred in Victorian England whereby the pastimes of the aristocracy became the serious professions of the middle classes. Evangelical ideas played an important role in shaping the Victorians' attitude to these four major areas of life. They were instrumental in establishing the reputation for honest dealing which characterized Victorian businessmen and which materially contributed to Britain's commercial supremacy in the nineteenth century; they helped to create a professional civil service and an ethic of public administration which were the envy of the world; they contributed to the development of militarism in Victorian England; and they played a major part in transforming politics from centring around the private interests and ambitions of those engaged in it to being about the debate and settlement of the great issues and causes of the nation. In every case, the principles of seriousness had triumphed because they happened also to be the principles of worldly success.

Evangelicalism, W. E. Gladstone once commented, 'did not ally itself with literature, art and general cultivation; but it harmonized very well with the money-getting pursuits.'[1] The large number of Evangelicals engaged in business and commerce in the first half of the nineteenth century would seem to bear out his remark. Among the Clapham Sect, the Wilberforces and Thorntons derived their wealth from the Baltic trade through Hull while the Grants, like many other Evangelicals, had extensive financial interests in the East India Company (opponents of the Evangelicals claimed that they were only interested in abolishing the slave trade because it would bring ruin to the rival West India interest). The two most celebrated fictional portrayals of Clapham Evangelicals, Disraeli's Falconet and Thackeray's Thomas Newcome, were respectively a prosperous East India merchant and a partner in a highly successful firm of cloth factors. Among the many family firms run by Evangelicals in the early nineteenth century were Huntley & Palmers, the Reading biscuit manufacturers, Crossley Brothers of Manchester, and Guinness, the famous Dublin brewers. Evangelical banking families included the Barclays, the Hoares, the Barings, the Gurneys, the Smiths, the Martins, the Laboucheres, the Williams and the Deacons.

It is not difficult to see the conduciveness of Evangelicalism to business and commercial activity. The argument of Max Weber's great work, *The Protestant Ethic and the Spirit of Capitalism*, that the development of large-scale entrepreneurial activity in the sixteenth and seventeenth centuries was helped by the puritan values and behavioural system associated with Protestant Christianity, is equally applicable to the growth of business and commerce in the nineteenth century. The notion of stewardship, to which both puritans and Evangelicals strongly adhered, and which held that it was the individual's duty to harbour the material resources of the world and to cause them to multiply for the greater glory of God, clearly encouraged the assumption of an entrepreneurial role. Like puritanism, Evangelicalism rationalized and justified worldly success. Its teaching that everything which happened on earth was a manifestation of the workings of Providence tended to equate success with virtue and its stress on the good that could be done by investment in charitable and philanthropic projects provided a further justification for amassing large fortunes. The lengthy sections of his *Enquiry* which Thomas Gisborne devoted to business and commerce encouraged Evangelical participation in these professions by pointing out the opportunities which they presented for exercising the Christian virtues and by establishing the proper behaviour for a Christian engaged in them.

Evangelicalism had something even more positive to offer to those engaged in the money-getting pursuits. The values and behaviour which were extolled by Gisborne and other Evangelical moralists were not only appropriate for serious Christians; they were also necessary for commercial success. The ideal life as put forward by the Evangelicals, in which constant application and activity guarded the soul against the sin of sloth, and a task shirked or an appointment missed meant sure retribution from above, could almost have been designed deliberately for businessmen and financiers. So could the Evangelical values of accountability, regularity, honesty and integrity. In declaring that 'a strict and active principle of probity will teach the trader to be scrupulously observant even of his verbal engagements in all pecuniary and mercantile transactions, and carefully to guard against exciting expectations of any kind, which there is not a fair prospect of his being able to satisfy,' Gisborne was not just expounding pious platitudes, he was talking sound commercial sense.[2] It is true that for those engaged in commercial activities which involved risk-taking and tycoonery, Evangelical values were of no use. But for those in banking and other forms of trading where success depended on a reputation for honest dealing and sound credit-worthiness, they were extremely important. Significantly, more Evangelicals seem to have gone into banking than into any other area of business or commerce and those who entered the profession seem to have been almost universally successful.

The career of Henry Thornton the younger shows the extent to which adherence to Evangelical values, and especially to the principle of integrity, could contribute to worldly success. In 1825 Thornton became a partner in the banking house of Pole, Thornton and Company in which his father had once been a partner but which was now in serious financial difficulties, having an inadequate amount of cash in hand. With the firm on the edge of bankruptcy, Thornton asked for help from the Bank of England. John Smith, the Evangelical proprietor of a rival banking house, was so impressed by Thornton's evident integrity that he stood surety for a Bank of England loan to get the Company out of trouble. Pole, Thornton and Company revived but crashed again with the general collapse of country banks in 1826 and its affairs had finally to be wound up. Henry Thornton's personal reputation for honesty stood so high, however, that he was asked to join the new banking house of Williams Deacons. The other partners in the new venture, Henry Labouchere, Charles Williams, Alexander Baring and Mr Deacon were all Evangelicals and they had no difficulty in raising capital and becoming one of the most successful private banks in England.

Williams Deacons is only one of several major London banks which remain to this day as a monument to the sound commercial advantages of Evangelical integrity. The others are Martins, Barings, Smith St Aubyn's, and Samuel Hoare & Company. All of them flourished because the principles and practices of their Evangelical founders made for highly successful banking. When Henry Thornton joined his Evangelical partners to start their new banking house in 1826, his sister Marianne wrote to Hannah More: 'It is the greatest comfort to know that these are all good men, so whatever else happens there will be no iniquity to mourn over as in the last case, and they are such a prudent lot that I was telling Nurse I don't think a Bill will ever get signed, they will look it over so long first.'[3] Wilberforce wrote to a friend: 'I am happy to be able to tell you that I have every reason to believe that while Henry will gain great credit, he will lose no money.'[4] It was this mixture of righteousness and prudence which made the Evangelicals such successful bankers and businessmen and which helped to give Victorian England the reputation for honest trading and impeccable creditworthiness which was so important in contributing to making it the leading financial and trading nation of the world.

Along with banking, the Civil Service seems to have been a popular career with Evangelicals, especially from around the time of Victoria's accession. We have already come across two prominent Evangelical civil servants: Sir James Stephen, the Under Secretary at the Colonial Office from 1836 to 1847, and W. J. Orsman, the costermongers' missionary in the 1860s who was a clerk in the Post Office. Others included Stevenson Blackwood, a leading lay preacher and mission-room teacher who was Secretary to the Post Office; G. E. Woodward, a noted philanthropist who regularly gave away a tenth of his annual income to charity, who was a clerk in the Navy Ordnance Department; Edward Rudolf, the founder of the Church of England Children's Society, who was a secretary in the Office of Works; and Sir Charles Trevelyan, Assistant Secretary to the Treasury from 1840 to 1859 and co-author of the famous Trevelyan–Northcote report of 1853 which paved the way for the establishment of the modern Civil Service in Britain. It was particularly appropriate that Trevelyan should have been an adherent to vital religion, since the creation of the professional civil service in the mid-nineteenth century with which his name is so closely associated was partly brought about through the introduction and implementation of Evangelical values.

Evangelicals had a powerful interest in seeing the emergence of a professional Civil Service in England. They strongly disapproved of the corruption and partiality which prevailed among government servants in the late eighteenth and early nineteenth centuries, and were actively involved in the movement for economical reform which sought to eliminate abuses and establish purer standards in public administration. In 1799 Charles Grant instituted a massive attack on the prevailing practice of buying and selling offices in the East India Company and he is generally credited with establishing the high standards of honesty and purity which later characterized the Indian Civil Service. Sir Charles Middleton, Comptroller of the Navy from 1778 to 1788, was the first head of a government department to apply the principles of economical reform. He did away with many abuses in the organization of the Navy, including the practice among dock workers of taking home 'chips', an allowance which had been so liberally interpreted that large planks were being carried away across two men's shoulders. In Parliament, the Saints campaigned vigorously for a purer administrative system. Wilberforce drew up a lengthy list of matters which he wished to see rectified, ranging from the 'buying of commissions in our army' to 'the not punishing abuses and misconduct in executive servants and the appointing to important situations unfit persons on account of their families, connexions and co.'.[5] Henry Bankes, an Evangelical M.P., led a strong and sustained attack on sinecures and on the practice of granting public offices in reversion so that they were passed from father to son as pieces of hereditary property. By 1810, thanks partly to Evangelical pressure, the sale of clerkships and the system of paying officials by means of fees and perquisites had been abolished in nearly every government department and the foundations laid for a purer system of public administration.

The subsequent development of a professional Civil Service in

10 'Making Decent!' Etching by George Cruikshank, 1822. Wilberforce
holds his hat over the fig-leaf on the Achilles statue erected in honour
of the Duke of Wellington in Hyde Park

11 Ragged School in George Yard, St Jude's, Whitechapel, 1859

12 Hannah More

13 The first picture in a missionary magazine, the *Missionary Register* of April 1816, representing a scene in West Africa

14 A missionary teaching on the roof-top of an Indian house. Illustration in the *Missionary Magazine*, July 1856

15 'Family Prayers'. Painting by Samuel Butler, 1864

England almost certainly owed something to Evangelical ideas. The principles of integrity, impartiality and unflinching application to duty which characterized the nineteenth-century Civil Service were also the principles of Evangelical Christianity. The model civil servant, reliable, punctual, respectable and undeviatingly honest, was almost identical to the ideal of the Christian gentleman as portrayed in the Evangelicals' manuals on conduct. The section in Gisborne's *Enquiry* on the duties of executive officers of government reads like a handbook for aspiring civil servants. It is an incitement to industry, incorruptibility, economy and minute attention to details of administration. No man should take a position in the public service, Gisborne counselled, unless he was convinced that his talents made him competent to fill it to the satisfaction and benefit of his country: 'Above all things he will scrupulously try himself in the balance of integrity, that he may discern whether he possess that upright simplicity and steadfast firmness of mind which may enable him to resist the allurements of personal emolument.'[6]

The importance of Gisborne's statements was not simply that they exhorted men to the qualities needed in an efficient, professional civil servant, but rather that they established public administration as a proper career for serious gentlemen and invested it with a distinct status and ideology. The key factor in the development of the civil service as a profession in the nineteenth century was the departure from the corridors of Whitehall of the well-connected place hunters and sinecurists who had filled them in the eighteenth century and their replacement by diligent and incorruptible clerks from the bourgeoisie. Evangelicalism assisted this trend away from aristocratic amateurism towards middle-class professionalism both by attacking the old order of civil servants and by exalting the values and life-style of the new. Evangelicals attacked the dominance of aristocratic personnel and principles in the early nineteenth-century Civil Service. Sir Charles Middleton criticized Admiralty colleagues 'who are at an office one day and following their amusements or private concerns another' and Sir James Stephen strongly condemned the gentlemen clerks in the Colonial Office who 'worked in the interval between their morning rides and their afternoon dinner parties'.[7] In their place, they called for the introduction of the serious middle classes into the Civil Service and championed the solidly bourgeois virtues of industry, respectability and integrity. In doing this, the Evangelicals played a crucial role in helping to develop the ethic of professional public service.

The work which civil servants, especially in lower grades, were called on to undertake in the nineteenth century was often dull. They were expected to perform routine tasks punctually and efficiently, to take orders rather than to give them, and to display industry and attention rather than originality or flair. By exalting the more humdrum virtues, and by stressing the deep seriousness and importance of the call to public administration, the Evangelicals helped to give civil servants a sense of pride in their work. Sir Charles Middleton once declared: 'Honesty and application will go a great way in carrying on public business; if they are wanting, all the talents which we hear so much of, will prove vain.'[8] Evangelicalism might also have been designed as an ideology for those whose success in work depended on the exercise of the virtues of regularity, sobriety and attention to duty rather than on intellectual brilliance or imaginative insight. Surely above every clerk's desk in the counting houses and government offices where the commercial and administrative achievement of the Victorians was wrought, there should have hung a framed copy of Hannah More's commendation of the humdrum virtues:

> Perhaps mediocrity of parts was decreed to be the ordinary lot by way of furnishing a stimulus to industry and strengthening the motives to virtuous application. For is it not obvious that moderate abilities, carefully carried to that measure of perfection of which they are capable, often enables their possessors to outstrip, in the race of knowledge and of usefulness, their more brilliant but less persevering competitors?[9]

Just as the career of Henry Thornton shows the applicability of Evangelical values to successful commercial activity, so the career of another son of Clapham, Sir James Stephen, shows their contribution to the development of the professional Civil Service. Stephen was above all else the slave of duty, regularly applying himself to his work from six in the morning until late at night and using up ten-and-a-half reams of folio paper in sixteen months. His greatest single complaint about his colleagues was not their lack of intelligence or originality but their chronic unpunctuality in answering correspondence. He himself hoped to be remembered 'chiefly for rapidity of conception and execution – the things conceived and the things executed being however middling things – efforts of sagacity not invention; clear arrangement of obvious muddle'.[10] Stephen lauded the mundane and routine nature of the civil servant's work. It was he who created the two grades of mechanical and intellectual in the Civil Service and who formulated the modern concept of civil servants as anonymous purveyors of impartial and expert advice to ministers. 'You stand not in need of statesmen in disguise', he told the Royal Commission on the Civil Service in 1854, 'but of intelligent, steady, methodical men of business.'[11]

Stephen opposed the Trevelyan–Northcote reforms of 1854, which confirmed the end of the tradition of aristocratic amateurism in the Civil Service by establishing entry through competitive examination, because he feared that they would lead to the recruitment of men whose minds would be too brilliant and original for the job they would be doing. In the event, competitive examinations brought into the Civil Service men with precisely those attributes which Stephen himself applauded. The civil servants of the latter part of the nineteenth century were predominantly from the middle classes, and often from Evangelical backgrounds. They had been brought up at home and at school to the disciplines of hard work and regularity. They regarded their job as a vocation. For them public service was not simply a source of personal gratification or gain; it was a matter of absolute moral duty. In fashioning this ethic of public service which made British administration the envy of the world, the Evangelicals had played no small part.

The large number of Evangelicals who served in the armed forces in the nineteenth century has already been alluded to. In part, this may perhaps have been a consequence of the very considerable evangelistic efforts which were made among soldiers and sailors in the early nineteenth century. A rather more likely explanation, however, is that the values and style of conduct adopted by Evangelicals made them particularly well suited to a military career. Thomas Gisborne had gone to some lengths to establish soldiering as a profession fit for serious men by proclaiming that there were such things as just wars and arguing that the serving officer had a high and noble calling to act with justice and mercy towards his opponents and to encourage religion and morality among those under his command. In a funeral sermon on Sir Henry Havelock, the most famous of all the Evangelical soldiers of the nineteenth century, the Revd Andrew Reed of the Bedford Chapel equated the qualities which made a good soldier with those that made a good Christian. These were, he said, implicit obedience to his leader, strength against temptation, willingness to undergo any sacrifice, bravery in the face of all dangers and determination to vanquish the foe. Certainly, Evangelicals made good soldiers: there is a celebrated story that when the General commanding the British forces in the Burma campaign of 1825 urgently needed to put crack troops into the field, he ordered 'Turn out Havelock's saints; he is always ready and his men are never drunk.'

The example of Evangelical soldier heroes like Havelock undoubtedly helped to foster the spirit of militarism which existed in Victorian England. The most popular and influential of the Great Lives written by Evangelical propagandists featured military heroes. Although they were intended primarily to show that there was no incompatibility between adherence to Evangelical Christianity and the profession of soldiering, many went beyond this and positively glorified war and conflict. A large number of the workers engaged on building the Crystal Palace are said to have enlisted in the Crimean forces after reading Catharine Marsh's *Memorials of Captain Hedley Vicars*. That great hymn of the Church Militant, *Onward Christian Soldiers*, was written in 1864 by an Evangelical curate, the Revd Sabine Baring-Gould, for the children of his Yorkshire village mission to sing as they marched up the hill to join the children of the local parish church for Sunday worship. It is difficult to avoid the impression that Evangelicalism, with its language of war and conflict and its stress on order and discipline, was at least partly responsible for the militarism of the Victorians.

Politics was another career which attracted many Evangelicals in the early nineteenth century. Over a hundred of them sat in the House of Commons in the fifty years before the passing of the Great Reform Bill in 1832 and an equal number were active in the House of Lords. They included not only the two great leaders of the Evangelical movement, Wilberforce and Shaftesbury, and the famous Saints of the Clapham Sect, but also Spencer Perceval, Prime Minister from 1807 to 1812; Lord Harrowby, who was called on to become Premier in 1812 and again in 1828; Nicholas Vansittart, Chancellor of the Exchequer from 1812 to 1822; Henry Bathurst,

Colonial Secretary from 1812 to 1827; Henry Goulburn, Chancellor of the Exchequer from 1828 to 1830 and from 1840 to 1846; and Charles Grant the younger, Colonial Secretary from 1835 to 1839. Evangelicalism could very nearly claim a second Prime Minister in the Fifteenth Earl of Derby, but he abandoned his early adherence to vital religion before he became Premier in 1852.

The attraction of a political career to Evangelicals is obvious. Membership of Parliament gave them an unrivalled platform from which to disseminate their views throughout society and a chance to shape the attitudes and behaviour of the country. Wilberforce regarded Parliament as 'the moral mint of the nation in which moral and political principles receive their stamp and currency'.[12] Through politics the Evangelicals believed that they could fight the great evils and injustices in society that offended their Christian consciences, and could work for the triumph of justice and humanity. After thirty-seven years in the House of Commons Wilberforce reflected: 'What various and extensive occasions of benefiting their fellow creatures are presented to M.P.s in this highly favoured country.'[13] The opportunities for usefulness which were open to a politician seemed almost unlimited. On the day that he became an M.P., Thomas Fowell Buxton noted in his diary:

> I see the vast good which one individual may do. My prayer is for the guidance of God's Holy Spirit; that, free from views of gain or popularity, that, careless of all things but fidelity to my trust, I may be enabled to do some good to my country, and something for mankind, especially in their most important concerns.[14]

Those Evangelicals who entered politics in the late eighteenth and early nineteenth centuries were appalled at the prevailing contemporary view of Parliament as an arena for place-hunting and faction-fighting rather than as a forum for the serious discussion and settlement of the affairs of the nation. Wilberforce complained that the House of Commons was 'degraded by the languor with which public interests are treated, compared with the animation called forth by petty party and personal squabbles'.[15] Evangelical M.P.s were particularly concerned about the fact that it was party considerations rather than principle which determined the votes and behaviour of most contemporary politicians. Wilberforce never forgave his close friend William Pitt for continuing the system of governing by influence and patronage, rather than basing his following in Parliament around issues of principle when he became Prime Minister in 1784. Many of the Evangelical M.P.s themselves eschewed party ties and maintained a strict independence so that they could speak and vote on every issue as their consciences directed. On two occasions, Evangelical politicians resigned over matters of principle: James Stephen quitted Parliament in 1815 when the Government refused to support his Bill to establish a register of slaves in the West Indies, and Charles Grant the younger resigned from Wellington's Administration in 1828 when it refused to disenfranchise the corrupt borough of East Retford. Evangelical M.P.s subjected every issue on which they were called to deliberate in Parliament to one simple question—was it morally right? After entering the anti-Government lobby on one occasion, Henry Thornton recorded in his diary, 'I voted today so that if my Master had come again at that moment I might have been able to give an account of my stewardship.'[16]

The presence of a significant number of M.P.s with so radically different a concept of their duties and responsibilities from that which prevailed among most politicians could not fail to have an effect on the House of Commons. There is no doubt that the Evangelicals contributed to bringing about two of the most important changes which occurred in English political life in the early nineteenth century: the transformation of Parliament from a gentlemen's club primarily concerned with the private interests of its members to a national assembly legislating for the public good, and the development of political parties based on shared principles and policies rather than on ties of family connection or personal interest. There were, of course, numerous other factors at work in producing these changes. The complex problems of an industrialized society demanded that Parliament legislate on a wide range of social and economic matters which it had never hitherto regarded as its province. The economical reform movement systematically reduced the power of patronage and influence in political life, while the growing political consciousness of the middle classes and the increasing agitation for Parliamentary reform forced politicians to concern themselves less with their own narrow interests and more with affairs of public importance. None the less, it is possible to identify a specific contribution which the Evangelicals made to the development of the legislative function of Parliament and to the growing power of principle in English politics in the early nineteenth century.

Evangelical M.P.s were among the first successfully to introduce into Parliament the discussion of major issues of principle and to base a call for legislation on the rightness of the cause itself rather than on an appeal to narrow self-interest. The subjects which interested them and on which they initiated debates were fundamentally different from those predominantly agricultural and fiscal questions which had occupied most of Parliament's time in the late eighteenth century. In fighting for and securing support for the abolition of slavery and the protection of factory workers, the Evangelical M.P.s had not only widened Parliament's sphere of interest beyond the narrow concerns of its members; they had also established its duty to legislate in the interest of humanity and justice. Reflecting on the successful outcome of the Saints' 1813 campaign to get the missionary clause inserted into the East India Charter, Wilberforce noted: 'When I consider what was the state of the House of Commons twenty-five years ago, and how little it would then have borne with patience what it heard not only with patience but acceptance during the late discussions, I cannot but draw a favourable augury for the welfare of our country.'[17] The activities and example of the Evangelical M.P.s, and especially of Wilberforce himself, had been instrumental in widening the perspectives of Parliament and in giving it a concern with morality and principle. On the eve of Wilberforce's departure from the House of Commons in 1825, after forty-five years as an M.P., one of his fellow Saints remarked to him: 'It must be a satisfaction to have observed that the moral tone of the House of Commons, as well as of the nation at large, is much higher than when you first entered public life; and there can be no doubt that God has made you the honoured instrument of contributing much to this great improvement.'[18]

Even more impressive than the Evangelicals' achievement in giving a new seriousness to Parliament's deliberations was the change they wrought in the style and behaviour of politicians in the early nineteenth century. It is no coincidence that the age of Fox gave way to the age of Peel during the period when Evangelical influence was at its height. By a combination of example, exhortation and subtle argument, the Evangelicals set out to remove from public life the colourful, wild-living, swashbuckling figures who dominated English politics in the late eighteenth century and replace them by sober and serious men. Few people were more urgently or more earnestly called to seriousness by the Evangelicals than the nation's political leaders and few responded to the call more enthusiastically than they did. By the middle of the nineteenth century it was clear to the most cynical politician that the only sure way to win popular esteem and electoral success lay in conforming as closely as possible to the model of the Christian Statesman that the Evangelicals had established.

The Evangelicals had an unmitigatedly low view of politicians in the early nineteenth century. It was based on the undeniable fact, noted by William Roberts in a long section devoted to politics in his *Portraiture of a Christian Gentleman*, that most men 'take up the profession of politics, not as a field of duty or usefulness, but as the road to eminence, profit or power'.[19] Specifically, Evangelicals attacked in the behaviour and attitudes of contemporary politicians the predominance of the same aristocratic values that they objected to in other walks of life. They disliked the prevailing principle of honour, which led political leaders to shield those of their colleagues whom they knew to have done wrong, and the overriding concern of politicians with popularity and reputation. 'In the place of the love and fear of God', Gisborne complained,' they substitute the love of applause and the fear of shame. In the place of conscience they substitute pride.'[20] Evangelicals criticized politicians particularly for being concerned with grandiose schemes of national aggrandizement and neglecting more important, if less spectacular, domestic concerns. Wilberforce declared his wholehearted contempt for 'those mistaken politicians, the chief object of whose admiration, and the main scope of whose endeavours for their country, are extended dominion, and commanding power, and unrivalled affluence, rather than those more solid advantages of peace, and comfort and security'.[21]

Predictably, the Evangelicals called for the adoption of a very much more serious approach to the politician's office than that which prevailed among their contemporaries. In a lengthy section of his *Enquiry* on the duties of politicians, Gisborne demanded that the prospective entrant to Parliament should carefully examine his motives: 'If he is impelled by a desire to gratify ambition, pride, or envy, or to promote the private interest at the expense of the public good, let him eradicate from his breast the unChristian principle, before he indulges a thought of further perseverance in his design.' If, however, he could satisfy his conscience on these points and was genuinely convinced that his desire to go into politics stemmed from 'an earnest zeal to promote the good of his country and of mankind by public exertions and private example,' then he might put himself forward as a candidate for election, making sure that the appeal which he addressed to the voters was scrupulously honest. Once elected to Parliament, model politicians would display 'patient industry, inflexible integrity, abhorrence of party spirit and care to guard against prejudices'.[22] It would be difficult to find a greater contrast to the way in which most contemporary politicians behaved.

In establishing their ideal type of politician, the Evangelicals substituted solid bourgeois values for the aristocratic attributes that had hitherto characterized the profession. In the place of private and family interest, Sir Thomas Dyke Acland demanded, 'let the real stay and reward be public opinion founded on character ... it ought to be the only fit object of a country gentleman's ambition.'[23] Criticizing the arrogance and haughtiness of contemporary politicians in 1832, Lord Henley, a Conservative peer of strong Evangelical persuasion, called on 'those who ride in the high places of the earth' to become 'more humble and tolerant, more attentive to the just demands of the governed, more observant of those claims which the varying conditions of society are daily advancing'.[24] Nearly thirty years earlier, Wilberforce had commented on the contemporary state of politics to a friend, 'it is not in fact talents in which we are chiefly wanting, but resolute integrity.'[25] Integrity was the principle on which the Evangelicals again and again insisted that politicians should base their behaviour, instead of on the false notion of honour. Listing it as the chief qualification for political life, Henry Thornton explained: 'by this term I mean an honest determination to perform our political duty though the performance of it should be prejudicial to our general reputation and also to our worldly interest and even though it should endanger our very seat in parliament.'[26]

Evangelicals demanded even more than seriousness and resolute integrity from politicians. They insisted that they be practising Christians. 'The British Statesman, or senator', William Roberts declared in his *Portraiture of a Christian Gentleman,* 'cannot be truly great in separation from Christian piety.'[27] Roberts created the ideal of the Christian Statesman which the Evangelicals were determined by their own example and through propaganda to see accepted and established as a model to be followed by all politicians in the land. Few men came as near to representing the ideal as the Seventh Earl of Shaftesbury and it is fitting that he should have given the most comprehensive definition of the qualities that made up the Christian Statesman. In a solemn entry in his diary in 1827, Shaftesbury noted:

> I have decided in my own heart that no one should be Prime Minister of this great country, unless deeply imbued with religion; a spirit which will reflect and weigh all propositions, examine each duty, and decide upon the highest; be content to do good in secret, and hold display as a bauble compared with the true interests of God and the kingdom; have energy to withstand political jobbing, and refuse what is holy as a sacrifice to faction. He must calculate advantages to arise in a century, and not shows to glitter at the moment; he must appoint that which is best, and not that which is most capable of appearing so. He must leaven every deed with the feeling of religion.[28]

Examining the qualifications of the great political leaders of the past fifty years for being regarded as Christian Statesmen, William Roberts dismissed Pitt and Fox as falling far short of the ideal but found much to praise in the attitudes and behaviour of Spencer Perceval and of the recently deceased First Earl of Liverpool, Prime Minister from 1812 to 1827. A generation later, he would have found in the characters of Peel and Gladstone an even more conspicuous demonstration of the Evangelical virtues. The fact was that a remarkable transformation occurred in the style of political leadership in England around the time of the Napoleonic wars. The leading politicians of the first half of the nineteenth century were on the whole duller, more sober, more industrious and more honest than those of the previous half century. Perceval, Liverpool, Peel and Gladstone were serious men in a way that Fox and Pitt had not been. All four were strong Christians who came from Evangelical homes. The Evangelicals' ideal had triumphed: Victorian England, it seemed, was destined to be ruled by Christian statesmen.

Why did political leaders become more serious in the early nineteenth century? To a large extent it was because the problems of a rapidly industrializing society demanded constant and detailed attention in both Parliament and government. The vast increase in legislative and administrative activity which occurred in this period forced politicians to take their duties very much more seriously. This, however, does not fully explain why so many of the leading politicians of the early nineteenth century conform so closely to the stereotype of the Christian Statesman. The example and exhortation of the Evangelicals played a considerable part, not least in showing politicians how to regain the confidence and popularity of the people who, under Evangelical influence, were becoming increasingly dissatisfied with the attitudes and behaviour which prevailed in public life.

There is no doubt that many politicians were stirred and shamed into becoming more serious by the example of Evangelical M.P.s. Charles Greville, the cynical and worldly Whig diarist, noted after reading Sir James Stephen's essay on Wilberforce and the Clapham Sect in 1838 that 'a certain uneasy feeling, a conscience-stricken sensation, comes across my mind ... I see men who filled with glory their respective stations either in active or contemplative life; and then I ask myself the question how have I filled mine ... an humble station indeed, but one which might have been both useful and respectable if it had been filled as it ought.'[29] Wilberforce was the commonest hero in Victorian school textbooks and there must have been many eager and earnest young M.P.s who embarked on their political careers in the later nineteenth century, as Disraeli's Falconet did, with the example of his career ever before their eyes. Sir James Mackintosh, a radical Whig who worked closely with the Saints in the campaign for penal reform, wrote of Wilberforce in 1807:

Who knows whether the greater part of the benefit that he has conferred on the world may not be the encouraging example that the exertions of virtue may be crowned by such splendid success? Hundreds and thousands will be animated by Mr. Wilberforce's example, by his success, and by a renown that can only perish with the world, to attack all the forms of corruption and cruelty that scourge mankind.[30]

As Mackintosh's remark suggests, it was the success as much as the integrity and noble deeds of the Evangelical M.P.s which impressed contemporary politicians. Heedless of worldly fame and applause though the Saints might have been, they had certainly won their full share of it. Henry Thornton refused to give the traditional guinea a head to the voters in the notoriously venal borough of Southwark, yet they elected him as their representative in three successive Parliaments. Wilberforce hardly ever visited Yorkshire, he never once went to the race meetings and social gatherings which the county's M.P. was expected to attend, nor did he ally himself with a local aristocratic house or attempt to build up a following; yet for twenty-eight years he held the largest constituency in the country against powerful challenges. In the election of 1807 the funds to pay for his campaign, which totalled £28,600 against the £200,000 spent by his two opponents, were raised entirely from unsolicited voluntary contributions from supporters throughout England. In 1847 the future Lord Shaftesbury was elected M.P. for Bath with a large majority despite breaking the cardinal rule of nineteenth-century electioneering by not spending a single penny during the campaign on beer. Clearly, seriousness was an asset at the polls.

The fact was that the leading Evangelical politicians commanded tremendous popular support in the early nineteenth century, particularly among the middle classes. We have already seen how participation in the Evangelical societies and in the great campaigns to abolish slavery and press for humanitarian legislation increased the political as well as the moral consciousness of the middle classes, turning them into dedicated followers of Wilberforce and other Evangelical leaders. This happened at a time when public confidence in the existing political system and in politicians generally was at a particularly low ebb. The middle classes especially felt totally alienated from and contemptuous of the goings-on in Parliament in the early nineteenth century. Mostly deprived of the vote until given it in 1832 to prevent them in their despair from joining with the lower classes in a revolutionary alliance, they viewed with increasing hostility and impatience the corrupt dealings and self-interested stances of most contemporary politicians. It was not surprising that Wilberforce and his Saints strongly appealed to the middle classes as representing a purer and higher ethic in public life,

nor that the Evangelical politicians for their part took up the griev-
ances and frustrations of the people and incorporated them in their
own call for a more serious approach to politics.

During 1831, as the Great Reform Bill made its painfully slow and
often checked progress through Parliament, the *Christian Observer*
carried a series of articles on the political state of the nation. The
sympathies of the leading journal of enlightened Evangelical opinion
were clear from the opening words of the first article which expressed
fellow feeling for 'the large class of persons [who] have long viewed
with extreme disapprobation the venal and interested plans of
parties in parliament, the profligacy of unmerited pensions and
sinecures: and the prejudiced and selfish opposition to measures of
undoubted public benefit' shown by most politicians.[31] Two extracts
from later articles indicate why many Evangelicals strongly supported the 1832 Reform Bill in the belief that, quite apart from its
political aspect, it was a measure of considerable moral significance
and a positive inducement to more serious politics:

> Hitherto, the great majority of the respectable, substantial, loyal,
> peaceable, moral, religious and intelligent part of the public, the
> leading householders of our parishes and the persons looked up to
> in their neighbourhoods as the moral strength of the country,
> have been almost wholly unrepresented. One of our chief hopes,
> in reference to a reformed parliament, is that it will be chosen
> chiefly by the great bulk of the middle classes of society, among
> whom lies most of the piety and good sense and right feeling
> of the country.[32]

> It is clear that the future labours of the Legislature will be most
> laborious; and as every Member has now a constituency who
> will expect his diligent attendance upon his parliamentary
> duties, there will eventually be an utter extinction of that large
> class of senators who were mere idlers, assuming the office only
> as a sinecure honour, or in order to vote occasionally on a party
> question. The majority of the members must now of necessity
> be working men, and also men who take an interest, whether for
> good or evil, in the public proceedings.[33]

To a large extent, the *Christian Observer* was right in its predic-
tions. After 1832 English politicians had to pay more heed to the

demands of those who elected them. The people who got the vote in that year were for the most part from the middle classes and many of them were under strong Evangelical or Nonconformist influences. It was hardly surprising that politicians anxious to win the support of these newly enfranchised voters heeded with particular attention the advice of the Evangelicals and tried consciously to model themselves on them. Two particular attributes of the Saints seemed to have won especially strong support from the middle classes and therefore appeared well worth imitating by politicians after 1832. These were their capacity for introducing moral issues into politics and the absolute purity of their own lives.

There is no doubt that part of the reason for the strong support which Evangelical politicians won from the middle classes derived from their conception of politics as a series of great moral crusades. Parliament was for them a mighty instrument to right the wrongs of the nation and of all mankind. In their campaign against slavery in particular, the Evangelical M.P.s had transformed the traditional idea of political activity by whipping up the righteous indignation of hundreds of thousands of voters over a great cause. They had at the same time become national heroes. The Evangelicals themselves were fully aware of the temporal advantages to be gained by politicians who espoused moral causes. Wilberforce wrote to Henry Brougham, the Whig M.P., in 1827 in an effort to persuade him to join the Abolitionist movement: 'were it only for the place to be occupied in the page of History, it would be a distinction to be coveted, that while all around you had been using their influence for purposes of personal advancement, you had been rendering yours subservient to the far nobler purpose of redressing the wrongs of a no small proportion of the family of Men'.[34]

Victorian politicians were not slow to see the advantage to be gained by appearing as champions of moral causes. When Richard Cobden was deciding how best to organize his campaign for the abolition of the Corn Laws in 1840 it was the strategy employed by the Evangelicals in their crusade against slavery that he decided to follow. 'It appears to me', he wrote to a friend, 'that a moral and even a religious spirit may be infused into the topic and if agitated in the same manner that the question of slavery has been, it will be irresistible.'[35] The reason why so many of the great political campaigns of the Victorian period, though wholly secular in purpose, were pursued as though they were moral crusades and conducted in the language of the Bible, and why, as the historian W. E. H. Lecky complained in the 1870s, 'lofty maxims and sacred names are invoked in parliament much more frequently than of old,' was quite simply that politicians had come to appreciate how many votes there were to be won from appearing to be serious men.[36]

Nineteenth-century politicians seeking popular acclaim found that the possession of a pure and wholesome private character was almost more essential than involvement in a moral cause. The importance of this attribute was clear from the time that Evangelicalism first started to influence popular attitudes in England. In 1809 James Stephen told Spencer Perceval: 'There is a great and growing reliance on private character as a ground of political judgement . . . The people look much to, rely much upon, that which they can best understand, the character which a statesman bears in the relations of private life, and in that which we all bear to God.'[37] Charles James Fox was perhaps the first English politician to suffer as a victim of his countrymen's new-found obsession with the private morality of their leaders and to discover that marital fidelity and moderate living were of infinitely more importance for political advancement than oratorial ability or administrative competence. His persistent failure to achieve office was due in large measure to popular disapproval of his dissolute and loose habits. The most mediocre Evangelical politicians, on the other hand, found themselves universally applauded and acclaimed for the purity of their character. Nicholas Vansittart was a near disaster as Chancellor of the Exchequer, yet, as a contemporary commented, 'the primitive simplicity of his character procured him many friends, and his white hair and unworldly gentleness acquired the sort of reverence men are accustomed to feel for a saintly priest.'[38] Spencer Perceval hardly had an original idea in his head, yet he became one of the most popular Premiers of the early nineteenth century because, as Henry Brougham rather acidly reflected, 'his whole character was eminently fitted to command the respect and win the favour of a nation whose prejudices are numerous and deep rooted, and whose regard for the decencies of private life readily accepts a strict observance of them as a substitute for almost any political defect, and a compensation for many political crimes.'[39]

After 1832 private character counted for even more among

politicians. 'Most powerful indeed would be the moral lesson', thundered the *Record* after the passing of the Reform Bill, 'if it were only publicly understood that there are hundreds of thousands of conscientious electors, far removed from all political factions, who will never give their vote for any man of known immoral life; or who is ascertained to hold infidel or sceptical sentiments in religion; or who arrayed himself on the side of impiety or blasphemy.'[40] Victorian politicians understood it only too well: there were remarkably few public figures in the later nineteenth century who let a whiff of scandal about their private lives and character reach the ears of the public. In his novel *Sybil* (1848) Disraeli made much of the obsession of contemporary politicians with not offending Evangelical standards of taste and propriety. The following exchange is typical:

Lord Marney: 'This is a domestic country, and the country expects that no problem should take household office, whose private character is not inexpungable.'
Tadpole: 'Private character is to be the basis of the new government. Since the Reform Act, that is a qualification much more esteemed by the constituency than public service. We must go with the times, my lord. A virtuous middle class shrinks with horror from French actresses; and the Wesleyans, the Wesleyans must be considered.'
'I always subscribe to them,' said his lordship.[41]

In another scene in *Sybil*, Tadpole calls on his colleagues to get the Prime Minister 'to make some kind of a religious move ... if we could get him to speak at Exeter Hall, were it only a slavery meeting, that would do'.[42] The Evangelicals may have demonstrated to politicians that middle-class electors were not to be influenced by liquor or bribery, but they had at the same time shown them how they could be won over by ostentatious piety and affected seriousness. Not a few nineteenth-century politicians deliberately involved themselves in popular moral causes or assumed conspicuously pious attitudes in the same calculated and cynical spirit as Tadpole. In 1821 Lord Lauderdale told Earl Grey that 'as I like to be in the fashion I thought that at a time when you and Lord Holland with his three hundred and ten reasons in favour of reform were paying court to the radicals, I would take a little touch of the Methodists', and that he had therefore liberally peppered a political address with

Biblical references.[43] Palmerston made his patronage of serious candidates for the Episcopate a major point of his campaign in the 1857 election. There were undoubtedly votes to be won by pondering to Evangelical prejudices and votes to be lost by ignoring them. The *Record* attributed the unseating of Dr Lushington and Lord John Russell in the General Election of 1830 to the fact that they had lost votes for respectively referring contemptuously to the Home Missionary Society and bringing into dispute 'the interesting and consolatory doctrine of a particular Providence'.[44]

Undoubtedly one of the effects of the Evangelical impact on English politics was to increase the amount of cant and hypocrisy displayed by politicians. But this was not the most important feature of the Evangelicals' legacy to Victorian public life. Their great achievement was to have established politics as an honourable profession for honest men rather than as a playground for party hacks. Other groups had contributed to this development. The economical reform movement had removed most of the pickings to be made out of politics and the radicals had attacked the corruption of the eighteenth-century political system and raised the cry of reform. The Evangelicals, however, by their example and their exhortation, probably did more than any of their contemporaries to make politics a serious calling. It is predominantly their influence and achievement which explains why it was that the leading politicians of the Victorian age were on the whole more honest, more highly principled and more moral than those of the eighteenth century.

When they had completed their five-volume life of their famous father in 1838, Robert and Samuel Wilberforce sent a copy to the earnest young W. E. Gladstone, who had recently decided after much conscience-searching that the Almighty had called him to a political rather than an ecclesiastical career. 'The sketch which it gives of a public man holding fast to high principles and living in the fear of God', Samuel Wilberforce wrote in a note accompanying the book, 'will, I have no doubt, be interesting to you, and must, I think, be useful to those whose lot it is to be thrown into the midst of the same tempestuous scenes.'[45] The recipient of their gift, who was himself the product of a stern Evangelical upbringing, hardly needed the example of Wilberforce to encourage him to see the solemn duties and responsibilities of his calling. Gladstone's deep personal piety, his impeccable private life and his practice of fixing on great issues and causes on which he whipped up the moral indignation of the electorate with the oratory of a revivalist preacher, made him the epitome of all that the Evangelicals and the English public asked for in their politicians. No other Victorian came as close to the ideal of the Christian Statesman – nor did any achieve half his popularity. In its obituary notice, *The Times* identified without hesitation the ultimate source of his appeal:

> It is obvious that, in a country where seriousness is a great force, this must have proved to Mr. Gladstone a source of strength.[46]

10

Home and Family

Evangelicalism was above all else the religion of the home. It idealized and sanctified family life. 'Domestic happiness', wrote William Cowper in *The Task*, was the 'only bliss of Paradise that has surviv'd the fall'.[1] The Evangelical tract writers maintained the same theme. Hannah More criticized those women who forsook the solid comforts and duties of home for the specious joys of watering places and pleasure gardens. Thomas Gisborne called on husbands and fathers to quit gaming clubs and political societies and 'join the family circle in the winter evenings' perusal of the selected portion of history, poetry, or other improving or elegant branch of literature.'[2] William Roberts urged the Christian gentleman to make his home and family his dearest concern and to remember that 'a vagrant charity but ill compensates for a deserted hearth, a distracted economy and a loose domestic government.'[3] The Evangelicals themselves were devoted to their homes and they set a pattern of family life which was taken as a model by the middle classes. Characteristically, Wilberforce resigned the Parliamentary representation of Yorkshire in 1812 so that he could devote more time to his children. The Evangelicals succeeded in establishing the home as the centre of nineteenth-century English life. The Victorians' strong conviction that only within the bosom of the family could virtues be cultivated and the ideal life be led derived in very large measure from their influence. So also did the oppressiveness and terror of many Victorian childhoods.

At the centre of life in all Evangelical households stood the institution of family prayers. One of the first actions of those converted to vital religion was to gather their families together for daily

179

worship. To help them there were numerous published collections of family prayers, the most popular of which was written by Henry Thornton and published after his death, going through thirty-one editions in two years. According to G. W. E. Russell, the use of Thornton's *Family Prayers* was a distinctive sign of Evangelicalism. Family prayers were a formidable occasion; they regularly lasted up to an hour and involved the whole household, including the servants. They often occurred not once but twice in the day. Wilberforce noted in his private journal in November 1785, a few weeks after his conversion, 'began this night constant family prayer, and resolved to have it every morning and evening.'[4] This description of the morning's devotions by a subsequent visitor to the Wilberforces accords closely with the picture given a generation later by Samuel Butler in his painting 'Family Prayers':

> About a quarter before ten o'clock, the family assembled to prayers, which were read by Wilberforce in the dining room. As we passed from the drawing room I saw all the servants standing in regular order, the women ranged in a line against the wall and the men the same. There were seven women and six men. When the whole were collected in the dining room, all knelt down each against a chair or sofa, Wilberforce knelt at a table in the middle of the room, and after a little pause began to read a prayer, which he did very slowly in a low, solemnly awful voice.[5]

During the nineteenth century the practice of having family prayers spread to non-Evangelical households. The Revd Charles Sumner succeeded in making it fashionable when, as chaplain-in-ordinary to the Royal Household, he persuaded George IV to institute family prayers at Buckingham Palace. By the end of the century the practice had become so common in middle-class families that the Provost of King's College Cambridge could write in a circular letter to undergraduates about morning chapel in 1889, 'You, most of you, come from homes where family prayers are the custom.'[6] It is not difficult to see why family prayers had become so popular. Like the other practice which the Evangelicals reintroduced into English life, that of saying grace before and after meals, it strengthened family bonds and reinforced the position of the head of the household. There were few occasions on which a Victorian father could assert his dominance over his wife, his children and his servants so effectively as when he led them in family prayers. Thackeray went so far as to suggest in Chapter XIV of *The Newcomes* that the whole practice was designed principally to confirm the authority of the master over his servants 'who answer the bell for prayers as they answer the bell for coals'.

Family prayers were only one of many trials which had to be endured by children in Evangelical families. The Evangelicals' attitude towards their children was in keeping with their belief in the importance of a closely knit family. They generally shunned the conventional boarding school education for their sons and daughters and instead employed private tutors, usually clergymen who were renowned for their seriousness. Wilberforce decided against sending his sons to a public school from a consideration 'of its probable effects on eternal state', and chose rather to educate them at home where, as Gisborne put it, 'many temptations to vice from the contagion of corrupt examples are avoided.'[7] Most other Evangelicals did the same. In 1825 a contemporary observer attributed the decline of Harrow School to the fact that 'the religious world, as represented by Mr. Wilberforce and his associates, had declared against the prevailing system.' In the rare cases where the children of Evangelicals were sent away to school, it was always to establishments which were impeccably serious in character. One such was the school for clergy daughters presided over by William Carus Wilson at Cowan Bridge in Yorkshire, to which the Brontë sisters were sent and which formed the model for Lowood School in *Jane Eyre*. At such places there was no danger either of contamination by worldlings or of a watering down of the severe training in abstinence and self-denial which the Evangelicals believed to be proper for their offspring.

At home, the lives of Evangelical children were hedged around on all sides by restrictions and prohibitions. The dominant theme of childhood in a serious family was summed up in the little sermon which Harriet Martineau was taught to repeat at the age of three by her Evangelical nurse: 'dooty fust and pleasure afterwards'. Serious parents were specifically enjoined by Hannah More not to indulge their offspring, lest they come to connect 'happiness with gluttony and pleasure with loitering, feasting or sleeping', but rather to train them early on in the principles of discipline and self-restraint.[8] Most reponded to this demand with alacrity and sub-jected their children to a rigorously puritanical regime in which everything was restricted and controlled. Evangelical children found that their choice of friends was regulated and that they were denied many of the normal pleasures and pastimes of childhood. Many boys suffered, as Samuel Wilberforce did, from parental insistence that their choice of playmates should be based 'on Scriptural precepts'; while for girls, ball-going, extravagant clothes, and hair arranged in curls or ringlets were strictly taboo. Several children of Evangelical families were forcibly enrolled into 'voluntary' associations like the Bond of Joy into which Mrs Pardiggle recruited her son, Alfred, and whose members pledged themselves to abstain from cakes and tobacco. Sometimes, good behaviour would be recognized with a small monetary reward, but immediate moral pressure was invari-ably brought to deprive the unlucky child of his hard-earned penny. G. W. E. Russell, who remembered with particular ire the impound-ing of the money which he won as a child in 'the race game' for the missionary box, recalled his aunt composing the following lines for the benefit of her young relations:

Would you like to be told the best use for a penny?
I can tell you a use which is better than any —
Not on toys, not on fruit, nor on sweetmeats to spend it,
But over the seas to the heathen to send it.[9]

Nearly all Evangelical parents imposed stringent restrictions of what their children should be allowed in the way of reading matter. In homes from which card games, visits to the theatre, and other diversions had been banned, reading was naturally one of the main occupations and it was particularly important to ensure that the literature on which children were brought up was of a suitably 'serious' kind. Fairy tales and novels were not generally to be found on the nursery shelves in Evangelical homes — nor were editions of the classics, except in heavily Bowdlerized versions. In their place were the improving stories written by Mrs Sherwood and Charlotte Elizabeth Tonna, the volumes of the *Christian Family Library* which Edward Bickersteth started in 1832, and, later on, the *Boy's Own Paper* (soon followed by the *Girl's Own Paper*) estab-lished by the Religious Tract Society in 1878 'to illustrate by practical example the noblest type of manhood and the truest

Christian devotion'.[10] The diet of 'serious' reading matter on which Evangelical children were brought up did not simply consist of these sentimental and often second-rate publications, however. It also included the works of Bunyan, Milton and Cowper and, of course, the Bible. One of the main reasons why the Victorians were able to digest, and enjoy, the heavy prose of such writers as Carlyle, Mill, Arnold and Ruskin was because so many of them had developed an early acquaintance with 'serious' literature in their Evangelical childhoods.

The restrictions and prohibitions to which Evangelical children were subjected through the week were nothing to those that they suffered on Sundays. Virtually every enjoyable pastime was forbidden them on the Sabbath. Toys and games were locked away. Readers of *The Way of All Flesh* will remember that in the Pontifex household all traffic on the toy railway was prohibited despite the children's promise that they would run only Sunday trains on it. No hot food was allowed on the Sabbath except for an egg at breakfast; G. W. E. Russell remembered from his childhood a Sunday menu for 'cold beef, salad, cold sweats'. Reading matter was even more rigorously censored than during the week. Newspapers were strictly taboo on Sundays in most Evangelical homes and in their place serious families took *Sunday at Home*, *The Family Treasury of Sunday Reading* or *The Sunday Review* which were all started by Evangelical publishers in the 1850s. Other activities were frowned upon. In 1821 John Henry Newman was called downstairs after Sunday dinner to give his opinion as to whether it was sinful to write letters on the Sabbath after his brother had refused to copy one for his father. John Ruskin's mother turned all the pictures to the wall on Sundays lest their bright colours should distract her children from their contemplation of man's sinful state. It was small wonder that, as Ruskin later recalled, echoing the experience of countless other Evangelical children in the nineteenth century, 'the horror of Sunday used even to cast its prescient gloom as far back in the week as Friday – and all the glory of Monday, with church seven days removed again, was not equivalent for it.'[11]

Sabbath observance was the focal point of Evangelical family life. It shows more clearly than anything else the strength and the weakness of the Evangelical family – its closely knit and protective nature, and its puritanical oppressiveness. It is worth quoting at some length two very different pictures of Sunday in an Evangelical home to illustrate this. The first, presenting the ideal Sabbath as conceived by the Evangelicals, comes from a tract published by the Religious Tract Society entitled *Sunday Afternoon with Mama*:

Sunday was a happy day to little Kate and Ernest. Shall I tell you how they spent it? On Saturday evening just before bedtime, they always helped their nurse to put away in the nursery cupboard all their toys and their 'week-day' Picture Books, and then from a drawer below was taken first a box of movable letters, which Kate and Ernest were only allowed to use on Sunday. The children were very fond of putting these letters together so as to form words, and they often were able to spell a verse from the Bible in this way. Besides the letter box, in the Sunday drawer were kept two large Picture Books, with large coloured pictures of Bible scenes. One of these belonged to Katie, and the other to Ernie, and there were some smaller books as well, with pretty Bible stories, and sweet hymns in them. All these were taken out of the drawer on Saturday night, and put away again on Sunday night because if Katie and Ernie had had these letters and books every day they would perhaps have grown tired of them and had no fresh books for Sunday.

Dear Mama always tried to make Sunday a very happy day for her children; and when they were not happy, I think it must have been either when they were not very well, or not very good. In the morning they went to the House of God with their papa and mama, and although they did not know all that was said, yet they tried to behave well, that they might not disturb other people. When all the people knelt in prayer, their mama had told them that they could think a little prayer in their heart, and that, though they did not speak, God would hear what their hearts said to Him.

On Sundays Katie and Ernie had the pleasure of dining and taking tea with papa and mama, instead of in the nursery as in other days; and though they were very fond of nurse, and quite happy with her, this was a great treat. But it is about their Sunday afternoon with mama that I am going to tell you. Katie and Ernie spent them alone with her. Nurse and all the other servants but one went to worship God, and papa went to the

ragged school, to teach some poor little boys who had not kind
fathers or mothers at home to tell them how the Lord Jesus
loves little children. Sometimes Katie and Ernie read to their
mama from one of their Sunday story books. Then she read to
them and they learned a short text, or one or two verses of a
hymn. But what they liked best was listening to the stories
their mama told them from the Bible. When papa came home he
often had something to say about the poor little ragged boys in
his class. Katie and Ernie often asked a great many questions
about them at tea-time. After tea Mama opened the piano, and
sang with her children some sweet children's hymns.

Then nurse came to call the children to the nursery, and after
a happy talk with her, and kneeling down and thanking God for
all his love and care during the day and asking him to watch
them through the night, Kate and Ernest were almost ready for
bed, and soon might be seen fast asleep on their little pillows.

The second description of the Evangelical Sabbath comes from
the pen of one of its fiercest critics, Charles Dickens. In Chapter III
of *Little Dorrit*, Arthur Clenman is prompted by the sound of
church bells in London to reminisce about the Sundays of his
childhood:

'Heaven forgive me,' said he, 'and those who trained me. How I
have hated this day.' There was the dreary Sunday of his
childhood, when he sat with his hands before him scared out of
his senses by a horrible tract which commenced business with
the poor child by asking him in its title, why he was going to
Perdition? – a piece of curiosity that he really in a frock and
drawers was not in a condition to satisfy – and which, for the
further attraction of his infant mind, had a parenthesis in every
other line with some hiccupping reference as 2 Ep. Thess., c. iii,
v. 6 & 7. There was the sleepy Sunday of his boyhood, when,
like a military deserter, he was marched to chapel by a picquet
of teachers three times a day, morally handcuffed to another
boy; and when he would willingly have bartered two meals
of indigestible sermon for another ounce or two of inferior
mutton at his scanty dinner in the flesh. There was the inter-
minable Sunday of his nonage; when his mother, stern of face
and unrelenting of heart, would sit all day behind a Bible –

bound, like her own construction of it, in the hardest, barest, and straitest boards, with one dinted ornament on the cover like the drag of a chain, and a wrathful sprinkling of red upon the edges of the leaves – as if it, of all books! were a fortification against sweetness of temper, natural affection, and gentle intercourse. There was the resentful Sunday of a little later, when he sat glowering and glooming through the tardy length of the day, with a sullen sense of injury in his heart, and no more real knowledge of the beneficent history of the New Testament, than if he had been bred among idolaters. There was the legion of Sundays, all days of unserviceable bitterness and mortification, slowly passing before him.

The restrictions and prohibitions which had surrounded their early lives left many of those brought up in Evangelical households with a feeling of oppression and bitterness which lingered long into adulthood. But they did not leave so profound a mark as the constant reminders of their own sinfulness and depravity to which they were subjected. This message was rammed home at every opportunity. Addressing parents in her *Strictures on Female Education* Hannah More asked, 'is it not a fundamental error to consider children as innocent beings, whose little weaknesses may perhaps want some correction, rather than as beings who bring into the world a corrupt nature and evil dispositions?'[12] Mrs Sherwood's *The Fairchild Family*, first published in 1818 and infinitely the most popular children's book in the first three decades of Victoria's reign, set out to convince its young readers of their depravity by means of such apparently spontaneous exchanges as the following:

'Papa', said Lucy, 'may we have some verses about mankind having bad hearts?'
'Yes my dear,' answered Mr. Fairchild.
Then each of the children repeated a verse from the Bible to prove that the nature of man, after the fall of Adam, is utterly and entirely sinful. (Chapter 11)

Charlotte Elizabeth Tonna's popular *Short Stories for Children* laboured the same theme. One of them, for example, which was about the rescue of a boy and girl who had fallen into a lake in an effort to climb on to their father's boat, concluded:

If God had not taken pity on these faulty children, they would have been deep in the cold water, dead and stiff before night; and if the Lord Jesus did not show compassion to you, and offer you salvation through his precious blood, you would have no way of escape from the far more deep and horrible pit that burns with eternal fire.[13]

The terrors of Hell were very real to Evangelical children. All of them could have answered only too well the awful question which Mr Brocklehurst put to Jane Eyre when he was told by her guardian that she was not always a good girl: 'Do you know where the wicked go after death?' A large number of Evangelical tracts for children featured the stories of infant Sabbath breakers and 'naughty children addicted to falsehood and deceit' who had died suddenly and who were destined for eternal perdition. William Carus Wilson, on whom Charlotte Brontë had based Mr Brocklehurst, specialized in producing these terrifying children's stories which dwelt almost exclusively on death and the horrors which could follow it. His theme is summed up in a verse from a typical story, *The Bad Boy*, in his best-selling collection, *The Child's First Tales*:

> There is an hour when I must die,
> Nor do I know how soon 'twill come;
> A thousand children, young as I,
> Are called by death to hear their doom.[14]

The concentration of Evangelical tract writers on the themes of death and hell directly inspired the Victorian cult of deathbed morality. The Evangelicals believed that there were important moral lessons to be learned from witnessing and studying the manner of death of both sinners and the saved. In *The Complete Duty of Man* Henry Venn urged parents to bring their children at the earliest possible opportunity to the deathbeds of friends and relatives. Many Victorian children were early brought into contact with the experience of death, and made to feel the crucial importance of ordering their own lives with the end constantly in view, and in preparation for a happy eternity. More seriously, they were also often preoccupied with guilt and fear induced by the acceptance of Evangelical teaching on depravity. Henry Manning recalled that he was so terrified at being told at the age of four that 'God had a book in which he wrote down everything we did wrong' that 'I remember being found by my mother sitting under a kind of writing-table in great fear.'[15] Charles Kingsley commented on his Evangelical childhood: 'believing, in obedience to my mother's assurance, and the solemn prayers of the ministers about me, that I was a child of hell, and a lost and miserable sinner, I used to have accesses of terror, and fancy that I should surely wake next morning in everlasting flames.'[16] The Brontë sisters experienced for the rest of their lives the dread of damnation and the fear of the terrible fate which awaited them after death which had been implanted in them as children by the teaching of their Evangelical father and of a Methodist aunt. Samuel Butler reflected in *The Way Of All Flesh* that Evangelicalism probably had a good deal to do with the unhappy relations which often existed between Victorian parents and children:

> The general impression it leaves upon the mind of the young is that their wickedness at birth was but very imperfectly wiped out at baptism, and that the mere fact of being young at all has something with it that savours more or less distinctly of the nature of sin. (Chapter VII)

There is no doubt that the experience of being brought up in an Evangelical home could be profoundly depressing and even terrifying. Most of the features of Victorian childhood which we regard as being particularly oppressive were introduced by the Evangelicals — the rigid observance of the Sabbath, the denial of pleasures and the equation of enjoyment with sin, the stress on conformity and obedience to authority, and the overwhelming preoccupation with death and hell. Certainly some of the worst cases of parental cruelty and indifference to children on the part of the Victorian middle classes were to be found in Evangelical homes. The childhood sufferings of Augustus Hare, who later became a famous liberal Victorian churchman, at the hands of his Evangelical aunt provide a particularly grim example. She killed his favourite cat, regularly locked him for hours in the vestry of her husband's church at Herstmonceaux in Sussex, and delighted in putting delicious puddings in front of him which he was obliged to take off untasted to the poor of the village. It was little wonder that many of those brought up in Evangelical homes revolted against the religion of their parents.

Not all Evangelical childhoods were like Augustus Hare's, however. The Thornton children led blissfully happy lives at their home at Battersea Rise in Clapham, playing with the equally happy young Wilberforces and Macaulays next door. They even took part in fancy-dress parties: Marianne Thornton's diary records one in 1808 to which she came as Mrs Slipslop, Samuel Wilberforce as the Pope, and Tom Macaulay as Napoleon. For all the terror that she inflicted in the hearts of other children, Mrs Sherwood was loved and revered by her own daughter, Sophia. Victoria de Bunsen, the daughter of Lady Victoria Buxton, recalled even the Sundays of her Evangelical childhood with affection and asked: 'who could have been nurtured and taught by so saintly and beautiful a mother or have been told of God and Christ and trained so fully in the right way?'[17] George Gilbert Scott simply thanked God for his pious and excellent parents and for his blessed and happy childhood.

The fact was that most of the offspring of Evangelical families in the nineteenth century derived something very much more positive from their upbringing than just a lingering sense of guilt and fear. They got a rigorous and thorough education, a high degree of self-discipline and self-respect, and a strong urge to do good in the world. They also gained a great deal from the example of personal holiness and service to others which they saw displayed in the lives of their parents. G. W. E. Russell once commented that he had witnessed in the Evangelical home in which he was brought up 'an abiding sense of religious responsibility, a self-sacrificing energy in works of mercy, an evangelistic zeal, an aloofness from the world, and a level of saintliness in daily life, such as I do not expect again to see realized on earth'.[18] Recalling his upbringing among the Clapham Saints, Henry Venn's nephew, John, wrote:

> These wise men never endeavoured to mould our unformed opinions into any particular pattern. Indeed it was needless for them to preach to us. Their lives spoke far more plainly and convincingly than any words. We saw their patience, cheerfulness, generosity, wisdom and activity daily before us, and we knew and felt that all this was only the natural expression of hearts given to the service of God.[19]

With the example of their parents' lives constantly before them, it is not difficult to see why so many children of Evangelical families, and especially of the members of the Clapham Sect, went on to become leading figures in the public and intellectual life of Victorian England. They had grown up among men and women who were dedicated both to the service of the community and to the serious study of the human condition. The atmosphere in most Evangelical households in the early nineteenth century, and particularly in the homes of the Clapham Sect, was one of intellectual rigour and intense involvement in public affairs as well as of deep piety and firm discipline. From an early stage Evangelical children were introduced to serious ideas and concepts, and were involved in the discussion and formulation of major projects for the improvement of mankind. At the age of three John Ruskin delighted his parents by climbing on to a chair and preaching a little sermon which embodied the essentials of the Evangelical call to seriousness: 'People, be dood. If you are dood, Dod will love you; if you are not dood, Dod will not love you. People, be dood.' Charles Kingsley was a year older when he delivered his first sermon from the nursery. Robert Peel was made as a boy to repeat verbatim to his father the morning and evening sermons which he had heard in church every Sunday. Thomas Macaulay made his literary debut at the age of fifteen in the *Christian Observer*, which his father edited, and his first public speech nine years later at the May meeting of the Society for the Abolition of Slavery. It was in such suitably 'serious' ways that the offspring of Evangelical families first developed their talents.

Evangelical children were given a further powerful encouragement to embark on useful careers by constant lectures from their parents on the dangers of passing their time unprofitably. When he went up to Cambridge as an undergraduate in 1818, Thomas Macaulay was told by his father not to accept wine invitations or attend dinner parties as they were a waste of time and led only to sinful excesses. William Wilberforce gave his son Samuel a long list of do's and don't's when he went to Oxford in 1823. It included a strong warning against taking part in the common undergraduate practice of holding Sunday breakfast parties, which he considered 'very injurious and less excusable because at that early hour of the day the spirits of young men especially can need no such cordial'.[20] Forty-four years later Sir James Stephen urged his son, James Fitzjames, then an undergraduate at Cambridge, to avoid participating in Sunday evening Shakespeare clubs and other 'dull, profitless, and dissipated and mischievous activities', and instead to 'establish a small club to drink tea together with any other solace of the same kind after Sunday evening Chapel, having for its object to purpose a new translation of some part of the New Testament.'[21] All three sons took heed of these parental strictures and spent their student days in serious study and activity, to the considerable profit of their future careers.

Evangelical parents did not simply tell their children not to waste time. They positively encouraged and exhorted them to lead useful lives. Victoria de Bunsen recalled that her mother 'never counselled soft things. Rather she spurred to endeavour. When one hoped that one's lurid account of a full day had satisfied even her demands, she would end up with, "But couldn't you get in some little bit of *practical* work? Couldn't you visit a hospital, for instance?".'[22] Wilberforce wrote to his son Samuel on the eve of his departure for Oxford:

> You, as my son, will be tried by a different standard from that which is commonly referred to, be judged by a more rigorous rule ... remember that you have my credit in your keeping as well as your own ... Aim high. Don't be satisfied with being hopeful ... How little do you know to what services Providence may call you.[23]

It was a powerful incitement to make a mark on the world. Many of those Evangelical children who attained literary or public distinction in the Victorian age were driven throughout their lives by a fear of being found wanting in their parents' eyes and of living unworthy of their own high calling.

Perhaps the most valuable gift which those brought up in Evangelical homes obtained in their childhood was the love of their parents. The numerous letters which Evangelical mothers and fathers wrote to their children were often full of censure and admonition but they were also shot through with deep compassion and affection. Evangelical families were bound together by very strong ties of love. They exhibited a unity of purpose and a depth of fellowship which provided a model of the stereotype Victorian happy family group engaged together in the pursuit of some innocent recreation around the hearth. 'I still hear the voices that joined in part-songs there on a winter's evening,' Henry Moule reflected nostalgically on the family gatherings of his childhood in his father's Dorset vicarage.[24] The strong stability which characterized the life of Evangelical families derived partly from this deep mutual love and affection and partly from an overwhelming sense of peace and resignation in the face of the trials of this world and a sure confidence in the world to come. The Evangelicals were certain that those who lived and died in faith would meet together in Heaven, never again to part. This was the strongest bond which united them with their loved ones. In 1797 William Hey, an Evangelical magistrate from Leeds, called his numerous children together for the last time before they went off into the world to pursue their various callings: 'Although we shall not all meet again here', he told them, 'it will be of no consequence. We will meet in another world around the throne of God.'[25]

This certainty about the after-life was the corollary of the Evangelicals' obsession with death. As they sat beside the deathbed of a loved one, the Evangelicals knew that their estrangement would only be brief and they knew also that the soul was about to make a journey to a happier land. In an age when death could strike suddenly and often, this double certainty was a source of profound strength and consolation. 'I shall not look for you in vain at the last,' says the dying Mr Trynan to Janet Dempster in the closing scene of *Janet's Repentance*. 'No, no', comes the unfaltering reply, 'I shall be there. God will not forsake me.' As she nursed through sickness the one child who remained to her after her five others had died, Catharine Tait, the deeply Evangelical wife of the famous Victorian Archbishop, asked herself:

> Should I take the choice upon myself, and crave at any cost the life of this sweet child now so precious to us? I thought of the home in Heaven to which Chatty and Susan were gone, and then I thought of the very brightest home I might hope to secure for this little lamb on earth. If her Home in Heaven was ready, should I wish to keep her here? No.[26]

It was this deep faith which was ultimately the most precious legacy of an Evangelical upbringing. Reflecting in his autobiography on his Evangelical childhood, the historian E. L. Woodward confessed that it had meant that 'to the last day of my life I shall never travel by train on Sunday without a slight feeling of guilt. Also I shall never escape from a slight twinge of reproach that I chose an easier and more selfish career than that of a missionary in Darkest Africa.' But, he concluded:

our own tranquil life and pleasures, all very simple, were so deeply happy that even today I assume every family to be united, and I find it difficult to believe that all my contemporaries do not look back, as I look back, without any sense of bleakness or frustration, to these unending but long ended years of childhood.[27]

In his autobiography, G. W. E. Russell recalled:

My home was intensely Evangelical and I lived from my earliest days in an atmosphere where the salvation of the individual soul was the supreme and constant concern of life ... May my lot be with these evangelical saints from whom I first learned that, in the supreme work of salvation, no human being and no created thing can interfere between the soul and the Creator. Happy is the man whose religious life has been built on the impregnable rock of that belief.[28]

II

A Serious Generation

Many of the children of Evangelical families in the nineteenth century remained in the faith of their parents. The Venns, the Elliotts and the Bickersteths continued to produce Evangelical clergymen right through Victoria's reign, while among the laity the Thorntons, the Buxtons and the Ryders clung to the tenets of vital religion well into the twentieth century. Bishop Handley Moule kept true to his father's faith; so did George Gilbert Scott. But an alarmingly high number of children deserted the Evangelical fold. Three of Wilberforce's sons, as well as his son-in-law Henry Manning, followed John Henry Newman into Roman Catholicism. Samuel, the only Wilberforce son to remain an Anglican, was certainly not on the Evangelical wing of the Church. Archibald Tait became a Broad Churchman and W. E. Gladstone a High Anglican. Thomas Macaulay was in adulthood only a nominal Christian. Samuel Butler, George Eliot, Leslie and James Fitzjames Stephen and Francis Newman renounced Christianity altogether and became atheists.

There were good reasons why sensitive and intelligent men and women brought up as Evangelicals should have abandoned the religion of their parents in the mid-nineteenth century. As we have seen, Evangelicalism was by this time less a vital religion than a dry and formal creed. Those brought up in Evangelical homes who became Catholics or atheists in the 1840s and 1850s were reacting not only against the endemic narrowness and oppressiveness of their parents' faith but also against a new obscurantism and fanaticism which had only recently crept into it. Belief in the literal authority of the Bible and the imminent second coming of Christ which became standard Evangelical doctrines in the early part of Victoria's reign made it difficult for many people to remain in the faith. Evangelicalism in the second half of the nineteenth century was very different from what it had been in the first: there was a good deal more cant and a great deal less practical piety. Among the clergy there were more Chadbands and Honeymans and fewer Amos Bartons. 'Where are the people who are at once really religious, and really cultivated in heart and understanding?' Sir James Stephen asked in 1845; 'the people with whom we could associate as our fathers used to associate with each other ... No Clapham Sect nowadays.'[1] Many people deserted Evangelicalism during Victoria's reign because they felt it had changed its character.

Although they might depart far from the faith of their childhood, those who were brought up as Evangelicals in the nineteenth century retained one enduring characteristic of their parents' religion. They were, without exception, intensely serious men and women. 'Mean and ignoble as our middle class looks,' Matthew Arnold commented in 1866, 'it has this capital virtue, it has seriousness.' Arnold defined this seriousness, which he attributed to the influence of the Evangelical or Nonconformist upbringing which most middle-class Victorians had experienced, as 'an energy driving at practice, a paramount sense of the obligation of duty, self-control, and work, and an earnestness in going manfully with the best light we have'.[2] Nowhere were these particular attributes more clearly displayed than in the lives and attitudes of those children of Evangelical families who went on to achieve public and intellectual distinction in the nineteenth century. These particular eminent Victorians were a supremely serious generation.

Of those famous Victorians brought up as Evangelicals who renounced their parents' creed but still remained Christians, W. E. Gladstone was almost certainly the supreme exemplar of Evangelical seriousness. Although he became a High Churchman, Gladstone retained to the end of his life the ethical and moral beliefs to which he had been brought up by his strongly Evangelical parents. His impeccable private life and his conception of politics as a moral crusade made him, as we have seen, the closest approximation among all Victorian politicians to the Evangelicals' ideal of the Christian Statesman. To the end of his life, he remained obsessed with Evangelical notions of accountability and judgment. He told his brother Robertson, 'the great matter is to hope, pray and strive that we may be able when the great day comes to give an account ... which shall shew that we have been, however feebly, endeavouring to do the will of God in procuring good and trying to curb evil among His creatures.'[3] Above all, Gladstone clung to a view of life which was deeply and uncompromisingly serious. He summed it up in an address to the boys of Hawarden Grammar School in 1877: Be inspired with the belief that life is a great and noble calling; not a mean and grovelling thing that we are to shuffle through as we can, but an elevated and lofty destiny.[4]

The continuing legacy of Evangelical seriousness is shown equally strongly in the life of Samuel Wilberforce. At the age of fourteen Wilberforce solemnly dedicated himself to a career in the Church, 'that I might do my best to extend God's kingdom upon the earth'.[5] For the rest of his life, he was an obsessive worker who filled every moment of the day with useful activity. His habit of writing letters while on train journeys caused one correspondent to address a note to him, 'S. Oxon., Esq., Rail, Nr. Reading'. As Bishop of Oxford from 1845 to 1869, he transformed the episcopal office from being an administrative sinecure. He introduced the modern concept of bishops as the spiritual and pastoral fathers of the clergy and people and the voice of the Church in the secular affairs of the nation. So scandalized was Wilberforce by the lack of preparation and devotional exercises given to ordinands in the Church of England that in 1854 he established at Cuddesdon the first purpose-built theological college in the country. He was a strong advocate of the cause of foreign missions and a frequent speaker in the House of Lords on penal reform and other humanitarian matters. In 1848 he showed his strong attachment to the principle of voluntary philanthropy established by his father's generation of Evangelicals when, together with W. E. Gladstone, he was instrumental in setting up the Church Penitentiary Association for the Reclamation of Fallen Women.

Thomas Babington Macaulay clung only tenuously to the Christian faith but he retained throughout his life strong marks of the seriousness of his upbringing. Evangelical sexual morality gripped him so strongly that his emotional life centred entirely around his sisters. Macaulay imposed on himself the highest standards of conduct in both private and public life and acted in both as a perpetual slave to his conscience. He once stated: 'It is necessary to my happiness that I should possess, in Parliament or out of it, the consciousness of having done what is right.'[6] He expected other men to do the same. The vehement censures which Macaulay delivered on his contemporaries in his great Parliamentary speeches and on the figures of the past in his celebrated historical writings, were the supreme expression of his Evangelical temperament. The deep seriousness of purpose which infused Macaulay's whole life meant, as John Morley put it, that 'to him criticism was only a tribunal before which men were brought to be decisively tried by one or two inflexible tests, and then sent to join the sheep on the one hand, or the goats on the other.'[7] But it meant also, as Sir George Trevelyan pointed out, 'that one, whose judgements upon the statesmen of many ages and countries have been delivered to an audience vast beyond all precedent, should have framed his decisions in accordance with the dictates of honour and humanity, of ardent public spirit and lofty public virtue'.[8]

Other famous Evangelical sons who relinquished their parents' faith for different forms of Christianity continued to display unmistakable signs of their serious upbringing in later life. Charles Kingsley retained from his childhood in his father's vicarage a strong sense of the sanctity of family life and a deep commitment to humanitarian endeavour. John Henry Newman, who underwent a full-blooded conversion to vital religion at the age of fifteen, continued to hold to many of the Evangelical doctrines of his youth even after he became a Cardinal in the Roman Catholic Church. His strong belief in judgment and providence, his stress on the individuality of the soul, his firm commitment to the notion of sanctification, and above all his insistence that only through the operations of each man's conscience could the existence of God be proved, were all legacies from his early Evangelical years. John Ruskin fiercely attacked the narrowness and oppressiveness of the faith that he had been brought up in but he inherited the Evangelicals' determination to work for others and their insistence that moral considerations should override purely aesthetic ones in matters of art and taste. His remark on Millais' painting 'Mariana in the Moated Grange' shows him to be a true disciple of Evangelical seriousness: 'If the painter had painted Mariana at work in an unmoated grange, instead of idle in a moated one, it had been more to the purpose – whether of art or life.'⁹

Those from Evangelical backgrounds who renounced Christianity altogether displayed in some ways an even greater seriousness in their attitude and behaviour than those who remained believers. They became agnostics or atheists only after agonizing searchings of conscience and because they felt that they could no longer honestly call themselves Christians. Less serious men and women affected by similar doubts would have remained as nominal Christians, as many eighteenth-century clergymen had done, not bothering about the hypocrisy involved. Not so that distinguished group of Victorian thinkers, brought up as Evangelicals, who renounced conventional Christianity and who exemplified the great crisis of faith through which so many people passed in the nineteenth century. Although they rejected the theology and the dogma of Evangelicalism, they clung tenaciously to its morality and its ethical assumptions. Indeed, they devoted their lives to trying to find a rational, non-supernatural basis for serious behaviour.

The first famous figure to make the journey from Evangelical certainty to honest doubt in the nineteenth century was Francis Newman, the younger brother of John Henry. Francis began life as an even more ardent Evangelical than his elder brother. In 1827, at the age of twenty-two, he went as tutor to the household of Lord Congleton in Dublin, determined to convert the Catholic Irish to vital Christianity, and three years later he travelled to Baghdad as a missionary. His faith was shaken, however, when he returned to England and became a University lecturer in classics. He found himself unable to accept the literal authority of the Bible. In particular, Newman objected to the doctrine of the after-life. He was not just concerned, as many contemporaries were, about the standard Christian picture of Hell as a place of eternal torment; he was equally worried about the traditional view of Heaven as a place of eternal repose. This, he believed, could only distract men from the important obligations in this life. Newman actually criticized the Christian concept of Heaven because it was too comfortable and complacent:

It is certainly too monotonous for an Eternity ... to make a new life desirable it must give us something to do, something worth

198

striving for, and a career by which we may improve in virtue ...
If we are to increase in virtue we need occasion for self-denial,
self-control, and self-sacrifice. But these cannot exist where
there is no want, no offence, no pain. Want and pain, toil and
trial, cannot be wholly banished out of my Heaven.[10]

George Eliot forsook the Evangelical faith in which she had been
brought up and became a rational agnostic at much the same time as
Francis Newman did. As a girl she had been a devoted adherent to
the principles of vital Christianity. In 1838, at the age of nineteen,
she wrote to her Evangelical governess about her hero Wilberforce
and prayed: 'Oh that I might be made as useful in my lowly and
obscure station as he was in the exalted one assigned to him.'[11] In
another letter she confessed that she would not be sorry if the only
music which she ever heard again was the music of church worship.
Three years later she rejected Christianity in a conversion which was
almost as cataclysmic as those which had brought others to vital
religion. As a result of reading two detailed works of Biblical criticism, Charles Hennell's *Inquiry Concerning the Origin of Christianity*
and Strauss' *Life of Jesus*, George Eliot came to feel that she could
no longer accept the Christian religion. Her overriding objection to
it was that by emphasizing the will and acts of an omnipotent Deity,
it extinguished the possibilities of human love and service. She
rejected Christianity not to espouse a philosophy of hedonism or
self-indulgence, but for the far harder task of trying to lead a selfless
and moral life without any Divine assistance. 'Heaven help us! said
the old religion,' she wrote in 1853; 'the new one, from its very lack
of faith will teach us all the more to help one another.'[12] George
Eliot's subsequent life was devoted to searching for a substitute to
the Christian notions of God and the after-life which would make
men behave seriously and responsibly. She found it in a reassertion of the Evangelical concept of duty and the development of a
new religion of humanism.

The next important secessions from Evangelicalism to agnosticism occurred some thirty years later than the apostasies of George
Eliot and Francis Newman. James Fitzjames Stephen and his
younger brother Leslie were members of the second generation of
descendants from the original members of the Clapham Sect. Their
father, Sir James Stephen, had himself expressed grave doubts

about the new doctrines being adopted by his Evangelical contemporaries in the 1830s and 1840s and developed a personal version of vital religion in which human depravity played a much smaller part, and Divine love a much greater one, than in the traditional Evangelical creed. Sir James Fitzjames Stephen, who was a distinguished lawyer and was married to the daughter of J. W. Cunningham, the Evangelical Vicar of Harrow, felt unable in the late 1860s to continue even in his father's watered-down version of the Christian faith. His seriousness, however, gave him a determination to maintain a scrupulous adherence to the duties which attached to religious belief. Stephen tried desperately to find something which would take the place of Christianity for himself and others and encourage men to lead noble lives. He sought it in the Law, in the gospel of work and in the concept of duty. Ultimately, he argued, men must live as though they believed there was a purpose and an end to life even if they had profound doubts as to what these were. 'Let us dream no dreams and tell no lies,' he wrote in 1873 explaining his agnostic position, 'but go our way, wherever it may lead, with our eyes open and our heads erect.'[13]

Leslie Stephen, who is probably best remembered now as the founder of the *Dictionary of National Biography* and the father of Virginia Woolf, became an agnostic soon after his brother. In 1873 he published his *Essays on Freethinking and Plainspeaking* and two years later he renounced his Anglican orders. For him, as for many other Victorians, the doctrine of original sin had proved the great stumbling block to accepting Christianity. He found it impossible to square with his faith in human nature and his strong ethical beliefs. Like the other Evangelical converts to agnosticism, Leslie Stephen applied himself to finding a new sanction for altruistic and moral behaviour to replace the old supernatural one. In his *Science of Ethics* he set out to prove why men should wish to be good even if they did not believe in an after-life. He pinned his faith on an evolutionary law of morality, arguing that all men had a moral principle implanted in them as part of the ordinary course of human development, and so attempted to give seriousness a scientific basis.

The last and perhaps the most important of the famous converts from Evangelicalism to agnosticism in the nineteenth century was the Oxford philosopher, T. H. Green. Green was the son of a Yorkshire Evangelical clergyman, as was F. H. Bradley, another well-known Victorian philosopher; 'I gathered', his tutor at Balliol College later recalled, 'that like many other earnest men, he had come from an Evangelical home.'[14] Green was different from George Eliot and the Stephen brothers in that he did not reject Christianity altogether. He simply abandoned his belief in its miraculous elements without ever giving up the basis of Evangelical piety which lay at the root of his life. As another of his tutors recalled, 'At no time did Green lose, if I may so say, his effective desire for spiritual advancement in the ordinary Christian sense, and his complete belief in the code of ethics universally accepted as Christian as a practical guide for conduct.'[15] What he did was to redefine Christianity in such a way that its ethical and moral teaching could be accepted by those who could not accept its supernatural aspects. For Green the essential attribute of the true Christian was not subscription to certain beliefs and dogma, but rather having a proper relationship with God. 'Faith', he wrote, 'is a personal and conscious relation of man to God, forming the principle of a new life.'[16] Green defined this relationship in terms of conscience and duty. God, he argued, dwelt in every individual, taking the form of his higher self. It was by responding to this higher self, and leading a life of self-sacrifice, love and service to the community, that man fulfilled his divine and his human destiny. This was the root of Green's philosophy of idealism.

Green's idealist philosophy answered directly to the great dilemma of those many Victorians who found themselves unable to believe in Christianity and yet who wanted desperately to preserve its moral teaching. He shared with most of them the Evangelical upbringing which implanted high and noble ideals and established the individual conscience as supreme ruler and guide. Like them, he cared most for the central questions, 'What is knowledge, desire, will, duty, conscience? What is for man the highest good, the all-embracing end?'[17] Like them, he wanted passionately to believe in God and in a purpose for man's existence on earth, and yet found himself in all honesty unable to accept the supernatural elements in Christianity. Green provided a way out of the Victorian crisis of faith. He told his contemporaries to be good citizens, responding to their higher natures and obeying the gospel of duty and service. It was hardly an easy way out. The creed which the agnostics preached was, in a way, far more demanding than that of the Evangelicals. They called their fellow men to lead lives of service and self-sacrifice without any prospect of reward at the end. It was a serious call indeed.

The common feature that characterizes all those eminent Victorians who have been discussed here is their shared belief in the deep seriousness of life, the momentousness of personal choice and the importance of the responsibilities and duties of the individual. Not one of them was cynical or flippant. This was the measure of the seriousness which had been implanted in them, as in countless of their contemporaries, by the power and influence of Evangelicalism. In Chapter Nine of *Janet's Repentance*, George Eliot tried to sum up the effect which Evangelicalism had on the fictitious village of Milby. There could be no better description of its impact on the Victorians:

Evangelicalism had brought into palpable existence and operation in Milby society that idea of duty, that recognition of something to be lived for beyond the mere satisfaction of self, which is to the moral life what the addition of a great central ganglion is to animal life. No man can begin to mould himself on a faith or an idea without rising to a higher order of experience: a principle of subordination, or self-mastery has been introduced into his nature; he is no longer a mere bundle of impressions, desires, and impulses. Whatever might be the weaknesses of the ladies who pruned the luxuriance of their lace and ribbons, cut out garments for the poor, distributed tracts, quoted Scripture, and defined the true Gospel, they had learned this – that there was a divine work to be done in life, a rule of goodness higher than the opinion of their neighbours.

Abbreviations

Acland MSS. | The papers of Sir Thomas Dyke Acland in the Devon County Record Office, Exeter.
Brougham MSS. | The papers of Henry Brougham in the library of University College, London.
C.M.S. MSS. | The papers of the Church Missionary Society.
Green MSS. | Papers relating to T. H. Green in the library of Balliol College, Oxford.
Grey MSS. | The papers of Earl Grey in Durham University Library.
Harrowby MSS. | The papers of the Harrowby family in Sandon Hall, Staffordshire.
Perceval MSS. | The papers of Spencer Perceval in the British Museum.
Stephen MSS. | The papers of the Stephen family in Cambridge University Library.
Thornton MSS. | The papers of the Thornton family in Cambridge University Library.
Wilberforce MSS. | The papers of William Wilberforce in the Bodleian Library, Oxford.
Wrangham MSS. | The papers of William Wilberforce in the possession of C. E. Wrangham, Esq., Rosemary House, Catterick, Yorkshire.
Hansard | *The parliamentary debates from 1812 onwards,* printed by T. C. Hansard.
Parl. Hist. | *The Parliamentary History of England from the earliest period to 1803* (36 vols, 1816).

Notes

Except where otherwise stated, the place of publication of all books referred to below is London.

Introduction

1. *The Correspondence of Lucy Aikin & W. E. Channing*, ed. A. L. Le Breton (1874), p. 315.
2. Quoted in O. F. Christie, *The Transition from Aristocracy, 1832–1867* (1927), p. 174.
3. Quoted in G. R. Balleine, *A History of the Evangelical Party in the Church of England* (1909), p. 50.
4. S. Butler, *The Way Of All Flesh*, Chapter XVIII.
5. C. Kingsley, *Yeast* (4th edn, 1859), vii.
6. G. W. E. Russell, *Lady Victoria Buxton* (1919), p. 73.

Chapter 1: *Vital Religion*

1. W. Wilberforce, *A Practical View* .... (7th edn, 1798), p. 91.
2. H. More, *An Estimate of the religion of the fashionable world* (new edn, 1808), p. 146.
3. E. Hodder, *The Life and Work of the Seventh Earl of Shaftesbury* (popular edn, 1888), p. 527.
4. H. More, op. cit., p. 307.
5. G. Russell, *A Short History of the Evangelical Movement* (1918), p. 140.
6. T. R. Birks, *A Memoir of the Revd E. Bickersteth* (1852), I, 39.
7. Quoted in D. Newsome, *The Parting of Friends* (1966), p. 49.
8. W. Wilberforce, op. cit., p. 95.
9. Ibid., p. 97.
10. A. W. Brown, *Recollections of the conversation parties of the Revd Charles Simeon* (1863), p. 328.
11. Acland MSS., Box 5/1.
12. *Some Account of the life and writings of Mrs. Trimmer* (1814), p. viii.

13. Thornton MSS., 1/R, f.7.
14. Wilberforce MSS., e. 11, f. 27.
15. J. C. Gill, *The Ten Hours Parson* (1959), p. 39.
16. T. R. Birks, op. cit., II, 194.
17. G. Russell, *Lady Victoria Buxton* (1919), p. 35.
18. W. Urwick, *Biographical sketches of the late J. D. La Touche* (Dublin, 1868), p. 231.
19. E. Hodder, op. cit., p. 720.
20. W. Carus, *Memoirs of the life of the Revd Charles Simeon* (3rd edn, 1848), p. vi.
21. J. Foster, *On Some of the causes by which the Evangelical faith has been rendered less acceptable to persons of cultivated taste* in *Essays to a Friend* (1805), II, 36.
22. E. Sidney, *The Life of the Revd Rowland Hill* (1834), p. 198.
23. Quoted in N. St John Stevas, *Obscenity and the Law* (1956), p. 31.
24. R. I. and S. Wilberforce, *The Life of William Wilberforce* (1838), IV, 389.
25. *Falconet*, Chapter II; *The Vicar of Wrexhill*, ii, 86; G. Russell, *The Household of Faith* (1902), p. 235.
26. H. More, op. cit., p. 68.
27. R. I. and S. Wilberforce, op. cit., I, 106.
28. G. Gilbert Scott, *Personal and Professional Recollections* (1879), p. 33.
29. G. Russell, op. cit., p. 227.

Chapter 2: *Converting the Nation*

1. R. I. and S. Wilberforce, *The Life of William Wilberforce* (1838), IV, 227.
2. Quoted in W. L. Burn, *The Age of Equipoise* (1968), p. 271.
3. J. B. Braithwaite, *Memoirs of J. J. Gurney* (Norwich, 1854), I, 267.
4. T. R. Birks, *A Memoir of the Revd E. Bickersteth* (1852), I, 3.
5. J. S. Reynolds, *The Evangelicals at Oxford, 1735–1871* (Oxford, 1953), p. 83.
6. H. More, *Works* (1833), I, 249.
7. *Memorials Personal to Lord Gambier*, ed. G. Chatterton (1861), I, 266–7.
8. W. Jones, *Jubilee Memorial of the Religious Tract Society* (1850), p. 634.
9. *The Mendip Annals*, ed. A. Roberts (1859), p. 8.
10. *Hints on the Establishment of Sunday Schools* (1835), p. 15.
11. J. M. Weylland, *A thought for the world* (1878), p. 25.
12. E. Hodder, *The Life and Work of the Seventh Earl of Shaftesbury* (popular edn, 1888), pp. 747–8.

13. Ibid., p. 358.
14. Quoted in C. Binfield, *George Williams and the Y.M.C.A.* (1973), p. 120.
15. E. Hodder, op. cit., p. 749.
16. C. Marsh, *English Hearts and English Hands* (1858), p. 353.
17. *Mendip Annals*, p. 109.
18. *Edinburgh Review*, xcviii (October, 1853), 280.
19. H. More, *Works*, II, 287.
20. W. Wilberforce, *A Practical View* ... (7th edn, 1798), p. 3.
21. *Memoirs of the life and correspondence of Hannah More*, ed. W. Roberts, (2nd edn, 1834), III, 322.
22. W. Cowper, *The Task*, Book IV, ll. 88–93.
23. A. O'Callaghan, *The Bible Society against Church and State* (1817), p. 4.
24. J. H. Pratt, *Eclectic Notes* (2nd edn, 1865), p. 394.
25. W. L. Burn, op. cit.

Chapter 3: *Assault on the Church*

1. Quoted by D. Newsome, *The Parting of Friends* (1966), p. 52.
2. *The Autobiography of Arthur Young*, ed. M. Betham-Edwardes (1898), p. 400.
3. T. Gisborne, *An Enquiry Into the Duties of Men* (1795), II, 5.
4. B. W. Mathias, *Twenty One Sermons* (Dublin, 1838), p. 8.
5. *The principal clergy of London* (manuscript dated 1844 in the Bodleian Library, Oxford), f. 19.
6. L. E. Binns, *Religion in the Victorian Era* (1935), p. 44.
7. W. Carus, *Memoirs of the Life of the Revd Charles Simeon* (3rd edn, 1848), p. 554.
8. H. C. G. Moule, *Memories of a Vicarage* (1913), p. 54.
9. *The Vicar of Wrexhill*, II. 261
10. H. Moule, op. cit., p. 40.
11. Quoted in A. Cockshutt, *Anglican Attitudes* (1959), p. 52.
12. *Edinburgh Review*, xcviii (October, 1853), 280.

Chapter 4: *A Mission to the Heathen*

1. *Jane Eyre*, Chapter XXII.
2. *Memorials Personal of Lord Gambier*, I, 234.
3. Quoted in G. Moorhouse, *The Missionaries* (1973), p. 50.
4. *The First Ten Years Quarterly Papers of the C.M.S.* (1826), p. 5.
5. *Punch*, vi (1844), 210.
6. The most recent is J. Gratus, *The Great White Lie* (1973).
7. C. Grant, *Observations on the state of society among the Asiatic subjects of Great Britain* (1793), p. 110.

8. E. Edwardes, *Memorial of the Life and Letters of Sir H B. Edwardes* (1886), II, 410.
9. J. Rosselli, *Lord William Bentinck* (1974), p. 210.
10. Quoted in M. Edwardes, *British Rule in India* (1967), p. 42.
11. *A brief view of the present state of the C.M.S.* (1826), p. 10.
12. Quoted in *Britain pre-eminent; studies of British world influence in the Nineteenth Century*, ed. C. J. Bartlett (1969), p. 142.
13. G. Moorhouse, op. cit., p. 23.
14. C. Grant, op. cit., p. 94.
15. E. Hodder, *The Life and Work of the Seventh Earl of Shaftesbury* (popular edn, 1888), p. 695.
16. A. R. Ashwell and R. G. Wilberforce, *The Life of Samuel Wilberforce* (1880), II, 197.
17. *12th Anniversary Report of the C.M.S.* (1812), p. 438.
18. E. Hodder, op. cit., p. 243.
19. C.M.S. MSS., C. H/O 24.
20. A Hinderer, *Seventeen Years in Yoruba Country*, ed. R. B. Hone (1872), p. 6.
21. C.M.S. MSS. C. H/052.
22. W. Brock, *A biographical sketch of Sir Henry Havelock* (1858), p. 1.
23. Quoted in M. Edwardes, op. cit., pp. 176–7.
24. Lawrence's dispatch on the elimination of all un-Christian principles from the Government of India, quoted in C. Aitchison, *Lord Lawrence* (1894), p. 118.

Chapter 5: *The War Against Vice*

1. R. I. and S. Wilberforce, *The Life of William Wilberforce* (1838), I, 149.
2. The Proclamation is printed in full as Appendix 3, No. 1 in the third volume of L. Radzinowicz, *A History of English Criminal Law* (1956).
3. T. Bowdler, *A Memoir of John Bowdler* (1825), p. 320.
4. *Hansard*, 1815, XXXI, 615.
5. *Parl. Papers*, 1817, VII (484), 479: Report of the committee on the state of the police in the metropolis.
6. *Christian Guardian*, April 1820, p. 159.
7. *Address to the public from the Society for the Suppression of Vice* (1803), part 2, p. 26.
8. *Hansard*, new series, 1823, viii, 711.
9. Quoted in P. H. Williams, 'Lotteries and Government Finance in England', *History Today*, vi (1956), 561.
10. *Par. Papers*, 1817, vii (484), 533.
11. Quoted in G. W. E. Russell, *A Short History of the Evangelical Movement* (1915), p. 133.
12. J. H. Pratt, *Eclectic Notes*, pp. 159–164.

13. *Parl. Register*, 1802, XVIII, 501.
14. *The Correspondence of William Wilberforce*, ed. R. I. and S. Wilberforce (1840), I, 373.
15. Wrangham MSS., Box 3.
16. *One Leg: the life and letters of H. W. Paget, First Marquess of Anglesey*, ed. Marquess of Anglesey (1961), p. 228.
17. H. Perkin, The Origins of Modern English Society (1969), p. 280.
18. G. R. Taylor, *The Angel Makers* (1958), p. 32; E. P. Thompson, *The Making of the English Working Classes* (Penguin edn, 1968), p. 451.
19. Quoted in G. R. Taylor, op. cit., p. 22.
20. *Correspondence of W. E. Channing & Lucy Aikin*, p. 29; J. T. Coleridge, *A Memoir of John Keble* (1870), p. 185.
21. *The Works of Sydney Smith* (1850), p. 134.
22. C. Dickens, *Sunday Under Three Heads* (1836), p. 22.
23. H. More, *Thoughts on the Importance of the Manners of the Great* (new edn, 1809), p. 78.
24. Ibid., p. 79.
25. Quoted in A. Smith, *The Established Church & Popular Religion, 1750–1850*, (1971), p. 51. See, for example, J. L. and B. Hammond, *The Town Labourer* (1917), Chapter XI, and E. P. Thompson, op. cit., p. 61.
26. R. I. and S. Wilberforce, op. cit., v, 40.
27. H. More, *Stories for the Middle Ranks and Tales for the Common People* (1818), I, 30–31.
28. Wilberforce MSS., c.3, f. 13.
29. Quoted in W. L. Mathieson, *England in Transition, 1789–1832*, (1920), p. 155.
30. *Hansard*, 3rd series, 1831, VIII, 421.
31. H. More, *Works* (1834), II, 221–236.
32. *Hansard* 1819, XII, 135.
33. *Black Dwarf*, v (1820), 112.
34. Wrangham MSS. Wilberforce to Major Cartwright, April 14th, 1807.
35. R. I. and S. Wilberforce, op. cit., II, 384–5; III, 6.
36. *Christian Observer*, XVIII (1819), 624.
37. *The Works of Sydney Smith*, p. 130.
38. *Parl. Hist.*, 1800, XXXV, 204; ibid., 1802, XXXVI, 845.
39. Thornton MSS., 1/R, f. 82.

Chapter 6: *Philanthropy and Paternalism*

1. E. Hodder, *The Life and Work of the Seventh Earl of Shaftesbury* (popular edn, 1888), p. 519.
2. H. Thornton, *Family Prayers* (1834), p. 137.
3. Quoted in N. Bentley, *The Victorian Scene* (1968), p. 194.

4. H. More, *Works* (1834), III, 81.
5. Quoted in M. Jaeger, *Before Victoria* (1956), p. 29.
6. *Correspondence of W. E. Channing & Lucy Aikin*, p. 396.
7. E. Hodder, op. cit., p. 350.
8. *Hansard*, new series, 1821, V, 900.
9. T. Gisborne, *An Enquiry into the Duties of Men* (1795), II, 377n.
10. E. Hodder, op. cit., p. 370.
11. Quoted in J. C. Gill, *The Ten Hours Parson* (1959), p. 82.
12. E. Hodder, op. cit., p. 226.
13. *Hansard*, new series, 1829, XXI, 981.
14. *Hansard*, 3rd series, 1832, XI, 385.
15. *Correspondence of W. E. Channing & Lucy Aikin*, p. 90.
16. S. Trimmer, *The Economy of Charity* (1787), p. 60.
17. *Mendip Annals*, p. 182.
18. Quoted in *Pressure From Without*, ed. P. Hollis (1974), pp. 175–6.
19. J. L. and B. Hammond, *Lord Shaftesbury* (new edn, 1969), p. 258.
20. E. Hodder, op. cit., p. 775.

Chapter 7: *The Age of Societies*

1. J. Stephen, *Essays in Ecclesiastical Biography* (new impression, 1907), II, 248.
2. C. S. Dudley, *An Analysis of the System of the Bible Society* (1821), p. 145.
3. J. E. Jackson, *Reasons for withdrawing from the Hibernian Bible Society* (Dublin, 1822), p. 8.
4. Quoted in E. M. Forster, *Marianne Thornton* (1956), p. 126.
5. *The Vicar of Wrexhill*, II, 70.
6. F. M. Holmes, *Exeter Hall and its Associations* (1881), p. 161.
7. *The Moonstone*, 'First Period', Chapter VIII.
8. J. Stephen, op. cit., II, 246–7.
9. *Blackwood's Edinburgh Magazine* (1824), pp. 686–7.
10. *Anti-Jacobin* (August, 1816), p. 782.
11. R. I. and S. Wilberforce, *The Life of William Wilberforce* (1838), IV, 124.
12. G. Stephen, *Anti-Slavery Recollections* (1854), p. 160.
13. Quoted in E. M. Forster, op. cit., p. 132.
14. *Culture and Anarchy*, Chapter One.
15. *Bleak House*, Chapter VIII.

Chapter 8: *The Cult of Conduct*

1. Quoted in E. M. Forster, *Marianne Thornton* (1956), p. 78.
2. B. W. Mathias, *Twenty One Sermons* (n.d.), p. 8.
3. C. Marsh, *Memorials of Captain Hedley Vicars* (1856), XI.

4. *Memoirs of the Life and Correspondence of Hannah More*, ed. W. Roberts (2nd edn, 1834), II, 305.
5. E. Hodder, *The Life and Work of the Seventh Earl of Shaftesbury* (popular edn, 1888), p. 676.
6. *The Gentleman's Magazine*, LIV (1784), pt. I, 412.
7. *Mendip Annals*, pp. 9, 151.
8. T. Gisborne, *An Enquiry into the Duties of Men* (1795), I, 4.
9. H. More, *Thoughts on the importance of the manners of the great*, p. 2.
10. T. Gisborne, op. cit., I, I.
11. Ibid., II, 217, 484.
12. H. More, *Works* (1834), III, 105.
13. Ibid., II, 319.
14. R. Hill, *An Address to persons or fashion concerning some particulars relating to Balls* (3rd edn, 1761), p. vi.
15. Wilberforce MSS., e. 11, f. 38.
16. T. Gisborne, *An Enquiry Into the Duties of the Female Sex* (1797). II, p. 213.
17. H. More, *Works*, III, 187.
18. *Correspondence of W. E. Channing & Lucy Aikin*, p. 398.
19. J. Bowdler, *Reform or Ruin* (3rd edn, 1797), p. 11.
20. W. Roberts, *The Portraiture Of A Christian Gentleman* (1829), p. 127.
21. *Memoirs Of The Life And Correspondence Of Hannah More*, III, 31.
22. Quoted in O. F. Christie, *The Transition from Aristocracy, 1832–1867* (1927), p. 210.
23. E. Hodder, op. cit., p. 315.
24. *Correspondence of Wilberforce*, I, 220.
25. J. Bean, *Zeal Without Innovation* (1808), p. 284.
26. *Edinburgh Review* (Oct. 1840), p. 41.
27. M. Arnold, *My Countrymen* (1866); J. S. Mill, *On Liberty* (1859), Chapter III.

Chapter 9: *Serious Cailings*

1. W. E. Gladstone, *Gleanings of Past Years* (1879), VII, 219.
2. T. Gisborne, *An Enquiry Into The Duties of Men*, II, 221.
3. Quoted in E. M. Forster, *Marianne Thornton* (1956), p. 121.
4. Wilberforce MSS., c. 1.
5. R. I. and S. Wilberforce, *The Life of William Wilberforce* (1838), II, 436–7.
6. T. Gisborne, op. cit., I, 225.
7. Quoted in O. MacDonagh, *A Pattern of Government Growth* (1961), p. 120. *The Letters & Papers of Charles, Lord Barham*, ed. J. K. Laughton (1907), II, 5.

8. *Memoirs of the Life and Correspondence of Hannah More*, ed. W. Roberts (2nd edn, 1834), III, 333.
9. H. More, *Works* (1834), III, 109.
10. Stephen MSS., Sir J. Stephen's diary, January 9th, 1846.
11. Quoted in G. Kitson-Clark, 'Statesmen In Disguise: Reflections on the history of the neutrality of the Civil Service', *Historical Journal*, II (1959), 23.
12. R. I. and S. Wilberforce, op. cit., II, 453.
13. Ibid., IV, 359.
14. Z. Mudge, *The Christian Statesman – A Portraiture of Sir Thomas Fowell Buxton* (New York, 1865), p. 85.
15. R. I. and S. Wilberforce, op. cit., II, 458.
16. Quoted in M. Hennell, 'A Little Known Social Revolution', *Church Quarterly Review*, CXLIII (1946), 199.
17. R. I. and S. Wilberforce, op. cit., IV, 125.
18. Ibid., V, p. 240.
19. W. Roberts, *The Portraiture of a Christian Gentleman* (1829), p. 67.
20. T. Gisborne, *The Principles of Moral and Political Philosophy Investigated* (4th edn, 1798), p. 74.
21. W. Wilberforce, *A Practical View*, p. 247.
22. T. Gisborne, *An Enquiry into the Duties of Men*, II, 186.
23. Harrowby MSS., 1st series, vol. xix, f. 284.
24. Lord Henley, 'A Plan of Church Reform' (2nd edn 1832), p. 7.
25. R. I. and S. Wilberforce, op. cit., III, 150.
26. Thornton MSS. 1/N, f. 22.
27. W. Roberts, op. cit., p. 71.
28. E. Hodder, *The Life and Work of the Seventh Earl of Shaftesbury* (popular edn, 1888), p. 33.
29. *The Greville Memoirs*, ed. L. Strachey and R. Fulford (1938), IV, 54.
30. R. I. and S. Wilberforce, op. cit., III, 302.
31. *Christian Observer*, XXX (1831), 188.
32. Ibid., p. 639.
33. Ibid., XXXII (1833), 634.
34. Brougham MSS., f. 10, 316.
35. Quoted in R. G. Cowherd, *The Politics of English Dissent* (1959), p. 132.
36. W. E. H. Lecky, *A History of England in the Eighteenth Century* (1899 edn), VII, 384.
37. Perceval MSS., 49183, f. 115, 136.
38. H. Morris, *The Founder and First Three Presidents of the Bible Society* (1895), p. 108.
39. H. Brougham, *Historical Sketches of Statesmen who Flourished in the time of George III* (2nd edn, 1839), I, 247.

40. *Record*, September 27th, 1832.
41. *Sybil*, p. 305.
42. Ibid., p. 301.
43. Grey MSS., Box 39, file 30.
44. *Record*, August 16th, 1830.
45. A. R. Ashwell and R. G. Wilberforce, *The Life of Samuel Wilberforce* (1880), I, 133.
46. *The Times*, May 20th, 1898.

Chapter 10: *Home and Family*

1. *The Task*, Book III, l. 41.
2. T. Gisborne, *An Enquiry* ... , II, 446.
3. W. Roberts, *The Portraiture of A Christian Gentleman* (1829), p. 63.
4. R. I. and S. Wilberforce, *The Life of William Wilberforce* (1838), I, 91.
5. Quoted in C. H. Smyth, *Simeon & Church Order* (Cambridge, 1940), p. 22.
6. Ibid., p. 20.
7. R. I. and S. Wilberforce, op. cit., III, 348; T. Gisborne, op. cit., II, 449.
8. H. More, *Works* (1834), III, 80.
9. G. W. E. Russell, *The Household of Faith* (1902), p. 242.
10. *The Story of the Religious Tract Society* (1898), p. 25.
11. J. Ruskin, *Collected Works* (1905), XXXV, 25.
12. H. More, *Works*, III, 47.
13. C. E. Tonna, *Short Stories for Children* (1832), I, 9.
14. Quoted in F. K. Brown, *Fathers of the Victorians* (Cambridge, 1961), p. 466.
15. L. Strachey, *Eminent Victorians* (1942 edn), p. 347.
16. C. Kingsley, *Alton Locke* (1881), I, 155.
17. G. W. E. Russell, *Lady Victorian Buxton* (1919), p. 215.
18. G. W. E. Russell, *The Household of Faith* (1902), p. 232.
19. J. Venn, *Annals of A Clerical Family* (1904), p. 174.
20. Wilberforce MSS., c. 1, f. 70.
21. Stephen MSS., Bundle 1, f. 19.
22. G. W. E. Russell, *Lady Victoria Buxton* (1919), p. 212.
23. Quoted in D. Newsome, *The Parting of Friends* (1966), p. 55.
24. H. C. G. Moule, *Memories of a Vicarage* (1913), p. 21.
25. J. Pearson, *The Life of William Hey* (1822), p. 297.
26. *Catharine & Craufurd Tait: A Memoir*, ed. W. Benham (1879), p. 327.
27. E. L. Woodward, *Short Journey* (1942), pp. 10, 14–15.
28. G. W. E. Russell, *Fifteen Chapters of Autobiography* (1915), pp. 21–23.

Chapter 11:   *A Serious Generation*

1. *Sir James Stephen. Letters with biographical notes*, ed. C. Stephen (1906), p. 87.
2. *My Countrymen; Culture & Anarchy*, Preface.
3. Quoted in S. G. Checkland, *The Gladstones, a family biography* (1971), p. 404.
4. J. Morley, *The Life of W. E. Gladstone* (1903), I, 184.
5. Wilberforce MSS. d. 9, f. 3.
6. Quoted in M. Jaeger, *Before Victoria* (1956), p. 142.
7. J. Morley, *Critical Miscellanies* (1903), I, 184.
8. G. O. Trevelyan, *The Life & Letters of Lord Macaulay* (new edn, 1961), I, 67.
9. *The Works of John Ruskin*, ed. E. T. Cook and A. D. Wedderburn (1902–12), XIV, 496.
10. Quoted in D. G. Rowell, *Hell & The Victorians* (Oxford, 1974), pp. 59–60.
11. J. W. Cross, *The Life of George Eliot* (1885), I, 35.
12. Ibid., I, 302.
13. J. F. Stephen, *Liberty, Equality & Fraternity* (1873), p. 354.
14. Green MSS., Recollections of W. L. Newman, f. 1.
15. Ibid., Recollections of Professor H. Nettleship, f. 35.
16. *The Works of T. H. Green*, ed. R. L. Nettleship (1885), II, 260.
17. Green MSS., Letter of C. S. Parker, f. 4.

Suggestions for Further Reading

Chapter 1: *Vital Religion*

J. D. Walsh, 'The Origins of the Evangelical Revival', in *Essays in Modern English Church History*, ed. G. V. Bennett and J. D. Walsh (1966).
D. Newsome, *The Parting of Friends* (1966), Chapters I–III.
L. E. Binns, *The Evangelical Movement in the English Church* (1928).
G. R. Balleine, *A History of the Evangelical Party* (new edn, 1951).
H. C. G. Moule, *The Evangelical School in the Church of England* (1901).

Chapter 2: *Converting the Nation*

F. K. Brown, *Fathers of the Victorians* (1961).
V. Kiernan, 'Evangelicalism & The French Revolution', in *Past & Present*, No. 1 (1952).
J. McLeish, *Evangelical Religion and Popular Education* (1969).
W. Jones, *Jubilee Memorial of the Religious Tract Society* (1850).
E. C. W. Stratford, *The Lords of Cobham Hall* (1959).

Chapter 3: *Assault on the Church*

G. Best, 'The Evangelicals and the Established Church in the early Nineteenth Century', in *Journal of Theological Studies*, x (1959).
C. H. Smyth, *Simeon and Church Order* (1940).
E. J. Speck, *The Church Pastoral Aid Society* (1881).
J. S. Reynolds, *The Evangelicals at Oxford, 1735–1871* (1953).
S. C. Carpenter, *Church and People, 1789–1889* (1933).
J. H. Overton, *The English Church in the Nineteenth Century* (1894).
O. Chadwick, *The Victorian Church* (1966), Vol. One.

Chapter 4: *A Mission to the Heathen*

E. Stock, *History of the Church Missionary Society* (4 vols. 1899–1916).
C. Hole, *The early history of the Church Missionary Society* (1896).

G. Moorhouse, *The Missionaries* (1973).
R. Coupland, *The British Anti-Slavery Movement* (2nd edn, 1964).
E. Stokes, *The English Utilitarians and India* (1959).
K. Ingham, *Reformers in India* (1956).
A. T. Embree, *Charles Grant and British Rule in India* (1962).
S. C. Neill, *Colonialism and Christian Mission* (1966).

Chapter 5: *The War Against Vice*

L. Radzinowicz, *A History of English Criminal Law* (1956), Vol. Three.
G. M. Trevelyan, 'Poetry & Rebellion' in *Clio, A Muse, & Other Essays* (1930).
E. P. Thompson, *The Making of the English Working Class* (1963).
B. Harrison, *Drink and the Victorians* (1971).
——, 'State Intervention and Moral Reform' in *Pressure from Without in Early Victorian England*, ed. P. Hollis (1974).
N. St. John Stevas, *Obscenity and the Law* (1956).
H. W. Moss, *Valiant Crusade: A History of the R.S.P.C.A.* (1961).
G. R. Taylor, *The Angel Makers* (1958).

Chapter 6: *Philanthropy and Paternalism*

K. Heasman, *Evangelicals in Action* (1962).
J. R. Poynter, *Society and Pauperism, 1795–1834* (1969).
G. Kitson Clark, *Churchmen and the Condition of England* (1973).
R. A. Soloway, *Prelates and People: Ecclesiastical Social Thought in England, 1783–1852* (1969).
G. Petrie, *A Singular Iniquity: the Campaigns of Josephine Butler* (1971).
J. T. Ward, *The Factory Movement, 1830–1855* (1962).
D. Roberts, *The Victorian Origins of the British Welfare State* (1963).

Chapter 7: *The Age of Societies*

W. Canton, *History of the British & Foreign Bible Society* (5 vols., 1904–1910).
W. T. Gidney, *History of the London Society for Promoting Christianity amongst the Jews* (1908).
F. M. Holmes, *Exeter Hall and its Associates* (1881).
H. Jephson, *The Platform, its rise and progress* (1892).

Chapter 8: *The Cult of Conduct*

H. Perkin, *The Origins of Modern English Society* (1969).
M. Jaeger, *Before Victoria* (1956).
M. Quinlan, *Victorian Prelude* (1941).
E. C. W. Stratford, *The Making of a Gentleman* (1938).

D. Spring, 'The Clapham Sect: some social and political aspects', in *Victorian Studies*, V, No. 1 (1961).
——, 'Aristocracy, Social Structure and Religion in the early Victorian period', in *Victorian Studies*, VI, No. 3 (1963).
W. L. Mathieson, *England in Transition, 1789–1832* (1920).
O. F. Christie, *The Transition from Aristocracy, 1832–1867* (1927).

Chapter 9: *Serious Callings*

G. Millerson, *The Qualifying Associations* (1964).
H. G. Nicholas, 'The New Morality', in *Ideas & Beliefs of the Victorians*, ed. H. Grisewood (1949).
S. G. Checkland, *The Rise of Industrial Society in England, 1815–1885*, (1964).
O. Anderson, 'The Growth of Christian Militarism in mid-Victorian Britain', in *English Historical Review*, lxxxvi (1971).
E. M. Howse, *Saints in Politics* (1953).
J. H. Grainger, *Character and Style in English Politics* (1969).

Chapter 10: *Home and Family*

V. Anderson, *The Northrepps Grandchildren* (1968).
E. E. Kellett, *Religion and Life in the Early Victorian Age* (1938).
H. L. Beales, 'The Victorian Family', in *Ideas & Beliefs of the Victorians*, ed. H. Grisewood (1949).
Mrs C. S. Peel, 'Homes and Habits', in *Early Victorian England*, ed. G. M. Young (1951), Vol. One.

Chapter 11: *A Serious Generation*

S. Meacham, 'The Evangelical Inheritance', in *Journal of British Studies*, iii, No. 1 (1963).
N. G. Annan, 'The Intellectual Aristocracy', in *Studies in Social History, a tribute to G. M. Trevelyan*, ed. J. H. Plumb (1955).
——, *Leslie Stephen* (1951).
S. G. Checkland, *The Gladstones, A Family Biography* (1971).
J. Clive, *Thomas Babington Macaulay, the Shaping of the Historian* (1973).
B. Willey, *Nineteenth Century Studies* (1949).
——, *More Nineteenth Century Studies* (1956).
W. E. Houghton, *The Victorian Frame of Mind* (1957).

Biographies of leading Evangelicals

R. Coupland, *Wilberforce – A Narrative* (2nd edn, 1945).
R. Furneaux, *William Wilberforce* (1974).
J. L. & B. Hammond, *Lord Shaftesbury* (1923).

SUGGESTIONS FOR FURTHER READING

G. Best, *Shaftesbury* (1964).

G. Battiscombe, *Shaftesbury: A Biography of the Seventh Earl* (1974).

M. G. Jones, *Hannah More* (1952).

E. M. Forster, *Marianne Thornton* (1956).

S. Meacham, *Henry Thornton of Clapham* (1964).

M. Hennell, *John Venn and the Clapham Sect* (1958).

J. C. Gill, *Parson Bull of Byerley* (1963).

D. Gray, *Spencer Perceval, the Evangelical Prime Minister* (1963).

M. Bevington (Ed.), *Memoirs of James Stephen* (1954).

T. R. Birks, *Memoir of Edward Bickersteth* (1852).

Index

Note : The names of Evangelicals appear in bold type

INDEX

Middleton, Sir Charles
(1726–1813), later 1st Lord
Barham, naval administrator, 51,
65, 160, 161, 162
Middleton, Lady, 58
Milbanke, Arabella, 34
Militarism, 164
Mill, John Stuart, 14, 183; quoted,
117–18, 154, 155
Miller, Rev. J. C. (1814–80), Vicar
of St Martin's, Birmingham, 66
Montgomery, Sir Robert
(1809–87), Indian administrator, 92
More, Hannah (1745–1833), author,
32, 43, 51, 55, 56, 58, 59, 111, 113,
124, 139, 179; quoted, 19, 30, 42,
45, 50, 51, 77, 110, 112, 113, 124,
132, 146, 147, 148, 150, 151, 152,
162, 186; *Village Politics* quoted,
113–14, 115
Morley, John, quoted, 197
Moule, Rev. Henry (1801–80),
Vicar of Fordington, Dorset, 68,
101
Moule, Rev. H. C. G. (1841–1920),
Bishop of Durham, 68, 194;
quoted, 71, 191
Mudie, Charles (1818–90), founder
of circulating library, 98
Munsterberg, Hugo, quoted, 123

Newman, Francis (1805–97), 194,
198–9
Newman, John Henry, 13, 183, 194,
197
Newton, Rev. John (1725–1807),
Curate of Olney, Buckinghamshire,
52, 60, 65, 103
Nicholson, Sir John (1821–57),
soldier, 92
Nightingale, Florence, 129
Noel, Rev. Baptist (1798–1873),
Minister at St John's, Bedford
Row, London, 46, 121
Noel, Caroline (1817–77), hymn-
writer, 65
Nonconformists, 41, 48, 62, 69, 75,
101

Obscenity, Evangelical attitude to,
98–9
Orsman, W. J., evangelist, 45–6,
120, 159
Oxford Movement, 71
Oxford University, 39

Paine, Thomas, 100, 108, 112
Palmerston, 3rd Viscount, 72, 105,
106, 177
Paternalism, 130–33
Peel, Sir Robert (1750–1830), M.P.
and industrialist, 127, 128, 142
Peel, Sir Robert, Prime Minister, 13,
127, 167, 170, 190
Pennefather, Rev. William
(1816–73), Vicar of St Jude's,
Islington, 123, 125
Perceval, Spencer (1762–1812),
Prime Minister 1809–12, 97, 128,
164, 170, 175
Peterloo Massacre (1819), 114, 116
Phillpotts, Bishop Henry, 71
Pitt, William, 30, 104, 111, 152, 166,
170
Place, Francis, quoted, 107, 114
Politics, Evangelical attitude to,
165–78
Pollok, Robert (1798–1827), poet, 98
Pratt, Rev. Josiah (1768–1844),
Secretary of C.M.S., 39, 62, 102
Prayer Book and Homily Society, 107
Prison reform, 127
Pritchard, George, Secretary of
Vice Society, 99

Racing, Evangelical condemnation of
101
Ragged schools, 46–7, 122, 131, 133,
147
Ragged School Union, 46, 47, 123,
140
Raikes, Robert (1735–1811),
promoter of Sunday schools, 44,
147
Ram, Rev. Stopford (1826–81),
Secretary of Church of England
Temperance Society, 101
Ramsay, Rev. James (1733–89),
Vicar of Teston, Kent, 86
Record, quoted, 31, 135, 176, 177
Reed, Rev. Andrew (1787–1862),
incumbent at Wycliffe Chapel,
London, 164
Reeve, Rev. John William
(1807–82), Chaplain to Queen
Victoria, 48
Reform Bill (1832), 173, 176
Religious Tract Society, 42, 43, 52,
136, 137, 146, 147, 182
Richmond, Rev. Leigh